THE POLITICAL ECONOMY OF WORK IN THE 21ST CENTURY

THE POLITICAL ECONOMY OF WORK IN THE 21ST CENTURY

IMPLICATIONS FOR AN AGING AMERICAN WORKFORCE

Martin Sicker

QUORUM BOOKS
Westport, Connecticut • London

Library of Congress Cataloging-in-Publication Data

Sicker, Martin.
    The political economy of work in the 21st century : implications for an aging American workforce / by Martin Sicker.
      p. cm.
    Includes bibliographical references and index.
    ISBN 1–56720–566–6 (alk. paper)
    1. Aged—Government policy—United States. 2. Aging—Economic aspects—United States. 3. Age distribution (Demography)—Economic aspects—United States. I. Title.
HQ1064.U5S533   2002
362.6′0973—dc21   2001058597

British Library Cataloguing in Publication Data is available.

Library of Congress Catalog Card Number: 2001058597
ISBN: 1–56720–566–6

First published in 2002

Quorum Books, 88 Post Road West, Westport, CT 06881
An imprint of Greenwood Publishing Group, Inc.
www.quorumbooks.com

Printed in the United States of America

The paper used in this book complies with the
Permanent Paper Standard issued by the National
Information Standards Organization (Z39.48–1984).

10 9 8 7 6 5 4 3 2 1

CONTENTS

INTRODUCTION

The average age of the population of the United States, and of other industrialized nations, is increasing. This is not only one of the consequences of a relatively low birthrate that is slowing population growth, it is also being brought about simply because people generally are living longer and healthier lives, a tribute to the advances in medical science and other environmental factors. Suffice it to note that in 1900 there were about 3,500 centenarians in the United States. Today the number is estimated to be about 66,000. We are becoming a progressively older society, and that fact presents a series of concerns that should engage our attention.

This was brought home to us most dramatically in late 1998 with the space odyssey of senior citizen John Glenn. As pointed out by one journalist, "the fact that a 77-year-old man is now orbiting the globe is a vivid reminder of the debate we're not having on earth. This, of course, involves America's inevitable aging."[1] That debate should be over what we must do to reconstitute our society, its values, policies and institutions, to meet the challenge before us. However, as a society, we have a tendency to avoid dealing with broad and seemingly overly complex issues, and only do so as infrequently as possible. As a result, the debate that is just beginning to take place in earnest has essentially been limited to that of how to respond to the anticipated growth in national expenditures for the elderly in the forms of Social Security and Medicare.

When Congress enacted Social Security in 1935 and set the age of retirement at 65, the average life expectancy was 62 years. Not surprisingly, the number of people in the general population over age 65 was quite small. By the time Medicare was enacted 30 years later, life expectancy had risen to 70 years. The age of eligibility was predicated on the assumption that almost everyone over 65 that was eligible for the benefit was probably in some stage of serious illness and incapacity and therefore dependent on others to a significant extent for their sustenance. Since the enactment of Medicare, life expectancy has risen to 76 years and may be expected to increase further in the decades to come. Clearly, the increase in life expectancy has significant implications for the level of national expenditures attributable to an aging population.

It is frequently suggested that the costs of Social Security and Medicare for a rapidly growing elderly population impose an increasingly heavy burden on younger workers who finance these programs through payroll taxes, those taxes levied directly on their earnings from employment. Assuming that current retirement trends persist, this dependency burden, the number of pension beneficiaries compared with the number of pension contributors, has been estimated as 23.8 per 100 in 1995, 24.4 in 2010 and 40.0 in 2030.[2] Moreover, and assuming that 1995 Social Security contribution rates as a percentage of wages remain constant, the balance of pension revenue and expenditures is projected to be 1.1 percent in the year 2000, 1.7 in 2010, and -2.2 in 2030.[3] It is the implications of these numbers that has become a matter of serious concern.

According to a 1998 Congressional Budget Office (CBO) report, the average person between the ages of 20 and 64 paid $8,100 in taxes and received $1,500 in direct federal benefits. By contrast, the average person between the ages of 65 and 79 paid $4,800 in taxes and received $12,000 in direct federal benefits, primarily Social Security and Medicare. In the CBO scenario, Social Security outlays would rise from 4 percent of gross domestic product (GDP) in 1997 to 7 percent in 2050. Medicare and Medicaid together would increase from 4 percent of GDP in 1997 to 10 percent in 2050. However, the long-term budgetary implications are made far more severe by the consideration that increased spending on retirement and health programs may be expected to lead to increased Federal budget deficits, a rising national debt and substantially higher interest payments on that debt. The 1998 CBO report estimated that the interest payments on the national debt would climb from 3 percent of GDP in 1997 to nearly 20 percent in 2050.[4]

The basic issue reflected by these data was stated succinctly and with clarity in a 1998 Urban Institute briefing paper. "The nation faces a great challenge as it moves into the 21st century. The elderly population will live longer on average and the numbers of elderly will rise. It is impossible to keep the promises made to them without large tax increases on the young, and even then, reducing the share of the budget spent on all other societal needs."[5]

These large intergenerational transfers and their fiscal consequences are held by some to be "neither defensible nor desirable."[6] Others, however, may as easily argue that such transfers are indeed both defensible and desirable. The true significance of these transfers and the amounts involved is not at all self-evident. On what basis does one conclude that a transfer payment to a non-working adult is too much or just about the right amount? How about transfer payments from working adults to non-working children? Would one make a similar argument about the level of such transfers being neither defensible nor desirable? As pointed out by historian Theodore Roszak:

The tie that binds the generations cannot be reduced to a neat fiscal formula. The discussion of entitlements is complicated by a biological fact that does not yield to a purely economic analysis. It is called "family." The people who are giving and taking, earning and spending, are relatives. As nature would have it, with the passage of time the babies grow up, get old, and retire. Despite all the groaning and gnashing of teeth we hear from the generational accountants, it pays to remember that nothing worse is happening here than that life is going on. The demographic configuration changes, but the underlying obligation of kin to kin continues.[7]

One might therefore argue that such intergenerational transfers are both necessary and desirable because our values dictate them. What is at issue here is not a value-free economic concern, as some analysts seem to imply. It is ultimately a question of values, for better or worse, that underlies most of the ostensibly economic decisions that government is called upon to make. Thus our values appear to dictate that those with moderate income should disproportionately bear the brunt of the costs of such income transfers. How else can one explain the limit on payroll earnings taxable for social security, which effectively taxes someone who earns $60,000 a year the same amount as it taxes someone earning two, three, four or more times as much. How else can one explain the payroll taxes for low earners that are sometimes greater than their income taxes? Moreover, it is somewhat disingenuous to argue that Medicare reimbursements represent intergenerational transfers to retirees. In fact, the money never passes into or through their hands, and they have little to say about how it is disbursed. Like all health insurance reimbursements, it is paid directly to doctors, hospitals, nursing homes, insurance companies, and pharmaceutical houses, most of which are organized as profit-making medical corporations of some kind. Partly because it is not a direct income transfer to retirees, business exploitation of Medicare has helped spur the growth of health care into a major national industry, employing a growing segment of the labor force, and producing a not insignificant part of the annual national income. This fact led Roszak to conclude that, "If Medicare is an income transfer engine, it is a pump that sucks taxes out of all of us and delivers them to some of the wealthiest people in America. If anybody is paying golfing fees out of Medicare, it is apt to be the CEOs of the nation's prospering health maintenance organizations."[8]

Viewed from this perspective, conflating Social Security and Medicare into a single category of income transfers to retirees makes little real sense. It would be equally as meaningful to include a pro rata portion of the national defense budget in the income-transfer category on the grounds that retirees are also consumers of national security.

In the final analysis, any level of transfer payments from one generation to another, or from one segment of the population to another, is primarily a political issue and only secondarily an economic one. Once the multifaceted political question is answered, economic considerations can play a significant role in determining the optimum course of action. Unfortunately, the current national debate over how to deal with the growing burdens of Social Security and Medicare seems to assume that it is fundamentally a value-free economic question, if indeed there is such a thing. Because of this approach, the political process that will settle the matter, at least for a while, is not dealing with what I would suggest are the critical longer range issues that should concern us as an aging society.

In any case, one of the approaches being suggested as a solution to the so-called income transfer problem is to redefine old age, that is, to push retirement and its associated benefits off to a later age. Deferring the normal retirement age will have a positive effect on the "dependency ratio" between the generations by increasing the size of the effective workforce, with older workers continuing to contribute their payroll taxes for an extended period of time. Douglas Hall and Philip Mirvis wrote in this regard: "Our overall feeling is that the combination of market forces and demographic trends means that the business sector and society as a whole will have no choice in the future but to employ and develop older workers more. Society simply cannot afford to support a growing number of retired people with a shrinking base of employed people."[9] Of course, the underlying assumption in this is that there will be a constant labor shortage over the next decades. Presumably, this will provide job opportunities for millions of older, well-educated, experienced baby boomers (those born during the two decades following the end of World War II) without placing them in competition with younger workers. If not, as Roszak put it, "we may find younger Americans wishing mightily that this was a 'nation of Floridas' where they could pack all the troublesome seniors off to anyplace well out of the job market."[10]

Not the least of the problems that will have to be addressed is that of expectations. For the last half-century, we have been erecting a social structure in which individuals have grown to expect to retire at progressively younger ages, to live longer in retirement, and to have increasingly higher levels of retirement and health benefits. In 1890, some 68 percent of persons over the age of 65 were still in the workforce. This number declined to 56 percent in 1920, to 41 percent in 1950, to 25 percent in 1970, to 12.2 percent in 1980, and to 10.9 percent in 1993. Toward the end of the century, participation rates rose to the 1980 level because of acute labor shortages in some areas. The passage on April 7, 2000 of the Senior Citizens Freedom to Work Act, which eliminated the earnings penalty for those between the ages of 65–70, may cause the participation rate to remain at about that level for some time. Nonetheless, reversing the retirement trend for those over 65 will not be easy and may not be accepted with equanimity by the best-educated and most politically active generation in our history. Moreover, even if the trend reversal takes place, it is uncertain that it will lead many older workers back to what they consider acceptable employment for any length of time.

The critical question is, will there be sufficient employment opportunities for a growing number of older workers in the workforce of the future? Perhaps! The evidence for a more positive response is far from clear or compelling. For one thing, it is quite clear that economists and businessmen do not share a common perspective on the question. A 1999 *Fortune* article put it rather bluntly. "America is no place to age gracefully. Of course, basketball players, dancers, and fashion models are finished young; mathematicians and chess players peak early too. So do construction workers and coal miners. Once you're 55, it's almost impossible to find a job in business. But a new trend is emerging: In corporate America, 40 is starting to look and feel old."[11]

It is ironic that at the same time that public policy is slowly raising the age at which older workers should leave the workforce, private (corporate) policy is lowering that age. As the current baby boom generation matures, demographic projections indicate that people aged 55 and older will constitute some 40 percent of the working age population by 2020. Moreover, the number of older workers who will need to remain in the workforce may well exceed that projection for a number of reasons. There is every expectation that the aging baby boom generation will be faced by rising health care costs, and that in contrast to many of today's older people, they will have smaller savings and household wealth upon which to rely. Moreover, because of the pattern of late marriages and deferred childbirth, many prospective retirees are likely to have children in or about to enter college, and will be faced by the constantly growing costs of higher education. It seems a certainty that an increasing number of older Americans will have little choice but to stay in the workforce beyond the current normal retirement age, if they can, simply to pay their bills.[12]

The burden of this book is to examine the prospective place of the aging worker in the employment environment of the 21st century. However, in doing so it will be necessary to cast doubt on some of the neoclassical economic ideas and assumptions that have become part of the conventional wisdom of our time. Foremost among these is the idea of "The Market," which, according to Harvey Cox, in an article that should be obligatory reading for anyone concerned about values in our society, has become the new theology of our time.

Since the earliest stages of human history, of course, there have been bazaars, rialtos, and trading posts—all markets. But The Market was never God, because there were other centers of value and meaning, other "gods." The Market operated within a plethora of other institutions that restrained it . . . only in the past two centuries has The Market risen above these demigods and chthonic spirits to become today's First Cause.[13]

The Market is now described as effectively endowed with the divine attributes of omnipotence, omniscience, and omnipresence which theologians previously reserved for God. "Current thinking already assigns to The Market a comprehensive wisdom that in the past only the gods have known. The Market, we are taught, is able to determine what human needs are, what copper and capital should cost, how much barbers and CEOs should be paid, and how much jet airplanes, running shoes, and hysterectomies should sell for." But how do we know what The Market wants us to do? In times past, seers and prophets went into a trance and then revealed the divine mood and will.

Today The Market's fickle will is clarified by daily reports from Wall Street and other sensory organs of finance. Thus we can learn on a day-to-day basis that The Market is "apprehensive," "relieved," "nervous," or even at times "jubilant." On the basis of this revelation awed adepts make critical decisions about whether to buy or sell . . . That The Market is not at all displeased by downsizing or a growing income gap, or can be gleeful about the expansion of cigarette sales to Asian young people, should not cause anyone to question its ultimate omniscience. Like Calvin's inscrutable deity, The Market may work in mysterious ways, "hid from our eyes," but ultimately it knows best.[14]

One of the fundamental tenets of belief in The Market is that business decisions and the interaction between individuals and firms are ultimately economically efficient. That is, as explained by Morris Altman, "it is assumed that market forces will invariably and in short shrift force delinquent economic agents, be they workers or management, into making the right choice—that is, the effort-maximizing choice. So, even if individuals choose not to conform to the neo-classical ideal, these dissidents are invariably pressured into doing so by market forces."[15]

However, there is good reason to question both the validity and utility of that notion. Firms and individuals today operate in an environment that is characterized more by radical uncertainty than calculable risk. Economic agents have never been able to anticipate all possible or even probable outcomes that may result from their decisions. As argued by one team of authors, "Economic agents rely instead on heuristics, habits, and routines. Their decisions are conditioned by taken-for-granted assumptions. Only when the environment changes in ways that challenge customary understandings do individuals and firms search more broadly for alternatives."[16] Even then, operating in an environment of radical uncertainty means that their choices among possible alternatives cannot really be optimized. A case in point is the rapid development of ever more advanced technologies, the implications of which are quite unpredictable, as evidenced by the demise of many companies that staked their future on new technologies. As Michael Mandel of *Business Week* put it, this unpredictability "flies in the face of conventional economic theory, which asserts that in a market economy businesses adopt the most efficient technology."[17]

Many economic theorists are engaged in modeling The Market, trying to ferret out its secrets, much as theologians try to do with regard to divinity. Both groups often have great influence on their respective adepts. However, modeling The Market does not in itself demonstrate that there actually is such a thing as The Market. Indeed, models of The Market may bear little resemblance to reality, and public and private policies predicated on them may not only prove to be wrong but also harmful. Despite this, neoclassical economic theorists and their acolytes continue to proclaim the truth of their visions in the face of evidence to the contrary. This is reminiscent of the perhaps apocryphal story told of the famous German professor of philosophy, G.W.F. Hegel, who was expounding his theory of the dialectics of history. When one of his students challenged him with the observation that the events of history did not seem to comport well with his theory, he responded that, in that case, it was just too bad for history.

An example of such a counterintuitive as well as counterfactual tenet is the bizarre neoclassical economic assertion that unemployment and leisure are substitutes, which means that all unemployment is voluntary. After all, the argument goes, if workers would accept a reduction in wages, in accordance with the dictates of The Market, those out of work would soon find employment. Their refusal to accept whatever wages are offered is therefore equivalent to a decision for leisure instead of employment. "In other words," economist Ravi Batra, an outspoken critic of neoclassical economics, writes, "a manager who is laid off from AT&T can always go to work at Burger King for $5 an hour. He or she need not be unemployed. Managers who don't accept the Burger King job are voluntarily unemployed and seek to enjoy leisure." However, the reality is that most people who have been managers for much of their working lives will be reluctant to take such fast food jobs except as a last resort. They will try to find work in the fields in which they have invested so much of their lives, perhaps accepting modest pay cuts, for as long as their savings and credit last, a process that can often take years. "Are they relaxing all this time and happy about their situation? Hardly. This is the practical reality that economics frequently ignores."[18]

The concern in this book is not for economic theory as such, but for those aging workers who are being blithely told that their reluctance to take jobs for which they are grossly overqualified is equivalent to a decision for leisure instead of work. It is concerned with the realities and uncertainties that aging workers will face in the decades to come.

NOTES

1. Robert Samuelson, "Plundering the Young," *Washington Post*, November 4, 1998. It is noteworthy that when this article appeared subsequently in the *Washington Post National Weekly Edition*, November 9, 1998, it was re-titled, "Redefining 'Elderly.' "

2. Murray Gendell, "Trends in Retirement Age in Four Countries, 1965–95," *Monthly Labor Review*, August 1998, Table 6.

3. Ibid., Table 7.

4. "Long-Term Budgetary Pressures and Policy Options" (Washington, DC: Congressional Budget Office, May 1998).

5. "Policy Challenges Posed by the Aging of America" (Washington, DC: Urban Institute, May 1998).

6. Samuelson, "Plundering the Young."

7. Theodore Roszak, *America the Wise* (Boston, MA: Houghton Mifflin, 1998), p. 32.

8. Ibid.

9. Douglas T. Hall and Philip H. Mirvis, "The New Workplace and Older Workers," in James A. Auerbach and Joyce C. Welsh, eds., *Aging and Competition: Rebuilding the U.S. Workforce* (Washington, DC: National Planning Association, 1994), p. 89.

10. Roszak, *America the Wise*, p. 39.

11. Nina Munk, "Finished at Forty," *Fortune*, February 1, 1999, p. 50.

12. Douglas T. Hall and Philip H. Mirvis, "Increasing the Value of Older Workers: Flexible Employment and Lifelong Learning," in James A. Auerbach, ed., *Through a Glass Darkly: Building the New Workplace for the 21st Century* (Washington, DC: National Policy Association, 1998), p. 38.

13. Harvey Cox, "The Market as God," *The Atlantic Monthly*, March 1999, p. 20.

14. Ibid., p. 22.

15. Morris Altman, "A High Wage Path to Economic Growth and Development," *Challenge*, January–February 1998, p. 93.

16. Stephen Herzenberg, John Alic, and Howard Wial, "A New Deal for a New Economy," *Challenge*, March–April 1999, p. 107.

17. Michael J. Mandel. *The High-Risk Society: Peril and Promise in the New Economy* (New York: Times Books, 1996), p. 106.

18. Ravi Batra, *The Great American Deception* (New York: John Wiley & Sons, 1996), p. 34.

I

THE REAL WORLD OF WORK AND RETIREMENT

One must work, if not by choice, at least by despair, since it is less annoying to work than to be amused.

—Charles Baudelaire

Given the centrality of work in our lives as individuals and collectively as a society and nation, it is rather surprising that relatively little public attention is directed to the manner and extent to which work and employment influence our social as well as economic well-being. Indeed, upon reflection it will be seen that work and employment affect virtually every aspect of our personal and communal existence in one way or another. As economic historian Paul McNulty observed:

Surely no other influence has broader implications for people's lives in modern society than their employment. It determines generally where and how they live and the kind of education their children receive, and it intimately affects most of their relations with the community and the larger society. Our most pressing economic problems—poverty and unemployment, inflation and the balance of international payments, the impact of technological change, the quality and direction of our educational programs, the problems of energy, environmental pollution, and resource conservation—are or are directly related to the problems of men and women at work.[1]

Although the terms *work* and *employment* are often considered synonymous and therefore are used interchangeably, there are significant conceptual distinctions between the two terms that merit our notice. Indeed, these distinctions should be taken into consideration in any discussion of the effects of changes in the work environment on individuals and society. In light of the dramatic developments currently taking place in the organization of economic life throughout the industrialized world, the distinctions between work and employment are becoming increasingly significant and are likely to remain so for the foreseeable future.

What are these distinctions? In essence, work is an activity, whereas employment is a status. Work is something that we do; employment is something that is done with us. Work is a productive activity that is most often subject to our individual control. Employment, particularly in modern industrialized societies, is a circumstance over which we generally have little influence and even less control. Put aside the fundamental question of whether human beings have an inherent need to work or whether such a perceived need is a result of social conditioning or economic necessity. The fact is that most people feel compelled to engage in some sort of productive activity, physical or mental, regardless of whether they are compensated for it monetarily. Indeed, there are many people who demonstrate greater commitment and devote greater effort to self-determined work for which they receive little or no monetary compensation than to the employment from which they derive their livelihood.

Millions of people in all walks of life volunteer their time, skills, and energies to perform a variety of tasks on behalf of others. These do invaluable work for the benefit of society but are not considered as employed by the people or institutions they serve. At the same time, all or most of these same people must also engage, or have been so engaged in the past, in remunerative employment, including self-employment, which compensates them with the income and benefits needed to sustain or improve their individual standards of living.

Moreover, there seems to be a clear link between work and self-identity that is especially prominent in American culture, as Barbara Rudolph pointed out in a 1998 book depicting the experiences of six people who were made redundant in a downsizing by a major American corporation. Rudolph noted "the fundamental connection between work and sense of self, between who we are and what we do. This peculiarly American link between work and identity dates back to Puritanism: the Yankee interpretation of the Calvinist link between work and virtue, between honest labor and a man's salvation. That heritage endures. In Chicago or San Jose, one stranger may ask another 'What do you do?' by way of greeting, but one is much less likely to hear this phrase in Paris, Dublin, or Hong Kong."[2]

The significance of this linkage is that work has great importance for people that may be substantially independent of monetary compensation for the effort expended. The point was made clear in the results of a 1995 national survey conducted by the Public Agenda Foundation. It disclosed that 69 percent of Americans asserted that work is something they enjoy, primarily because it gives them a sense of accomplishment. On the other hand, only 28 percent indicated that their primary purpose in working was to earn a living and that they would stop working if they could afford to do so.[3] Two 1998 national surveys of the so-called baby-boom generation, the 76 million people born between 1946 and 1964 that are expected to begin to retire in 2010, are particularly instructive in this regard. In both surveys only a relatively few respondents indicated that they expected to continue to work out of economic necessity. One study, conducted by the Gallup organization for the brokerage firm Paine Webber Inc., indicated that 60 percent of those surveyed wanted new jobs or aspired to develop businesses of their own, and 10 percent sought to achieve a balance between work and leisure. Another 15 percent of the respondents planned to continue working indefinitely, and only 15 percent indicated that they did not plan to work any longer. The second study, conducted by Roper Starch Worldwide Inc. for the American Association of Retired Persons (AARP), indicated that 35 percent intended to work part-time for their own enjoyment and 23 percent because of the desire for additional income, and 17 percent said they wanted to open their own businesses. Five percent indicated that they planned to seek different full-time employment, and as in the Gallup survey, about 16 percent did not plan to work any longer after reaching retirement age.[4]

These data, which clearly indicate an overwhelming commitment to continue to work in some capacity or mode after nominal eligibility for retirement, also reflect another serious but frequently unarticulated concern. And that is one that employers, as a rule, rarely if ever give any consideration to, namely, the enormous investment that many workers have in their professions and careers. Long years of study and apprenticeship, augmented by expertise developed through experience, often at high actual and opportunity costs, make it very difficult for many, and especially older workers, to simply switch gears and adopt an entirely different role. These considerations also have significant impact on the decision of older workers to retire voluntarily. As a former NASA executive is quoted as saying, "There's almost nothing in life as final as retirement. When you make that decision, chances are you can't go back. To give up that enormous amount of knowledge and experience and be afraid you'll never use it again is a great detriment to walking out the door."[5]

It is, therefore, overly simplistic to assume, as some economists and businessmen are wont to, that people work primarily to put bread on their tables. Although financial need may be a compelling reason for most to seek employment, it assuredly is not the only factor motivating people to work, whether for others or for themselves. This point is argued forcefully by Roger Terry:

Work has a practical purpose—to provide food, clothing, and shelter for the individual in society—but work is something more than mere utilitarian labor. Work has purposes beyond the economic fruits it produces. Work helps individuals define themselves, define their place in the world, fix their unique stamp upon the physical, social, intellectual, or cultural environment. . . . *When the acquisition of wealth or even basic necessities becomes our primary objective, the individual, by definition, is less important than the work he or she performs and thus becomes a mere resource to be used by the organizers of economic endeavor*[6] (emphasis added).

The important distinction between work and employment tends to be obscured to some degree by the circumstance that, in an increasingly complex society, there are many kinds of highly rewarding work that can only be done in the context of employment by relatively large organizations. For example, it would be very difficult if not impracticable for someone to do serious biomedical research outside the embrace of an institution that provided the necessary laboratory facilities and other support. And this constraint would apply equally to a scientist who had sufficient independent wealth to maintain a satisfactory standard of living without any additional income from remunerative employment and to a scientist who must be remuneratively employed in order to put bread on the family table.

Why are these distinctions becoming increasingly important to us at this time? The answer is because many of us are already experiencing a growing disjunction between our need or desire to work and available opportunities for appropriate employment, and many more may be expected to have this same disquieting experience in the decades ahead. The need or desire to work for monetary compensation no longer necessarily translates into a realistic opportunity to do so. Rephrasing this in basic economic terms, those wishing to work for remuneration represent the available supply of labor, whereas opportunities for employment reflect the demand for labor, and the character of the relation between the two, as will be seen, is changing in significant ways. As a result, one of the great challenges that will confront society in the 21st century will be the creation of meaningful and rewarding opportunities for work outside the traditional economic framework of employment. For it seems clear that, with regard to the latter, barring some extraordinary employment-producing circumstances such as a major war, the growing supply of labor will more than likely greatly exceed any anticipated demand.

This assertion is made notwithstanding official government estimates that present a far rosier picture of future employment. Those projections, however, are based on extrapolations of current survey and study data that seem remarkably out of touch with the emerging realities of the rapidly changing labor market. It is worth noting in this regard that some independent analysts have suggested that virtually all of the world's fundamental needs for food, clothing, shelter, and other basic amenities can be produced, using current technologies, by no more than 20 percent of the present world labor force. Similarly, a study by the International Metalworkers Federation forecast that, as a result of increasing automation in manufacturing, within 30 years as few as two percent of the present global workforce will be needed to produce all the goods needed to satisfy total market demand.[7]

If such projections are even partially valid, the concomitant challenge to all industrialized as well as industrializing societies will be to devise appropriate means of sustaining a reasonable standard of living for potentially very large numbers of surplus workers. At the same time, it will be socially necessary to provide appropriate outlets for meaningful work, whether monetarily compensated or not. It is because of these considerations that the distinction between work and employment, which for the greater part of the twentieth century was of little practical consequence for most people, has become increasingly important.

Until only a few years ago it was generally taken for granted, quite reasonably, that each of us would spend a good part of our lives working in the employ of someone else. In our youth we were prepared for such employment through basic education, training, and apprenticeship. A worker typically entered the labor force for a period of 40 to 50 years and looked forward, with or without much enthusiasm, to the day when one might be able to withdraw from such employment to a life of relative leisure. At that time, one would be free to undertake the kinds of work or other activity that might be found enjoyable and fulfilling during one's remaining years. This benign state of affairs was labeled "retirement," and in fact reflected a status previously enjoyed only by the wealthy elite throughout history. For most people, however, except for those few who are independently wealthy, this latter non-employed stage of the life course continues to be conditioned by one's history of employment.

The reason for this begins to become evident once it is recognized that a person's ability to sustain a life of relative leisure after leaving the labor force is critically dependent on the extent of the financial resources available to the prospective retiree to maintain any particular standard of living. For most people, such post-retirement financial resources represent current income derived principally from one or more of the following: social insurance, pensions, savings, and investments. But, as it turns out, the actual amount of income in retirement that can be realized from these sources is a direct consequence of the history and character of an individual's employment experience.

The amount of the public social insurance benefit (Social Security) that a person may expect, once having reached the age of eligibility, is directly related to the length and continuity of one's employment history. It is predicated on the level of employer-matched contributions made during the course of the individual's career as an employee. For that fortunate segment of the labor force whose members will receive a predetermined or defined private pension benefit, the amount of such benefit will also be directly related to the individual's employment and salary history. Finally, the very notion of saving and investing for one's retirement years presupposes the ability to have set aside a portion of current income, which was itself derived in greatest measure from paid employment.

One might therefore assume, with good reason, that a decision to withdraw voluntarily from the active labor force, from the field of remunerated employment, would reflect a prudent assessment of the implications of such a decision for one's future. At a minimum, in the absence of a compelling reason such as poor health, a decision to retire would presumably be based on an objective assessment of one's prospective financial viability and likelihood of being able to maintain a particular standard of living. In other words, the retirement income anticipated from these employment-based sources should suffice for one's expected needs over an extended period of time once current earnings from remunerated employment cease. Suffice it merely to note at this point that any discontinuities in one's employment history can have notable consequences for an individual's solvency in retirement. Moreover, it should be understood that the aggregate amount that one will need to sustain a desired standard of living will increase in tandem with an increase in the average life expectancy of those who reach traditional retirement age in relatively good health.

One might have expected, therefore, that such an assessment of long-term financial viability was a major consideration in the early retirement decisions that saw the number of men aged 55–64 in the labor force dwindle from 83 percent in 1970 to about 65 percent in 1995. Unfortunately, as some of those who voluntarily chose the option of early withdrawal from the labor force discovered to their regret, prospective retirees often seriously underestimate the amount of retirement income necessary to maintain their current lifestyles. In fact, according to the Employee Benefit Research Institute's 1997 Retirement Confidence Survey, 22 percent of current retirees reported a decline in their standard of living.[8]

Generally speaking, the amount of retirement income necessary to maintain a pre-retirement standard of living over an extended period of time is estimated to be between 60 and 90 percent of pre-retirement income. As may be expected, income replacement rates do affect retirement patterns; as the expected replacement rate increases, the probability that one will withdraw from paid employment before age 65 increases. According to one study, 22 percent of workers with an expected income replacement rate below 60 percent expected to stop working before age 65. This expectation increased to 29 percent for those in the 60 to 69 percent replacement range and to 30 percent for those in the 70 to 79 percent replacement range.[9] The problem, of course, is to properly assess the income replacement rate necessary to maintain a given standard of living and to ascertain whether that replacement rate is realistically achievable.

Assuming an annual pre-retirement income of $40,000, it has been estimated that maintaining the same standard of living in retirement would require that approximately 71 percent of that annual amount be replaced on an ongoing basis from other income sources. These sources have traditionally been described as the "three-legged stool" of retirement income security. This metaphor is intended "to symbolize a division of responsibility among collective and individual efforts in providing for retirement income."[10] For more than six decades the most significant of these "legs" has been Social Security, at least for most people. However, it is important to note that as a result of amendments to the Social Security Act the normal retirement age at which one becomes eligible for full benefits is scheduled to rise to age 66 by 2009 and to 67 by 2027. This escalation of the eligibility age will have its greatest impact on those born after 1946.

One may expect to derive approximately 44 percent of the income needed in retirement from Social Security, assuming a history of lifetime (40 years or more) full-time employment, and the remainder from pensions and savings. For someone with a preretirement income of $90,000, approximately 86 percent of this amount would have to be replaced in order to maintain the same standard of living. In this case, only 21 percent would be replaced by Social Security and 65 percent would have to come from pensions and savings. However, given some of the developments and trends in the workplace that will be discussed later, one may reasonably anticipate a declining prospect of deriving significant retirement income from pensions and savings for many current midlife and older workers. This, of course, will be true as well as for many younger workers who will join their ranks in the years ahead.

Those who are fortunate enough to see their preretirement real income exceed the middle class average will experience an increasing need for replacement income in retirement that will have to derive from sources other than Social Security, if they expect to be able to maintain their preretirement standard of living. But, since less than half of the private-sector workforce can expect a defined benefit pension, the level of personal savings, and the manner in which those savings are invested to maximize the rate of return, becomes a critical factor in the retirement-standard of living relationship.

Dallas Salisbury of the Employee Benefit Research Institute set forth the essence of the problem clearly and unequivocally. The fact that more individuals today are earning the right to private pension benefits than at any time in history is being offset by the increase in relatively short job tenures resulting from volatility in the labor market. This means that the benefits actually received will be relatively small unless individuals in this situation save at higher rates to offset low pension income. However, only about one-third of future pension beneficiaries are doing this. Another third is saving far less than they will need to sustain their standard of living in retirement, and the remaining third is not saving at all. Furthermore, Salisbury points out, "tax data show that over two-thirds of those who are paid a preretirement age lump-sum distribution do not save it for retirement but spend it instead. This suggests an added problem in terms of retirement timing. Although many of these individuals would not have had any benefit in an earlier time, when they spend a distribution they are assuring that they will be un-pensioned, for that employer, by their own behavior."[11] Further compounding the problem are the historically high debt burdens that individuals and families are carrying, coupled with the desire to maintain their current standard of living. An obvious consequence of this is that many individuals in this situation will have no realistic alternative but to continue working at least until they are eligible for full Social Security benefits, if not longer.

Unfortunately, the trends in personal savings are also not very encouraging. According to a November 1994 survey of full-time workers, the amount saved for retirement dropped 8 percent in 1994 and 34 percent over the preceding two years, notwithstanding the upturn in the economy during the same period.[12] A 1995 Merrill Lynch Retirement and Financial Planning Survey indicated that net household savings as a percentage of disposable income was a mere 4.6 percent, less than one-third of the comparable figures for Japan or France. Moreover, the study concluded that although about two-thirds of those surveyed indicated that they were saving for retirement, the amount actually saved was only about one-third of what would be needed to maintain their current standards of living in retirement.[13] In their 1996 report, Merrill Lynch indicated that as many as 58 percent of those surveyed expressed concerns about outliving the money they put away for retirement.[14]

These results are consistent with the findings of a 1993 government-sponsored survey, which concluded that 40 percent of persons aged 51 to 61 expected to have no retirement income other than their Social Security benefit.[15] Further corroboration of these findings is provided by a concurrent survey conducted by the American Association of Retired Persons. Exploring the question of prospective retirement, the AARP study reported: "Of the age-50-plus respondents employed or self-employed full time (29 percent of the total sample), less than half (48 percent) expressed confidence that they were saving enough money to live comfortably in retirement."[16] Similarly, a 1995 *Workplace Pulse* survey, conducted by the Employers Council on Flexible Compensation, indicated that about three-fourths of the respondents acknowledged that their savings were inadequate. "For many people, that means the standard of living that we are used to is going to have to decline in our remaining work years in order for us to have a decent standard of living in retirement."[17] In 1997, a *Workplace Pulse* survey indicated that as much as one-third of those surveyed expected their standard of living to decline in retirement.[18] Finally, sounding a note of significant concern, the 1997 Employee Benefit Research Institute's Retirement Confidence Survey concluded that: "Only 27 percent of working Americans have any idea of what they will need to accumulate in order to retire when and how they want. Only 36 percent, slightly more than one-third, have even tried to determine how much they need to save by retirement (only 21 percent of current retirees tried)."[19] Moreover, as amply demonstrated by a 1998 AARP publication, the situation is especially serious for women. They are twice as likely to be poor or near poor than men, and because they tend to earn less and spend fewer years in the workforce they also lag substantially behind men in the accumulation of assets for retirement.[20]

But why, we may ask, do American households now generally save less and less of disposable income? Only a few years ago, in 1992, the personal savings rate was an already meager 5.7 percent of income. The rate dropped to 2.1 percent in 1997 and to 0.5 percent in 1998.[21] In fact, in September 1998 the personal savings rate became negative for the first time since the 1930s. That is, people spent more than they earned after taxes.[22] Is it a matter of people not understanding the long-term implications of a failure to save for retirement? It would seem that this is not the case. The most basic answer appears to be that notwithstanding the more than doubling of aggregate household wealth between 1987 and 1998 the average family is drowning in debt. As of 1997, total household debt reached the unprecedented high of $5.4 trillion. The share of disposable income that the average household must pay to service its debts exceeds 18 percent, with families with low to moderate income paying substantially higher relative amounts. Information from the Federal Reserve Bank of New York indicates that, from 1989 to 1995, as the percent of households with credit cards increased from 56 to 67 percent, the share of cardholders with incomes below $25,000 increased from 22 to 28 percent. During the same period, the average credit card debt rose from $1,100 to $1,700, at the same time that the typical cardholder's liquid assets decreased more than 25 percent.[23]

Given these considerations, it should not come as a surprise for many workers, that concerns about retirement security have had to take a back seat to the more immediate problems of rising principal and interest payments that must be met. As one writer put it, "These folks are struggling just to stay ahead of the bill collector. Rising numbers of consumers are paying food and medical bills with credit cards. The upward spiral in personal bankruptcy rates suggests that this is not simply a matter of increased convenience, but rather a matter of pressing necessity."[24]

If, however, this trend toward diminished personal retirement savings continues in the years ahead, and there is little evidence to suggest that it will not, voluntary withdrawal from the labor force may soon become an unrealistic option for many aging workers. This will reverse the long-standing trend toward early voluntary retirement that has begun to level off in recent years, and which, according to some analysts, "seems to have come to an abrupt halt."[25] In fact, the labor force participation of persons aged 55 and older went up slightly in 1996 from what it was a decade earlier and is expected to increase by another 6.5 percent over the next decade. At the same time, the participation of persons aged 65 and older increased from 10.9 percent in 1986 to 12.1 percent in 1996 and is expected to rise to 12.6 percent by the year 2006.[26] It now seems rather clear that many older workers will have little choice but to remain in the workforce for longer periods of time. The critical question is whether they will be given the opportunity to do so, considering the dramatic changes that are currently taking place in the American economy.

As pointed out by Anthony Carnevale, chairman of the National Commission for Employment Policy, economic change in itself is nothing new. "What is new in this particular economic transition is the erosion of public confidence in the basic institutions customarily charged with guiding us safely through change. The persistent anxiety stems from a fundamental disconnect between the new economic realities and those institutions that prepare Americans for work, sustain them during their working lives, and provide for their retirement. As a result, Americans are anxious about their prospects and angry that the rules are changing in the middle of the game."[27]

In the pages that follow we will explore several aspects of these "new economic realities," the changes in the rules of the employment game, and their implications for the future economic wellbeing of an inexorably aging workforce.

NOTES

1. Paul J. McNulty, *The Origins and Development of Labor Economics* (Cambridge: MIT Press, 1980), p. 2.

2. Barbara Rudolph, *Disconnected: How Six People from AT&T Discovered the New Meaning of Work in a Downsized Corporate America* (New York: Free Press, 1998), p. 1.

3. "Americans and Welfare Reform: Work, Not Cost, Primary Issue," press release (Washington, DC: The Public Agenda Foundation, April 24, 1996).

4. Stan Hinden, "We're Retired—When We're Not at Work," *Washington Post*, December 13, 1998.

5. Peter Behr, "Program Taps NASA Retirees' Payload of Skills," *Washington Post*, September 29, 1998.

6. Roger Terry, *Economic Insanity: How Growth-Driven Capitalism Is Devouring the American Dream* (San Francisco: Berrett-Koehler Publishers, 1995), pp. 28–29.

7. William W. Winpisinger, *Reclaiming Our Future* (Boulder: Westview Press, 1989), pp. 150–151.

8. Employee Benefit Research Institute press release, April 17, 1997.

9. "Employee Benefits, Retirement Patterns, and Implications for Increased Work Life," *Issue Brief*, no. 184 (Employee Benefit Research Institute, April 1997).

10. Yung-Ping Chen, "Income Security for the Third Age," *Research Dialogues* (TIAA-CREF), no. 53 (December 1997), p. 6.

11. Dallas L. Salisbury, "Preparing for the Baby Boomers Retirement: The Role of Employment" (Washington, DC: U.S. Senate Special Committee on Aging , July 25, 1997).

12. "Working Americans' Retirement Savings Drop 34 Percent in Two Years," *Workplace Pulse,* press release (Colonial Life & Accident Insurance Company and the Employers Council on Flexible Compensation, December 6, 1994).

13. Lynnette Khalani, "Facing the Facts of Retirement," *Washington Post*, September 17, 1995.

14. Summary of survey results released on October 28, 1996.

15. Leslie Eaton, "Cloudy Sunset," *Barron's*, July 12, 1993, p. 8.

16. *Horizons* (Washington, DC: American Association of Retired Persons, February 1994), p. 4.

17. Albert B. Crenshaw, "When It Comes to Savings, There Is Still Much to Do," *Washington Post*, December 17, 1995.

18. Albert B. Crenshaw, "Younger Americans Saving More, Baby Boomers Less," *Washington Post*, December 9, 1997.

19. Employee Benefit Research Institute, press release, October 16, 1997.

20. "Saving for Retirement: How Are Women Doing?" *Working Age*, 14, no. 4 (November/December 1998).

21. Robert J. Samuelson, "'Hell No, We Won't Save!'" *Washington Post*, February 17, 1999.

22. "Saving Disgrace," *The Economist* (November 14, 1998), p. 80.

23. Gene Koretz, "A Rising House of Cards," *Business Week* (April 5, 1999).

24. Maria Fiorini Ramirez, "Americans at Debt's Door," *New York Times*, October 14, 1997.

25. Larry Williams, "Era of Early Retirement is History," *Denver Post*, November 30, 1997.

26. Bureau of Labor Statistics, *Monthly Labor Review* (November 1997), p. 28.

27. Anthony Carnevale, "Preface," *Declining Job Security and the Professionalization of Opportunity*, research report no. 95–04 (Washington, DC: National Commission for Employment Policy, May 1995), p. viii.

2

THE CHANGING EMPLOYMENT ENVIRONMENT

There is a certain relief in change, even though it be from bad to worse; as I have found in traveling in a stage coach, that it is often a comfort to shift one's position and be bruised in a new place.

—Washington Irving

One of the great promises of an increasingly high-technology and knowledge-based employment environment is the progressive elimination of the most onerous and tedious kinds of work. The combination of modern computers and industrial automation has significantly reduced the amount of physically demanding work in many occupational fields and routinely performs many of the repetitive and boring tasks that have tended to drive older workers from the labor force prematurely. It would therefore seem reasonable that more and more older workers would now choose to continue their employment, and thereby reduce the number of years in retirement for which they may lack sufficient income to maintain a desired standard of living. And, in fact, voluntary early retirement has leveled off and increasing numbers of older workers have indicated a desire to continue to be active in the labor force.

At the same time, however, that there have been positive changes in the nature of the work that growing numbers of employees of all ages are being asked to perform, other profound structural and attitudinal changes are reshaping the employment environment in unprecedented ways. Indeed, these changes promise to have dramatic long-term effects on our society, creating circumstances with which we presently appear to be ill equipped to cope. One of the more egregious of these changes, to be discussed at some length below, is an emerging trend toward growing involuntary partial or total withdrawal from the labor force. This tends to occur most frequently among increasingly younger mature workers, without regard to their potential for sustained economic viability as they age.

The critical changes taking place in the contemporary organization and design of remunerated work are all closely interrelated and, in the aggregate, constitute a virtual revolution in the nature of employment as it has been known in this country for most of the past century. They reflect a new approach to work and employment that is gaining growing acceptance in the business community as companies engage in a struggle for survival in increasingly competitive domestic and global markets for goods and services. This development and its impacts are being felt throughout the economy and also apply to the providers of many of those high value services that characterize the so-called information age.

The rapidity of the changes occurring in today's workplace contributes to a good deal of uncertainty if not confusion about the nature of the employment opportunities that will be available in the future. It is asserted by some that we are in the process of transitioning to a post-industrial society in which manufacturing, the production of tangible goods, will play a diminishing role in the creation of wealth, just as it already does in the creation of employment. According to the 1995 White Paper of the World Gold Council, "Several factors are responsible for today's chaotic environment, but by far the most powerful is a shift in the fundamental nature of our economic system. We are moving from a production-based industrial economy to an information-based network economy. And, as a result, the principles that have governed both business and society for the past two hundred years are becoming obsolete."[1]

Those who share this perspective tend to argue that the creation of wealth in the future will depend increasingly on the ability to develop and deliver high-value-adding services. The classical economic notion of wealth as the extent of one's tangible assets—the products of what is grown, mined, or manufactured—is no longer applicable or relevant. They assert that in the present and future economy, information rather than material goods will play the more highly valued role. Others reject this approach, insisting that the traditional notion of what constitutes wealth is as pertinent today as in the past, and will remain so in the future. Although this discussion may appear somewhat academic and remote from the prosaic realities of the contemporary world of business and employment, it is important to recognize that the underlying issue is not merely theoretical, one without practical consequences. At stake is the future of the national economy, and with it the future economic security of today's aging workforce and the families whose wellbeing is bound up with it.

One may be inclined to accept the validity of the World Gold Council's confident assertion that "in tomorrow's marketplace, information—gathered and transmitted through a vast network of interconnected computers—will be the most valuable currency of business." However, realism demands acknowledgment that no one has any true inkling as to when that "tomorrow" may be expected to begin. At present, the classical notion of wealth as a measure of tangible assets is still generally considered to be the basis of the monetary system, which is essentially a system designed to facilitate the exchange of quantifiable goods. Even though one may exchange money for ideas and information, the economic value of that exchange can only be assessed in terms of tangible goods that are grown, mined, or manufactured. It is as yet still very difficult to conceive of an economy that thrives on the basis of the exchange of one set of ideas and information for another.

It is noteworthy that even the World Gold Council implicitly acknowledges this in its statement that, "The companies that win will be those who most efficiently collect and use information to rapidly test new products, identify best-selling items, replenish stock and match marketing efforts to new consumer demands."[2] The fact is, the more an economy produces tangible and quantifiable goods, the more it can afford to exchange those goods for a wide variety of services, which include the creation, development, and transfer of ideas, knowledge, and information. Put differently, agriculture, mining, and manufacturing create the tangible wealth that the services sector of the economy, which includes high value knowledge and information services, redistributes. Or, as one industry consultant put it: "The service industries simply trade claims against already-created wealth."[3]

The issue is important because no one has yet satisfactorily explained how a society as large as that of the United States could conceivably sustain a high general standard of living that depended increasingly on the redistribution of the tangible wealth created by others instead of producing such wealth itself. I would suggest, however, that the prophets of the new economy are predicating their prognoses on the generally unstated assumption that the national economy of the United States is being subsumed into a world economy in which its advanced technological capabilities will give it a permanent comparative advantage. The problem, of course, is that there is little evidence that the nation, other than its international corporations, is prepared to allow anticipated but uncertain long term economic advantage to overshadow the political value assigned to American national independence and relative autarky for more than two centuries. As the European Union is positioning itself to compete directly with the United States in the very same areas of presumed comparative advantage, it might prove prudent to temper our post-industrial enthusiasm with some more sober thinking about the viability of our domestic economy under less favorable international circumstances.

The basis of America's substantial national wealth remains primarily in its enormous production of tangible goods. Indeed, productivity is so consistently high in agriculture and manufacturing that we can easily produce more than we can consume. Moreover, much of agriculture and manufacturing has been mechanized and automated. As a result, fewer and fewer workers are needed or employed in these high productivity sectors of the economy. This helps foster the illusion that, because so many more people are engaged in the provision of services than in the production of goods, it is the services sector of the economy that generates a major portion of our national wealth. Such an illusion is given legitimacy through our system of national accounting, which uses gross domestic product (GDP), the aggregate of goods and services produced, as the principal measure of national wealth.

Although there surely is some validity to the suggestion that certain high value information services are beginning to overshadow in perceived importance the traditional sources of wealth production in this and other industrialized countries, upon closer examination the proposition would appear to be somewhat overstated. After all, information is not very valuable in economic terms unless it can be conveyed to others in a usable form, and this usually involves the use of manufactured high technology products such as computers, modems, facsimile machines, optical readers, and other electronic devices. In other words, the distinction between information and material goods is not as clear as some contemporary theorists suggest. As a practical matter, the so-called information-based economy is predicated on the extensive and growing use of manufactured high-technology high-value products, without which the information itself might not exist or be available in many, if not most, cases. The fact is that the intellectual product of a hundred or more scientists, engineers, designers, and programmers may be incorporated into a miniscule computer chip that is relatively cheap to manufacture. Without that very tangible chip, the intellectual product itself would have very little, if any, exchange value.

The currently over-dramatized characterization of what constitutes wealth in the so-called information age also reflects a popular myth that tends to lead to a degree of complacency about contemporary developments in the economy. This myth views economic development as a decisive shift in the use of productive capacity from one dominant sector of the economy to another. Thus, agriculture is seen as having been replaced by industry, much of which is now being shifted to less developed economies as it is replaced in advanced societies by high-technology and value-added, knowledge-based services. However, critics of this formulation argue, "This is simply incorrect—as history and as policy prescription. America did not shift out of agriculture or move it offshore. We automated it; we shifted labor out and substituted massive amounts of capital, technology, and education to increase output."[4] And, they insist this is precisely what is happening in the industrial sector today.

Many of the value-added service jobs, which some suggest will replace lost manufacturing jobs, are actually complementary to, rather than alternatives for, goods-producing employment. In effect, these high-value-adding service jobs are tightly linked to manufacturing in the same way that crop dusting is linked to agriculture. They are, as one writer puts it, "functional extensions of an ever more elaborate division of labor in production. The shift we are experiencing is not from an industrial economy to a postindustrial economy, but rather to a new kind of industrial economy."[5]

Perhaps the most notable development in this new industrial economy over the past two decades has been the steady shift from labor-intensive industries to those that are increasingly knowledge-intensive, from the production of steel and machine parts to the manufacture of pharmaceuticals, electronic devices, and other high-technology products. It therefore seems increasingly likely, notwithstanding sporadic upsurges in domestic manufacturing employment, that labor-intensive production will continue to relocate to lower-cost labor markets, where companies with good management and trained workers have proven capable of producing high-quality goods.

What should be of even greater concern, however, are the long-term implications of the slow but continuing erosion of the domestic labor-intensive manufacturing sector for the complementary service jobs that are linked to the affected industries. As a rule of thumb, manufacturing industry analysts have asserted that each manufacturing job spawns as many as ten related service jobs, covering the range from marketing and sales to employee food service. If this industry estimate is generally reliable, the continuing shrinking of employment in the manufacturing sector can be expected to have a significant multiplier effect on the levels of unemployment and underemployment among those service-sector workers whose jobs remain contingent on labor-intensive manufacturing employment. It is noteworthy that, at this point, we do not know whether a similar purported relationship also exists within the service sector itself. In other words, we do not know how many related service jobs new computer-programming or investment-counseling jobs spawn.

Given what has already occurred in a number of low technology, labor-intensive industries, there is also reason to be concerned about the comparable movement of knowledge-intensive employment to lower-cost foreign labor markets, the serious economic consequences of which are already beginning to be experienced by some highly skilled domestic workers. As noted by economist Lester Thurow, "With our global economy, where anything can be made anywhere and sold everywhere, the supply of cheap, often well-educated labor in the third world is having a big effect on first-world wages."[6] For example, increasing numbers of computer software makers are already shifting software-programming work overseas to significantly lower cost high technology labor markets in Bulgaria, Russia, and India.

A 1995 report by the International Labor Office makes the reasons for the export of such high-technology jobs quite clear. "The comparative advantage that countries such as India possess in this line of activity is due to the investments of the country in higher education, which has produced information technology experts in large numbers and given the country a competitive advantage over others in terms of both efficiency and wage rates."[7] That such investment in higher education in the United States is lacking is evident in the common complaint of businesses, especially in the high technology field, that it is becoming increasingly difficult to recruit and retain skilled and well-trained workers. A 1998 Employment Policy Foundation report noted that "the greatest challenge that U.S. employers face with slow labor force growth and tight labor markets is meeting their needs for a higher skilled workforce. Thirty years ago, new entrants to the labor force typically had higher levels of education than the older workers who were retiring. That is no longer true . . . Improvements in skills sought by employers will have to come primarily through investments in the human capital of existing workers."[8]

Moreover, it has been asserted that many college graduates are entering the workforce with skills that are out of alignment with the needs of the contemporary workplace. This has led to expressions of serious concern about the American future by business spokesmen. Thus, Eric Stowe of the American Chamber of Commerce Executives offered the following prediction:

In the long-term, the mid 20th century profile of the United States being most competitive at the high skill level will be severely challenged by both our collective inattention to the educational needs of our domestic workforce, as much as by competition from external high-skilled labor forces. Because of this reality, local economies, and collectively the national economy, could face the prospect of declining competitive advantage which would have a deleterious effect on the overall economic well-being and quality of life of the community.[9]

This alleged shortage of technically qualified and skilled U.S. workers, itself a debatable proposition, suggests that if such workers were available in greater numbers the export of high technology jobs would diminish dramatically. According to one much-touted study, "If America is to retain these high-skilled, well-paying jobs (and not see them gravitate to places like Singapore, which are avidly bidding for them by upgrading the skills of local workers), more American workers will have to command the requisite workplace skills."[10]

There are at least two aspects of this alleged shortage that merit more critical examination. First, there is a problem of training and skills lagging technology. For example, in 1999 there was talk of a shortage of some 300,000 qualified network technicians and engineers to meet the burgeoning demand for business communication networks. The problem is that the technology involved is so relatively new that the company that is the leader in the field just recently began to decentralize its training and certification programs to a variety of educational institutions, including public high schools. Thus, there is a significant shortage, but it is clearly a temporary one. Second, the assumption that if the shortage was alleviated, assuming that there really is such a shortage, business would curtail the export of jobs abroad seems to contradict the realities of the contemporary business world. At the moment, the focus of American business clearly appears to be on reaping the benefits of lower wages overseas, even when the same skills are available domestically.

Robert Kuttner wrote in this regard, "the Vice President of GE told me he pays mid-level computer programmers about $80,000 a year, a good salary, but he can get the identical programming skills in India for $8,000 a year."[11] That this is more than a theoretical issue is made clear by a reliable press report that as of mid-1995 there were as many 75,000 Indian programmers working on computer programs destined primarily for the American market.[12] Indeed, by late 1998 there were numerous reports about thousands of low-cost software programmers in the city of Bangalore that were working for American companies to deal with the Y2K problem.

Moreover, one may reasonably anticipate further erosion of the current domestically lucrative field of software programming, if and when the outstanding issues with China about the piracy of intellectual property are resolved satisfactorily. (It is perhaps noteworthy that a first significant step in this direction occurred when the *China Daily* reported on February 15, 1999 that Microsoft had won a lawsuit against two Chinese companies that had illegally copied software for their own use.[13]) The tendency to move such highly sophisticated work to comparatively low wage foreign labor markets can be expected to accelerate significantly in view of the rapidly increasing availability of skilled workers in that country. It has been noted, for example, that tens of thousands of qualified software programmers are currently to be found just in the city of Beijing, skilled workers who would gladly work for only a fraction of the salaries typically received by programmers in the United States.[14]

Further exacerbating the problem in a growing number of instances, foreign technical workers are being trained on-the-job in the United States by the very people whose jobs they will subsequently take home with them to their countries of origin.[15] There is also a growing number of documented instances in which American companies are replacing well paid domestic workers with lower-cost foreign workers brought into the country under the HB-1 visa program. This program currently allows as many as 65,000 foreign computer programmers, engineers, scientists, and certain other specially qualified workers to enter the country each year on a "nonimmigrant" basis, for up to six years at a time. The rationale is to fill identified job vacancies in skill areas where there is supposed to be a shortage of qualified domestic workers. This alleged shortage has become a matter of contention between opponents and proponents of the special visa program. According to the AFL-CIO Executive Council, "Alarmist claims that our nation faces an extreme shortage of highly-skilled and professional workers to serve its growing information technology-based industries rest on studies initiated and supported by the very employers who stand to gain the most from an oversupply of I.T. [information technology] workers."[16]

Similarly, the AFL-CIO took strong exception to the attempt by some companies to take advantage of other guest worker immigration programs to hire foreign workers for jobs that can be adequately filled by domestic workers. A case in point was the attempt by the Avondale shipyard in Louisiana to seek HB-2 visas to hire foreign welders. "There is no convincing evidence of a shortage of welders. Avondale's efforts are a transparent effort to utilize immigration laws to pay substandard wages and are made even more outrageous by the firm's role as a major Navy contractor."[17]

Some suggest that there is no real shortage of appropriately qualified workers for most new jobs. Some 90 percent of the net increase of nearly 12 million newly employed adults between 1992 and 1998 had completed some college education and that more than half of them had earned at least a bachelor's degree. This contrasts dramatically with the situation in 1992 when only 53 percent of the workforce had some college education and a mere 27 percent held a bachelor's degree. Indeed, Robert Lerman of the Urban Institute argues that it is the availability of this educated domestic workforce that has kept wages from rising dramatically in the last few years. This is "because employers have not been facing the skill bottlenecks that normally set off inflationary wage-price spirals." [18]

At the same time, advocates for employers insist that the impact of the HB-1 program on domestic employment in the information technology field is negligible, claiming that only as few as 7,000 foreign scientists and technicians were employed through the mid-1990s. "On its face, it is hard to imagine that such a small number of temporary worker admissions could pose a significant threat to wages of U.S. workers in an occupation as large as IT, which has been and is expected to continue to grow rapidly."[19]

Nonetheless, the occasionally blatant corporate abuse of current immigration laws has been confirmed by the former Secretary of Labor, Robert Reich. "We have seen numerous instances in which American businesses have brought in foreign skilled workers after having laid off skilled American workers, simply because they can get the foreign workers more cheaply." A case in point is that of Sea-Land Services, a New Jersey-based shipping company that laid off 325 computer programmers, who earned an average annual salary of about $50,000, and replaced them with much lower-paid Filipino programmers supplied by a Manila-based software company.[20]

THE CONSEQUENCES OF A NEW ECONOMY

The immediate consequences of some of these far-reaching changes in the employment environment, changes that are taking place throughout the entire industrialized world to one degree or another, are increasingly frequent and result in extensive dislocations of workers coupled with di-minished prospects for their reemployment at previous levels of compen-sation. This has resulted in a downward pressure on earnings for large numbers of wage earners. The long-standing practice of paying above mar-ket wages in order to assure the retention of a skilled, competent, and loyal workforce—what labor economists refer to as "efficiency wages," which have historically contributed significantly to the economic well-being of many American workers—is rapidly disappearing from the work place. The current widespread fear of losing one's job has proven to be enough of a motivating factor for most employees to make the payment of premium wages unnecessary. As Robert Kuttner put it to a university audience, "In this economy almost no one has job security. Certainly not the traditional forms of job security—not factory workers, not corporate middle manag-ers, not doctors, nurses, school teachers, or civil servants. Just about any-body is vulnerable to be downsized, out-sourced, reengineered except, perhaps, college professors. The next time your economics professor tells you about the benefits of making labor markets more like product markets, you might want to suggest she set a good example by renouncing tenure and hiring a fresh graduate student at half the salary with twice the skills."[21]

The lack of traditional forms of job security has produced inordinately high anxiety levels in the workforce. A 1998 nationwide survey of workers indicated that 59 percent were very concerned and 28 percent were some-what concerned about job security in general, even though 55 percent said that they were very satisfied and 31 percent somewhat satisfied with their own job security. "People may be feeling more secure in today's strong labor market," concluded Carl E. Van Horn of Rutgers University, "but the percep-tion of declining job security in the economy is still very much alive."[22]

One highly significant outcome of the prevailing turmoil in the employ-ment arena is the growing number of workers who are structurally under- or unemployed, as well as others who have given up hope of finding suit-able employment and have dropped out of the labor force entirely. Many of these are mid-career and older experienced workers who often find it even more difficult than younger colleagues to discover an appropriate niche for themselves in a highly unstable employment environment. Moreover, it is not an unreasonable expectation that it may take as long as another two decades or more before the ongoing restructuring of business and the reorganization of work reach a relatively stable state. Accordingly, the greatest long term effects of these changes will be experienced by the baby boom generation that is now beginning to join the ranks of the older workforce in large numbers.

These workforce dislocations will effectively cause many displaced workers to face their mature years without adequate opportunities for meaningful and remunerative employment. Their situation may be exacerbated further by the concurrent loss of health, pension, and other employee benefits that have typically accrued to workers in the past as a consequence of their full-time permanent employment. This will result in seriously diminished prospects of economic security for these workers and their families.

It is important to note that these troubling developments are not confined to any particular category of worker or to any specific industry. Workers across the entire spectrum of the labor force are being affected by the turbulence in the contemporary employment environment. As one writer put it, "a changing economy is gradually linking educated managers and technicians with high-school-trained assembly-line workers and office clerks. The link is their common place in an increasingly competitive economy that no longer values workers as much as it once did. What they share, public opinion polls show, are feelings of uncertainty, insecurity and anxiety about their jobs and their incomes."[23] One such poll, conducted by the *Providence Journal* and Brown University, indicated that 58 percent of the workers surveyed felt that they were not sharing in their company's success; 42 percent said they were facing wage stagnation; and only half of the respondents thought their retirement would be as secure as that of their parents.[24]

The often dramatic changes taking place in the contemporary employment environment may be seen as manifestations of several fundamental trends that are unfolding simultaneously and interdependently to produce the traumatic effects that the workforce is currently experiencing. These trends include the radical restructuring of American business, the phenomenal growth of what has become known as the "contingent" or nontraditional workforce, and the unanticipated decline of the "corporate paternalism" that typified the past relationship of many employers to their employees.

NOTES

1. Cited in Oren Harari, "Let the Computers Be the Bureaucrats," *Management Review*, September 1996, p. 57.

2. Ibid., p. 59.

3. Kenneth J. McGuire, quoted by John J. Sheridan, "Manufacturing: The Global Economic Engine," *Industry Week*, May 20, 1996, p. 21.

4. Stephen S. Cohen and John Zysman, "The Emergence of a Manufacturing Gap," *Transatlantic Perspectives*, Autumn 1988, p. 9.

5. Ibid.

6. Lester C. Thurow, "Companies Merge; Families Break Up," *New York Times*, September 3, 1995.

7. *Promoting Employment*, Report of the Director-General, International Labour Conference, 82nd Session 1995 (Geneva: International Labour Office), p. 23.

8. "Major Challenge Facing Employers: A Higher Skilled Workforce," *E-Mail Trends* (Washington, DC: Employment Policy Foundation, November 16, 1998).

9. Eric Stowe, "Workforce—The Critical Challenge" (Address presented to the American Chamber of Commerce Executives, May 1998).

10. Richard W. Judy and Carol D'Amico, *Workforce 2020: Work and Workers in the 21st Century* (Indianapolis, IN: Hudson Institute, 1997), p. 16.

11. Robert Kuttner, "The New Economy: Where Is It Taking Us?" (Address presented at the Providence Journal/Brown University Public Affairs Conference, March 12, 1997).

12. Keith Bradsher, "Skilled Workers Watch Their Jobs Migrate Overseas," *New York Times*, August 28, 1995.

13. "The Politics of Piracy," *The Economist* (February 20, 1999), p. 64.

14. G. Pascal Zachary, "U.S. Software: Now It May Be Made in Bulgaria," *Wall Street Journal*, February 21, 1995.

15. G. Pascal Zachary, "Skilled U.S. Workers' Objections Grow As More of Their Jobs Shift Overseas," *Wall Street Journal*, October 9, 1995.

16. "No Shortage of High-Tech Workers" (Statement of the AFL-CIO Executive Council, March 20, 1998).

17. "Immigration and Guestworker Programs" (Statement of the AFL-CIO Executive Council, August 5, 1998).

18. Robert I. Lerman, "Wage Inflation? Not to Worry," *Washington Post*, October 26, 1998.

19. *Economic Bytes* (Washington, DC: Employment Policy Foundation, September 18, 1998).

20. William Branigin, "White-Collar Visas: Importing Needed Skills or Cheap Labor?" *Washington Post*, October 21, 1995.

21. Robert Kuttner, "The New Economy."

22. Carl E. Van Horn, quoted by Gene Koretz, "Which Way Are Wages Headed?" *Business Week*, September 21, 1998, p. 26.

23. Louis Uchitelle, "The Rise of the Losing Class," *New York Times*, November 20, 1994.

24. Cited in Kuttner, "The New Economy."

3

THE RESTRUCTURING OF AMERICAN BUSINESS

The law of the jungle is no longer valid, if it ever was. We all believe in stiff and healthy competition and many of us have learned that it does nobody any good to destroy his competitor. If we did not have the competition we would have to invent its equivalent. But we are also understanding with increasing realism that the well-being of worker and employer, of manufacturer and consumer, of economic and political life, are all bound up together.

—Erwin D. Canham

The ongoing transformation of the contemporary employment environment, and its desultory impact on large segments of the population, appears to be one of the possibly unintended but nonetheless predictable consequences of the fundamental restructuring of the nation's economic life that has been taking place for more than two decades. This restructuring has taken on two fundamental forms, financial and technological, both of which have significant implications for the labor force.

Rapid and often dramatic changes in corporate ownership structures and new organizational concepts produce intense pressures in financial markets to restructure. The United States underwent several waves of financial restructuring over the course of the twentieth century. Between 1896 and 1902, the corporate trend was toward horizontal mergers and acquisitions, raising concerns about the effects of monopoly power in the marketplace. From 1926 to 1933 the focus shifted to vertical integration of businesses through mergers and acquisitions to reduce uncertainty and transaction costs. From 1965 to 1969, the major emphasis was on the creation of conglomerates of unrelated businesses to smooth out corporate revenue streams. The notion that bigger was better became the conventional wisdom of the corporate world. However, around 1981 corporate leaders began to conclude that the earlier focus on diversification had produced adverse effects on the competitiveness of their firms. They reached the conclusion that they could improve their competitive position and profitability by divesting themselves of companies, divisions, and product lines that were peripheral to their core businesses. Corporations now began selling off many of the unrelated businesses that they had acquired in accordance with the earlier conventional wisdom, a process that is continuing into the twenty-first century.

To make a business or operation attractive to buyers, it was important to increase its profitability. This can be achieved most effectively and most quickly by cutting costs. Similarly, the best way for a business to avoid being sold off or, in the case of publicly held companies, being acquired through a hostile takeover, was to demonstrate that it would be difficult to raise its profitability. It became important to show that the acquiring company would derive no quick benefits from the acquisition. The best way to convey that message was to show that all the profit-consuming fat in the organization had already been trimmed before the takeover could be consummated. This would significantly reduce the attractiveness of the business to corporate raiders. And, since labor constituted about three-fourths of overall business costs, most of the trimming of fat would have to take place there.[1]

However, in contrast to earlier business restructurings, where production workers bore the brunt of the impact on employment, the new wave of reorganizations began to displace large numbers of white collar workers and managers as headquarters operations were reduced and many "back-office" functions were contracted out or eliminated.

With regard to technology-driven restructuring, it is noteworthy that a few far-sighted individuals, who foresaw and correctly assessed the labor force implications of what they called the "cybernation revolution," forecast this restructuring decades earlier. In March 1963, a group of distinguished scientists, economists, and academicians published an open letter to President John F. Kennedy in the *New York Times* that warned of the potential impact on the economy of the widespread use of computers and automation. They wrote: "A new era of production has begun. Its principles of organization are as different as those of the industrial era were different from the agricultural. The cybernation revolution has been brought about by the combination of the computer and the automated self-regulating machine. This results in a system of almost unlimited productive capacity which requires progressively less human labor."[2]

What precipitated this dramatic public expression of concern? Why did those scientists and economists believe this technological advance to be qualitatively different from the numerous others that had taken place over the course of the previous century? As Stephen Barley points out, we need to distinguish between two basic types of technological change. Most technological change is substitutional. That is, it allows "the replacement of an earlier technology with a more efficient successor," for example, the fountain pen for the nib and inkwell; the ballpoint for the fountain pen; and the jet for the propeller-driven plane. Technological substitutes have made work easier, reducing labor costs and providing for economies of scale. However, as Barley has said, "the effects of substitutional technologies tend to be confined to specific production processes within specific industries." Because of this, they have only limited impact on the economy as a whole. The second and much rarer type of technological change, which Barley calls "infrastructural," is very different in character. "In any historical era," Barley has noted, "infrastructural technologies form the cornerstone of a society's system of production. . . . When a society experiences a change in its infrastructure, far-reaching reverberations can be expected."[3] This happened in the eighteenth and nineteenth centuries with the Industrial Revolution as well as with the second industrial revolution of the late nineteenth and early twentieth centuries, when the use of electric power became widespread. The scientists who raised the alarm in 1963 foresaw the development of cybernation as the inevitable basis for another such infrastructural revolution that would have similar far-reaching reverberations. It would, in effect, permit industry to "replace its electromechanical infrastructure with a computational one."[4] Accordingly, when attempting to assess the impact of technological changes on the economy it is of utmost importance not to mistake an infrastructural technology for a substitutional technology.

Although President Kennedy became sufficiently concerned about the warning to establish a national Commission on Automation, Technology and Economic Progress to consider the implications of cybernation, the report of the commission was inconclusive and the matter was allowed to languish. The commission appears to have made the cardinal error of judging cybernation to be a substitutional technology instead of the infrastructural technology that it actually is proving to be. As a result, the problem that led that prominent group of thinkers to raise their voices in concern did not, as many hoped, go away. Instead, their predictions began to become transformed into reality, albeit not as quickly as originally anticipated. What they had not foreseen was the lag between the time when the potential of cybernation was recognized and when industry would begin to discover how to exploit that potential in the workplace. As Richard

Sennett observed, "it takes institutions a long time to digest the technologies they have ingested."[5] That is happening today at an accelerating rate. "Computers and robots are now doing the work of two or three people, helping to keep total wages in check and hold down inflation."[6]

Although we surely are still far from having exhausted the possible applications of cybernation to the world of work, there can be little doubt that we are already well past the point of no return on a path of radical and irreversible change. The seemingly inevitable modifications to the traditional relationship between production and labor in modern industrialized societies that have been precipitated by the cybernation revolution have also made it necessary to revise a number of long held assumptions that have underpinned conventional thinking about the universe of work and employment.

THE NEW SHAPE OF BUSINESS

Peter Drucker, perhaps the most influential business and management intellectual of the twentieth century, suggested that contemporary economic life has been restructured in a manner that challenges the utility of the analytical categories conventionally used to characterize the organization and functioning of a modern economy.

Economic growth can no longer come from either putting more people to work—that is, from more resource input, as much of it has come in the past—or from greater consumer demand. It can come only from a very sharp and continuing increase in the productivity of the one resource in which the developed countries still have an edge (and which they are likely to maintain for a few more decades): the productivity of knowledge work and of knowledge workers.[7]

In other words, the economic paradigm that we have long used as the intellectual framework for our assessments of the interplay of market forces and other social and economic factors can no longer serve as a reliable guide to understanding contemporary economic realities.

Within the newly reconfigured economy, the production of goods is becoming progressively more independent of the volume of labor devoted to the purpose than would be the case if that relationship had continued to function in accordance with the labor market assumptions of the traditional paradigm. This, in large measure, is a direct consequence of the increasingly effective use of both new and existing technologies to attain the persistent gains in productivity that have been realized over the past several decades. A given level of production is therefore achievable with consistently diminishing amounts of human labor. This has clearly proven to be the case in the computer industry itself, the driving force of the cybernation revolution, in which total employment declined by 26 percent between 1983 and 1995 and is expected to drop by another 25 percent by

2005.[8] One of the factors at work in the computer industry is the development of sophisticated software that is itself capable of producing in whole or in part other software programs. "Such technological progress increases productivity by requiring less labor; but in this case the labor to be eliminated is performed by skilled software engineers and programmers. In short, as the technology continues to develop, it can replace human labor in carrying out increasingly more complicated tasks."[9]

But, as argued by some observers, this does not appear to be very different from what has happened in the past. New or modified technologies have always had positive effects on productivity. Why then should we be particularly concerned about the consequences of the infusion of new technologies into the work place today? One response to this question is that what most distinguishes the present trend from what has occurred in the past is the relentlessness of the process. Whereas productivity gains in the past, with some exceptions resulting from the occasional introduction of some radically new or modified technologies, were primarily related directly to the *growth* of the workforce, in the present environment that relationship is deteriorating rapidly. Increases in productivity are becoming more and more related to factors other than the volume of labor which, generally speaking, is consistently declining in importance.

This process may be seen as having been at work in the agricultural sector of the economy. At the beginning of the twentieth century, agriculture still constituted the largest occupational category, with some 38 percent of the American labor force working on farms. By 1991, this number had been reduced to a mere 3 percent at the same time that agricultural productivity soared. The process repeated itself in the second half of the century in manufacturing, but this time at an even more accelerated pace.

Current productivity increases in the goods producing sector derive from a variety of factors, the most notable of which are advances in manufacturing technology, standardization of components and processes, and improvements in product design, all of which are being facilitated by the increasing sophistication of computers and automation. As a result, by 1993, the same volume of goods could be produced with less than two-fifths of the man-hours that would have been required in 1973. The implications of this for the workforce are rather far-reaching. According to Laurence C. Siefert, an AT&T vice president for manufacturing: "Manufacturing employment is primarily governed by technology, and new technology requires half the number of people in product assembly every six years."[10] He pointed out that AT&T's productivity increases averaged 10 percent a year for the preceding decade. In order to maintain a constant level of employment, it would be necessary for the company to increase its equipment sales by 10 percent a year. However, since its annual increase in equipment sales is only about half that amount, the number of AT&T employees engaged in equipment manufacture can be expected to continue to decline. For comparable reasons, there has been a net permanent loss of some 3 million jobs in the fields of manufacturing and mining since 1980, with no end of such manpower reductions in sight. To put this in a broader historical perspective, in 1950 nearly 40 percent of the American workforce was employed in manufacturing. By 1995 this number had dropped to less than 16 percent, and it is expected to decline further over the next several years to about 12 percent.

A Bureau of Labor Statistics (BLS) productivity report, the best in two decades, nonetheless exemplified this general trend for the year 2000. It reported a 7.1 percent increase in manufacturing productivity and a 6.0 percent growth in output, which was accompanied by a 1.1 percent drop in hours worked. In the general nonfarm business sector, there was a 4.3 percent increase in productivity and a 5.7 percent growth in output, accompanied by only a 1.3 percent increase in the hours worked.[11] Such data demonstrating the *inverse* relationship between productivity and employment are not at all unusual nowadays. Drucker therefore suggested that "we should stop looking at manufacturing employment as the economy's bellwether and should look at manufacturing output instead; as long as its volume continues to rise, the industrial economy is healthy almost regardless of employment."[12] In other words, as the labor component of productivity is diminishing in importance the capital component of productivity is growing in significance. The rub is that it is a lot easier to measure the productivity of labor than that of capital. It is for this reason that the available productivity data can be quite misleading for one who tries to obtain a reasonable picture of the contemporary American economy, particularly in comparison to other industrialized economies.

One of the unintended consequences of the effective uncoupling of labor from production is that it creates the possibility of a significant disjunction between the well-being of business and the well-being of the workforce. That is, business may prosper from the benefits of increased productivity at the same time that increasing numbers of workers become unemployed, underemployed, or experience wage loss, creating the anomaly described by Robert Reich, speaking as the Secretary of Labor: "In macroeconomic terms, the nation is prospering. But Americans do not live by macroeconomics. They live by home economics. They don't live by official statistics. They live by the number that matters most: the figure on their family paycheck. . . . Closing the gap between paychecks and profits is our great remaining challenge. The steady decline in the median wage and the widening gulf between the rich and the rest, threatens the stability and prosperity of our nation."[13] The issues of wages in the new economy and the growth of income inequality will be addressed at length in another chapter.

But, we may ask, why can we not sustain high levels of both employment and productivity simultaneously? The simple answer seems to be, as will be discussed in greater depth in the next chapter, that productivity is increasing at a relatively faster rate than production. In conditions under which the actual level of production or output may be artificially constrained as a result of external factors such as competition or market share limits, higher productivity per work hour will necessarily result in a diminished need for workers. Ultimately, this will cause a loss of employment for some and possibly an increase in underemployment for others who nonetheless may be retained by management for any of a variety of reasons. This situation has led some farsighted business executives to argue that current approaches to reinvigorating American manufacturing tend to miss the mark. This is because their emphasis is "on wealth maintenance through greater productivity—which gets translated by corporate management as laying off workers, rather than creating new wealth-enhancing strategies and new higher-paying jobs."[14] This argument implicitly recognizes that a growth in new, well-paying jobs is important for business because it is perhaps the only effective way to increase the domestic customer base for American products. It also suggests that it is more economically as well as socially beneficial to strive to expand wealth through increased production to satisfy growing market demand than to seek to maximize corporate profit through increased productivity alone.

The problem becomes clear when one considers the situation in the fall of 1998, following the "summer from hell" for the global economy. During that summer the American economy grew at a solid 3.3 percent rate at the same time that hourly wages rose 2.4 percent after inflation in a tight labor market. Profits, however, were declining despite the otherwise robust economy because of the practical inability to raise prices to keep up with the higher costs of production. This proved a boon for households that were receiving bigger paychecks and had more buying power because of the weak pricing of goods. In fact, households were pouring so much money into purchases that in September 1998, for the first time since the Department of Commerce started collecting the data in 1959, the savings rate was negative. The situation reflected what has been called a "reversal of fortunes between Corporate America and Household America."[15] However, instead of increasing production to meet the growing domestic demand, corporations began to cut back in order to increase their flagging profit margins and thereby reduce the pressure from an unforgiving Wall Street, even at the cost of slowing economic growth. By the end of October of that year, more than a half million job cuts were announced, and some 50,000 manufacturing jobs had already been lost. The irony of the situation is that, "With the trade deficit widening rapidly, manufacturing activity slowing for the past five months in a row, and capital spending slackening, the economy would be in a real down-draft were it not for freewheeling consumers."[16] However, even with regard to the latter the picture was darkening. By the end of the third quarter of 1998 the annual rate of wage growth had slowed to 2.8 percent, only about a half percent ahead of infla-tion. At that rate, real wages were not keeping pace with the growth in pro-ductivity.[17]

Although the preceding discussion has tended to focus on what may be characterized as the "paradox of productivity" in the manufacturing sector, these same trends are already becoming evident in the services sector, in which some 80 percent of the American workforce is employed. However, in considering developments in the growing services sector, it is important to recognize that "services" is a category that encompasses at least two very distinct subcategories. As Stephen Barley points out, "A crucial distinction must be made between 'jobs that most people can do for themselves but no longer want to' and 'jobs that most people couldn't do for themselves even if they tried.'"[18] The first category tends to include low-skill jobs, such as lawn care or those found in the fast-food industry. The second category tends to include high-skill jobs, such as health care delivery, legal services, financial management, and other professional and technical jobs requiring specialized education and training.

These two subcategories of service workers, as different as they are, are both being affected by changes in the employment environment, albeit for rather different reasons. The demand for "jobs that most people can do for themselves but no longer want to" will be affected primarily by the state of the overall economy. As long as large numbers of people continue to have the disposable income to avoid doing things that they prefer having others do for them, demand for low-skill service workers will be high. The situa-tion could change dramatically, however, should there be a significant turn-down in the economy. When money is tight, people mow their own lawns and prepare their own sandwiches.

Although the need for high-skill services is clearly growing, the employ-ment of high-skill workers may nonetheless be affected by rapid changes in technology, changes that may enable many people to do things for them-selves that they could not have done earlier. The average person need no longer turn to an accountant for tax-preparation or to an attorney for pre-paring a will. Inexpensive computer programs enable many people to do these things for themselves. The dramatic increase of high-value services on the Internet—from booking reservations to investing in the stock mar-ket—may be expected to have significant impact on the numbers of profes-sional service providers needed to satisfy customer demand. And even the number of service professionals in other service fields will be affected by the growing globalization of the economy and the workforce.

A report by the *Wall Street Journal* suggested that, "Much of the huge U.S. service-sector seems to be on the verge of an upheaval similar to that which hit farming and manufacturing, where employment plunged for years while production increased steadily." Technological developments are tak-ing place at such a rapid pace in the services sector that companies are able to "shed far more workers than they need to hire to implement the technology or support expanding sales."[19] The dilemma for the country, however, is that at present there is no other private sector of the economy that can absorb the growing numbers of workers that may be expected to be displaced from the service-sector.

But, if the employment picture is as described above, how can one explain the increasingly tight labor market that has persisted from 1999 to the present, with unemployment having dipped to the lowest level in almost three decades? One answer to this question may strike the reader as counterintuitive. It is simply that, despite the remarkable developments in high-technology, which we might expect would reduce the need for labor, the costs of the capital needed to take advantage of that technology have risen substantially faster than the costs of labor. The result has been that for the last decade there has been a deceleration in the rate at which business has been increasing its use of capital in production.[20] This may be the critical factor that explains why there was such a tight labor market at the beginning of the twenty-first century. Will this continue into the decades ahead? "In thinking about the future of work in America it is critical to realize that the increase in employment has come about because the growth of wages has been meager. And those who are raising loud hosannahs to high-employment in the mid-1990s are neglecting the disturbing fact that job growth has been high because wage growth has been extremely slow. The implication is that . . . employment has risen in the United States mainly because labor is cheap as compared to capital."[21] And, if this is the case, unless wages are kept depressed capital will become relatively cheaper and we will see substantial increases in worker displacement and unemployment.

Employment and the Small Business

The continuing restructuring and downsizing of large corporations, and their outsourcing of many functions, often to small specialized firms, has led many to believe that it is the small business entrepreneur who holds the key to the creation of the employment opportunities of the future. Indeed, entrepreneurship is currently being vigorously promoted as a principle means of creating niche employment markets for many displaced workers. Emphasizing this perception, President Ronald Reagan stated in 1985: "We have lived through the age of industry and the age of the giant corporation. But I believe that this is the age of the entrepreneur." A decade later, this idea seems to have caught fire in the global economy. As Bennett Harrison put it, "The story line was simple and straightforward: Small was bountiful. Small was beautiful. Small was *in*. Only it was not—and is not—true."[22]

A case in point is Korea, a major U.S. trade partner, which is undergoing a major restructuring of its economy triggered by the East Asian financial crisis of 1998. In its efforts to reduce the power of the giant conglomerates that have driven the Korean economy for decades, the government is looking to small business to fill the vacuum. Small businesses, about 2.5 million in 1999, and growing at the rate of some 2,000 a month, account for about half of Korea's GDP and employ two-thirds of the workforce. The cautionary note in this robust development is that "the ratio of new small businesses (excluding shops) to bankruptcies has hit record levels."[23] The data suggest that the large growth of small business may not be quite the employment panacea that enthusiasts claim it to be.

The limited U.S. data currently available seem to bear out the job generating capacity of small business. Between 1987 and 1992, 16.9 million new jobs were created by firms with fewer than 100 employees as compared with 5.1 million jobs created by companies employing more than 1000 workers.[24] Indeed, according to a September 1994 news release from the Small Business Administration (SBA), the smallest businesses (0–4 employees) created 2.6 million net new jobs between 1989 and 1991, whereas large companies (500+ employees) created a mere 122,000 jobs during the same period. But, as pointed out by the SBA's Chief Counsel for Advocacy: "The disturbing aspect of these new data is that all the other small business size categories—those with between 5 and 499 employees—showed net job losses during this period. Without the growth and expansion of the firms with 0 to 4 employees, the recession would have been much worse, and there could have been over 2 million more unemployed workers."[25] However, to put these data in perspective, it should be noted that although firms with 0 to 4 employees represent some 58 percent of all business establishments, in 1992 they employed only about 6 million workers or 7 percent of the private labor force. By contrast, about 44 percent of workers in the private sector, some 40 million people, were employed by organizations with 100 or more employees which represented only 2 percent of all private business establishments.[26]

Small business employment information for the period 1991 to 1995 also indicates that the bulk of overall job creation took place in small businesses. According to an SBA fact sheet, "From 1991 to 1995, based upon Dun and Bradstreet data by firm size, virtually all net new jobs were generated by small firms with fewer than 500 employees; large companies continued to downsize, and separations exceeded hires. Small microbusinesses with 1 to 4 employees generated about 35 percent of the net new jobs, while firms with 5 to 19 employees created another 32 percent of new employment opportunities."[27] In other words, 67 percent of all new jobs during that period were generated by businesses employing less than 20 workers.

However, one must use extreme caution in making use of such national data to draw conclusions about the role of small business as the solution to the problems of the contemporary labor market. As the SBA itself noted, "The small business share of net new jobs increases most rapidly during the recovery stage of a cycle, and during the earlier parts of the expansion phase of a cycle. As the economy approaches full employment during the latter stages of an expansion, larger firms tend to produce a larger share of jobs, while the small business share falls somewhat."[28] Indeed, it has been pointed out that, in 1992, at the beginning of the present business recovery, this thesis was already clearly demonstrable in the financial sector, including insurance and real estate, two fields with many small firms. In this sector, small firms accounted for some 98 percent of all businesses, but for less than one third of employment and less than one-fifth of total sales revenues. By contrast, financial, real estate, and insurance firms employing 500 or more employees made up only seven-tenths of one percent of businesses in the financial sector but accounted for 57 percent of employment and 72.3 percent of sales.[29]

Moreover, because much of what we know about small businesses derives by inference from the aggregate of reports filed by such firms on a state-by-state basis, there is double-counting whenever a firm operates or employs workers in more than one state. Another consideration of some importance is reflected in a report by the Inspector General of the Small Business Administration on the matter of channeling SBA loans to high-growth industries as an approach to increasing small business employment. "The available evidence indicates that only a small percentage of firms in any given industry accounts for most of its job growth; therefore, focusing business loans on industries believed to have high job growth potential may not, in fact, result in significant job creation. Identifying in advance the relatively few firms likely to create most of the jobs is difficult due to such uncontrollable factors as the highly volatile nature of businesses and the employment they create."[30]

The clear implication of all this is that small business as such may not be the job generator it is generally assumed to be, and that only a relatively small number of high growth firms account for much of the employment growth usually attributed to small business as a whole. Moreover, since the bulk of small business job creation is in the lower wage end of the service-sector such as retail sales and the food and beverage industry, it tends to be very local in nature. Workers displaced from well-paying jobs in large firms are unlikely to go through the expense and social disruption of relocating in order to obtain such comparatively lower-paying and inherently less stable employment.

There is also substantial evidence that small businesses destroy jobs at a much higher rate than large employers, and that they also experience such a high business failure rate that many of the jobs they do create turn out to be temporary in nature. According to the SBA, between 1989 and 1995, some 2.9 million small businesses were created and about 2.6 million failed.[31] A 1994 study conducted by the Census Bureau's Center for Economic Studies examined job destruction in the manufacturing sector. It found that "the job destruction rate averages 18.8 percent of employment per year for firms with fewer than 20 employees, 9.8 percent for firms with 500–999 employees, and 8.0 percent for firms with 50,000 or more employees."[32]

It has been estimated that 40 percent of the jobs identified in the Small Business Administration's database in 1980 were no longer in existence six years later. The authors of the Census Bureau study concluded, "newly created jobs by small employers are less likely to survive for one or two years than newly created jobs by larger employers." Moreover, "both existing and newly created jobs are less secure at small businesses than at large businesses, and once lost, small-business jobs are less likely to reappear."[33] These data are corroborated further by a 1991 study of business survival rates carried out for the Small Business Administration. It showed that the survival rate for businesses with 50 or more employees was double that of firms with 1 to 4 employees, and that the business survival rate tended to increase with the size of employment.[34]

In addition to these concerns about the extent and continuity of the employment opportunities created by small companies, there is also the issue, introduced earlier, of the levels of compensation offered through such employment. Small companies tend to pay significantly lower wages and salaries than large businesses, an average of about 30 percent less. There is even a greater disparity when the availability of employee benefits is taken into consideration. This is particularly true with respect to the provision of employer-financed health benefits, since large employers are able to take advantage of their high-volume purchasing power to obtain such benefits for their employees at lower rates than would normally be available to small companies.[35] The 1997 Economic Report of the President stated, in this regard, that "currently almost 15 percent of re-employed workers who had health insurance at their old jobs receive no such coverage from their new employers. However, this represents a considerable improvement from the early 1980s, when over one-quarter of previously insured displaced workers did not receive health insurance at their new jobs. Nevertheless, the costs of displacement are substantial for a large number of workers."[36] It therefore seems clear that although a large number of workers may be re-employed by small businesses after having been dislocated from jobs in larger firms, from which they received paid health benefits, the terms and conditions of such employment leave much to be desired.

The differences between employment by small and large establishments appear starkest when considering pension benefits. Although about 22 percent of full-time employees in small establishments participated in defined benefit pension plans, approximately 59 percent of full-time employees in large establishments participated in such plans.[37] Consequently, although small businesses may continue to offer the greatest number of job opportunities in the foreseeable future, those jobs offer significantly diminished prospects for personal economic security and stability, now and in the future.

Finally, the shift in job creation from large to small and frequently new businesses has an anomalous consequence for older workers. Small new businesses tend to emerge in competitive industries characterized by rapid development and change, and therefore offer employment opportunities primarily to people with the necessary skills, having very little capacity to provide the retraining required by many older workers displaced from more traditional industries and occupations.

As a practical matter, it is primarily the large firms, which are downsizing and restructuring, that have the wherewithal to provide the training and retraining required by the smaller businesses, which are proliferating. Although there were attempts in the 1980s to form industry-wide consortia to provide such retraining, with the sponsorship and support of major private foundations, this approach has never been pursued beyond the creation of a few local consortia of small businesses and education-and-training institutions.

NOTES

1. Peter Cappelli and Michael Useem, "The Different Forces and Faces of Business Restructuring," in *Through a Glass Darkly: Building the New Workplace for the 21st Century*, ed. James Auerbach (Washington, DC: National Policy Association, 1998), pp. 18–19. See also, Michael Useem and Peter Cappelli, "The Pressures to Restructure Employment," in *Change at Work*, eds. Peter Cappelli et al. (New York: Oxford University Press, 1997), pp. 32–38.

2. Cited in Jeremy Rifkin, *The End of Work* (New York: Putnam, 1995), pp. 81–82.

3. Stephen A. Barley, *The New World of Work* (London: British-North American Committee, 1996), p. 23.

4. Ibid., p. 24.

5. Richard Sennett, *The Corrosion of Character* (New York: W.W. Norton, 1998), p. 96.

6. John A. Challenger, "There Is No Future for the Workplace," *The Futurist*, October 1998, p. 17.

7. Peter Drucker, "The Future That Has Already Happened," *The Futurist*, November 1998, p. 16.

8. James C. Franklin, "Industry Output and Employment Projections to 2005," *Monthly Labor Review*, November 1995, p. 53.

9. Richard W. Judy and Carol D'Amico, *Workforce 2020: Work and Workers in the 21st Century* (Indianapolis, IN: Hudson Institute, 1997), pp. 19–20.

10. Cited in Louis Uchitelle, "Job Losses Don't Let Up Even as Hard Times Ease," *New York Times*, March 22, 1994.

11. "Productivity and Costs: Fourth Quarter and Annual Averages, 2000," USDL 01–56 (Washington DC: U.S. Department of Labor, Bureau of Labor Statistics), March 2001.

12. Peter F. Drucker, *Managing for the Future: The 1990s and Beyond* (New York: E. P. Dutton/Truman Talley Books, 1992), p. 134.

13. Robert B. Reich, "Frayed-Collar Workers in Gold-Plated Times: The State of the American Workforce 1995" (address to the Center for National Policy, Washington, DC, August 31, 1995).

14. John H. Sheridan, "Reengineering Isn't Enough," *Industry Week*, January 17, 1994.

15. James C. Cooper and Kathleen Madigan, "Don't Be Fooled by the Strong Data," *Business Week*, November 16, 1998, p. 39.

16. Aaron Bernstein, "A Strong Economy Needs Strong Wages," *Business Week*, November 16, 1998, p. 56.

17. "Jobs Picture" (Washington, DC: Economic Policy Institute), November 6, 1998.

18. Barley, *The New World of Work*, pp. 8–9.

19. "Retooling Lives: Technological Gains Are Cutting Costs and Jobs in Services," *Wall Street Journal*, February 24, 1994.

20. Lawrence Mishel, Jared Bernstein, and John Schmitt, *The State of Working America 1996–1997* (Armonk, NY: M.E. Sharpe, 1997), p. 22.

21. William Wolman and Anne Colamosca, *The Judas Economy: The Triumph of Capital and the Betrayal of Work* (Reading, MA: Addison-Wesley, 1997), pp. 78–79.

22. Bennett Harrison, *Lean and Mean: The Changing Landscape of Corporate Power in the Age of Flexibility* (New York: Guilford Press, 1997), p. 38.

23. "Worker Bosses," *The Economist*, March 6, 1999, p. 62.

24. "The Changing World of Work and Employee Benefits," EBRI Issue Brief Number 172 (Washington, DC: Employee Benefit Research Institute), April 1996, p. 10.

25. "New Data Show Smallest Firms are Nation's Greatest Job Creators," SBA 94–17 ADVO (Washington, DC: U.S. Small Business Administration), September 30, 1994.

26. William J. Wiatrowski, "Small Businesses and Their Employees," *Monthly Labor Review*, October 1994, p. 30.

27. "Facts About Small Business" (Washington, DC: U.S. Small Business Administration, Office of Advocacy, 1997).

28. Ibid.

29. Bennett Harrison, "The Dark Side of Business Flexibility," *Challenge*, July-August 1998, p. 120.

30. "Job Creation and the 7(A) Guaranteed Loan Program," Inspection Report (Washington, DC: U.S. Small Business Administration, Office of the Inspector General), November 1994.

31. Gene Koretz, "Cycles of Death and Rebirth," *Business Week*, November 16, 1998, p. 26.

32. Steven J. Davis, John C. Haltiwanger, and Scott Schuh, "Gross Job Flows in U.S. Manufacturing" (Washington, DC: U.S. Department of Commerce, 1994), p. 6.

33. Ibid., p. 25.

34. Joel Popkin et al., "Business Survival Rates by Age Cohort of Business," Small Business Research Summary—RS no. 122 (Washington, DC: U.S. Small Business Administration), n.d.

35. Kenneth Labich, "The New Unemployed," *Fortune*, March 8, 1993.

36. "Economic Report of the President," H. Doc. 105–002 (Washington, DC: U.S. House of Representatives), 1997.

37. Wiatrowski, "Small Businesses and Their Employees," p. 33.

4

GLOBALIZATION OF THE ECONOMY

If the economist's guiding principle of the rational pursuit of self-interest is to be believed, the extent of opposition to NAFTA should itself have been sufficient to cast doubt on the claim that the agreement would benefit the public.
—Thomas I. Palley

The effects on employment resulting from the uncoupling of labor from production have been exacerbated by the emergence of an increasingly globalized economy that includes an expanding global labor market. This is a relatively new development the implications of which appear to be poorly understood. In the past, when capital moved from the developed world to the underdeveloped or developing world, labor tended to move with it to a significant extent. American managers and skilled workers were relocated to office and plant sites wherever American capital went to assure that productivity goals were met. This is no longer the case. "In the old global economy, capital and labor moved together. In the new global economy, developed world capital globe-trots in a freewheeling way that was never before possible."[1]

As indicated earlier, there is a rapidly growing pool of skilled labor in many parts of the developing world that is comparable in many qualitative respects to the domestic American workforce and more competitive in terms of cost. The situation, as described by former labor spokesman

Thomas R. Donahue, is that "the world has become a huge bazaar with nations peddling their workforces in competition against one another, offering the lowest prices for doing business."[2]

In a growing number of instances, it is no longer essential for factories and certain kinds of service facilities to be located at any particular geographic location because of the availability there of large numbers of appropriately trained workers. It is becoming neither necessary nor expedient in a growing number of cases to manufacture goods domestically and then export them abroad. Today, production facilities can be located virtually anywhere in the world that provides an optimum trade-off between the costs of labor, transportation, and inventory, in serving a particular segment of the global market.

To some extent, this flexibility in location has also become feasible, because of advances in the fields of communications and transportation, for certain kinds of high-value-added services such as financial operations and other knowledge-based activities. "Informatics, of which computer-mediated processes are the most common in financial, retail, and wholesale services, permit production and services to be dispersed throughout the globe with impunity."[3]

This reality, however, is still being ignored by those who predicate their arguments on the rather rosy projections of future employment from the Bureau of Labor Statistics, which suggest that there will be 151 million jobs in the United States by 2006 and only 141 million people employed. This has led outplacement specialist John Challenger to state with unbounded optimism: "I see a future economy with continued worker shortages created by consumer demand, coupled with an employment population too small to meet it. The next generation of workers will continue to be a scarce commodity for employers."[4] The predicted consumer demand may possibly be there, but it is by no means certain, except for primarily low-value services, that such demand will be fulfilled through domestic employment. In this new global economic environment, as one writer describes it,

Companies are portable, workers are throwaway. The rise of the knowledge economy means a change, in less than 20 years, from an overbuilt system of large, slow-moving economic units to an array of small, widely dispersed economic centers, some as small as the individual boss. In the new economy, geography dissolves, the highways are electronic. . . . Companies become concepts and in their dematerialization, become strangely conscienceless. And jobs are almost as susceptible as electrons to vanishing into thin air.[5]

A case in point is Wall Street, that is, the concentration of exchanges and brokerages in the small area of Manhattan that could conceivably relocate elsewhere. In this regard, it is noteworthy that in late 1998 the state and city of New York were planning to pay up to $450 million to build a new trading area for the New York Stock Exchange, in addition to granting it $160 million in tax concessions. All this in order to keep the Exchange from moving away from Wall Street, where it has been for more than 200 years, and thereby retaining the thousands of jobs associated with it.[6]

Consumer advocate Ralph Nader similarly expressed concern over the labor market implications of increased globalization when asked to project the implications of current business trends over the next twenty-five years. "Industrial companies are more reliant [than was the case previously] on global economic forces and trends which . . . will lead to exporting more jobs to cheap-but-skilled labor using modern equipment in foreign countries." However, he also suggested that this might well entail serious political and economic implications for business. "The loss of allegiance to their country of origin and the mobility of capital will affect many large multinationals and raise serious questions of job flight—both blue collar and white-collar—in the political arena, especially for companies receiving corporate welfare from the local, state, and federal government."[7]

This issue is not yet the subject of any significant public discussion or debate, but is likely to become one in the next few years if the concerns about job flight materialize. Suffice it to note at this point that at the time that the vote on the North American Free Trade Agreement (NAFTA) was being considered by the Congress in November 1993, President Clinton asserted that, if the trade agreement passed, "we estimate America will add another 200,000 jobs by 1995 alone." The reality, however, is that by September 30, 1995 there was a documented loss of 42,331 jobs. This was widely acknowledged to be a conservative figure because it only included those who applied and had been found eligible, as a consequence of trade-related job displacement, for government job training, search, and placement assistance.[8] As of February 10, 1997, the Department of Labor certified that 107,632 workers had lost their jobs either because production had been shifted to Mexico and Canada, or because of increases in imports from those countries.[9] A year later, the official figure almost doubled to 210,000 job losses attributable to the treaty.[10] Independent analyses, however, suggest that almost 400,000 jobs had been lost by the end of the third year after NAFTA went into effect on January 1, 1994.[11] A subsequent study by the Economic Policy Institute suggested that between 1994 and 2000 as many as 766,030 actual and potential jobs were lost "because of the rapid growth in the net U.S. export deficit with Mexico and Canada."[12]

The conventional assumption is that these job losses were overwhelmingly in low-skill occupations and in labor-intensive low technology industries. However, the reality is that many of those certified by the Department of Labor as having lost their jobs because of trade-related factors came from high technology firms such as General Electric and Hughes Aircraft. It is also noteworthy that in February 1997, French-owned Thomson Electronics announced that it was closing its U.S. plants and moving its operations to Mexico.

It is indisputable that NAFTA has transformed the economy of Mexico, making it in effect a low-cost industrial power serving primarily the U.S. and Canadian markets. Moreover, "free trade with the U.S. and Canada is turning the country from a mere assembler of cheap, low-quality goods into a reliable exporter of sophisticated products, from auto brake systems to laptop computers. Since 1993, exports have more than doubled, to $115 billion. Manufactured goods now make up close to 90% of Mexico's sales abroad, up from 77% five years ago." Foreign investment in the country has more than doubled since NAFTA went into effect, the biggest attraction being Mexico's low-cost labor, averaging $1.60 an hour in manufacturing in 1998.[13]

Perhaps somewhat ironically, NAFTA may also be having a negative effect on employment in Mexico itself. According to Wayne Cornelius of the Center for U.S.–Mexican Studies at the University of California, San Diego, "since 1990, large-scale urban producers in Mexico have been restructuring (shedding labor) to become viable competitors in the liberalized North American trade arena." He asserts that this has resulted in the loss of hundreds of thousands of jobs.[14] At the same time, a survey of labor costs in the textile industry indicates that while hourly pay rates in the United States rose from $11.89 in 1994 to $12.18 in 1995, those in Mexico dropped from $3.22 to $2.27.[15] As indicated above, Mexican hourly pay rates in manufacturing appear to have dropped even further since 1995. Moreover, a 1995 study projected that, as a result of the "Uruguay Round" of the General Agreement on Tariffs and Trade (GATT), the United States would likely experience a long-term loss of some 36 percent of current job opportunities in light industry, primarily in clothing and textiles.[16] Carlos Salas of La Red de Investigadores y Syndicalistas Para Estudios Laborales (RISEL) summed up the situation in Mexico at the end of the twentieth century. He noted: "Official unemployment levels are lower now than before NAFTA, but this decline in the official rate simply reflects the absence of unemployment insurance in Mexico. In fact, underemployment and work in low-pay low-productivity jobs . . . actually has grown rapidly since the early 1990s." These and other considerations led him to conclude, "After seven years, NAFTA has not delivered the promised benefits to workers in Mexico, and few if any of the agreement's stated goals have been attained."[17]

Further compounding the problem for U.S. workers is the growing transfer of high technology and related jobs to newly industrializing countries as the price of entry into their markets. A case in point was the agreement by the Boeing Corporation to manufacture part of the airframes for their aircraft being sold to China in that country. It seems highly likely that China will use the transferred technology to assist it in developing its own aircraft industry to compete with Boeing both domestically and internationally. Nonetheless, corporate short-term bottom line interests seem to have overridden concerns about the longer-term implications of such technology transfers to managed trade countries. This particular transaction triggered a strike by some 33,000 Boeing workers who saw it as placing their jobs in jeopardy. As a spokesman for the striking workers put it: "Whether through arrogance, complacency or shortsightedness, we have consistently underestimated the ability of the rest of the world to be a serious commercial competitor in a high-tech industry."[18]

This situation, in the view of Peter Drucker, is the result not of economics or technology, but demographics. "The key factor for business will not be the *over*population of the world. . . . It will be the increasing *under*population of the developed countries. . . . The developed world is in the process of committing collective national suicide. Its citizens are not producing enough babies to reproduce themselves." A consequence of this is that those who believe that the United States can maintain its position as the dominant world economic power are deluding themselves, "because no developed country has the population base to support such a role. There can be no long-term competitive advantage for any country, industry, or company, because neither money nor technology can, for any length of time, offset the growing imbalances in labor resources." As amply demonstrated in East and Southeast Asia, "the training methodologies developed during the two world wars—mostly in the United States—now make it possible to raise the productivity of a preindustrial and unskilled manual labor force to world-class levels in virtually no time." [19]

It is highly significant that the size of the world's labor force has more than doubled from 1.2 billion to 2.7 billion workers since 1950, far outstripping growth in the number of jobs. It has been estimated that more than an additional 1.9 billion jobs will have to be created in the developing world alone over the next 50 years just to maintain current levels of employment. This had led some to assert that while population growth may boost the demand for labor, it will most assuredly increase the supply of labor. As population growth tips the balance in favor of the supply of labor over demand, the resulting labor surplus will have a significant impact on the well-being of workers. In such a situation, workers will have little bargaining power and will be compelled to accept whatever work is available, work longer hours for less pay and fewer benefits, and have even less control over their work lives.[20] Add to this the increasing technical competence of comparatively low-wage surplus workers in the *developing* world and it is plain to see the potential implications for workers in the *developed* world. "The magnitude of the global increase in workers available for global market production since the end of the cold war has yet to sink in, either in the intellectual community or among average Americans."[21]

The growing globalization of the economy is therefore having highly significant consequences, some quite unintended, for the organization and functioning of business, as well as for the economic stability and well-being of the workforce. For one thing, the relative ease with which capital and technology can be transferred across international borders has effectively severed the linkages between high technology, high productivity, and high wages. It is now possible, according to Klaus Schwab, president of the World Economic Forum, to have high technology, high productivity, and *low wages*.[22]

An example of this that seems certain to become a significant development in the years ahead is the emergence of centers of high value services provided by major American corporations that are located in India. GE Capital's international services division, dealing with mortgages and credit accounts, is located outside Delhi and grew from 50 to 700 employees in 1998 and is adding workers at a rate of 100 a month. Selectronic, a firm that has been operating in India for several years, takes doctors' dictation through a toll-free number, transcribes the recordings, and sends the results back as text to an American HMO. These are but two of a growing number of similar remote service operations to be found in the country. As the *Economist* noted in 1999, "Remote services may be a market in which India can beat the world. It has a vast population, rock-bottom wages, and a good grasp of English. . . . Many of those employed in the remote-services business would be deemed overqualified in the West. A certified public accountant working on account conciliation costs GE $15,000–20,000 a year. In America, a less qualified worker doing the same job would cost up to three times as much."[23] It has been estimated that the remote services business centered in India alone will be worth as much as $50 billion by 2010.

The implications of economic globalization for the labor force may perhaps best be understood by considering what is happening in other industrialized countries. Faced by relatively high domestic labor costs, according to a survey of 10,000 firms conducted by the German Chamber of Commerce and Industry, in 1993 some 30 percent of German manufacturers planned to shift some production out of the country to lower cost labor markets, primarily in Eastern Europe. As a result, German companies will have created about 250,000 jobs abroad annually for the of next several years.[24] This trend is particularly noticeable in the German automobile industry, which slashed its domestic workforce by 20 percent between 1991 and 1995, and is moving the development and production of many new models out of the country to lower cost labor markets.[25] Moreover, a 1995 report by the Organization for Economic Cooperation and Development (OECD) indicated that nearly half of all German investment abroad was in low wage countries outside of Western Europe. Some 10 percent of such investment was being directed to Central Europe to take advantage of its comparatively cheap labor, skilled automotive workers in the Czech Republic costing about half of comparable workers in Germany itself.[26]

Since 1990, the giant Swiss-Swedish engineering conglomerate Asea Brown Boveri Ltd. has eliminated some 40,000 jobs from its North American and Western European operations and created 21,150 new jobs in Eastern Europe, where labor costs were only 5 to 10 percent of what they are in Germany.[27] Similar developments are taking place in Japan, where the high costs of labor are driving a growing segment of its industry abroad, some of it to the United States, where the average costs of skilled labor were substantially lower, $17.10, compared with $21.42 per hour in 1994.[28] As a result, Japan's largest automobile manufacturer, Toyota, increased its 1993 overseas production of cars by 17% over the preceding year. Overall, Japanese car exports fell in 1993 by 15.9% in dollars, while car imports from the United States increased by 70.8%. Toyota alone expected to sell in Japan, each month, some 1,800 cars manufactured at its plant in Kentucky. Japan is undergoing a similar restructuring in its electronics industry, creating great domestic uncertainty about what to do with the increasing number of workers that will be idled by this export of jobs to lower cost labor markets.[29] Indeed, many Japanese economists are confidently predicting that such traditional workplace icons such as lifetime employment, low unemployment, and generous job benefits will begin to disappear over the next several years, a process that has already begun. As noted by Susumu Taketomi, managing director of the Industrial Bank of Japan, in 1993, "This is a very severe change, the kind of transformation that only takes place once every half century. This process will take at least five years, or even a decade. If we look into the 21st century, this is probably good. But in the process, we will have lots of pain."[30]

It is interesting to note that there is an additional reason why some major international corporations are expanding their operations in the United States, namely that domestic policies in their home countries are more protective of workers than they are in this country. "Compared to operating within most European or Asian societies, laying off workers is easier in America. If demand falls, the American system is more flexible. Just as Japan perfected the just-in-time inventory system, America is well on its way to perfecting the just-in-time workforce, notwithstanding the grim toll it takes on labor. The harsh truth is that it is a major productivity plus."[31]

There is, however, a glimmer of evidence that the tendency to shift employment to lower labor cost countries in the globalized market is being reconsidered by a number of international corporations. An example of this is Toyota, which established manufacturing and research operations in Canada. It resisted the temptation to shift these activities to the lower cost labor markets in the southern United States and Mexico that are now more readily available to them as a result of NAFTA. Instead, as of 1995, Toyota was increasing the annual production capacity of its Ontario assembly plant, all of such production to be designated for export to the United States. It seems, according to the *Economist*, that "these firms have discovered that the lure of low wages in the southern United States and Mexico can be outweighed by the productivity of a loyal, well-educated—albeit highly paid—workforce."[32]

There appears to be some research evidence to support this judgment. According to economist Stephen Golub of Swarthmore College, lower wages usually correspond to lower productivity so that, in the long run, there are few advantages in terms of actual costs per unit in lower wage labor markets. Thus, an examination of 1990 labor costs and productivity in four Asian countries, Korea, Thailand, Malaysia, and the Philippines, indicates those factory wages and other compensation ranged from 14 to 32 percent of that paid in the United States. However, actual unit labor costs in Korea are pegged at 71 percent of U.S. levels, rising to 86 percent in Thailand, and surpassing U.S. levels in both Malaysia and the Philippines.[33] As a result, relatively lower productivity in these countries would seem to narrow substantially any competitive advantage one may have assumed such lower cost labor markets would afford to manufacturers in the United States and other industrialized nations. It remains to be seen whether these differentials between labor costs per unit and productivity will continue to hold as these lower labor cost markets continue to modernize.

It should be noted, however, that in 1997, unit labor costs in the United States declined by only one percent, while those in Japan, Korea, and Taiwan fell (in U.S. dollar terms) by 12.7, 19.4, and 5.6 percent, respectively. Although much of this was attributable to depreciating currencies with respect to the dollar, it is noteworthy that even after adjustments for currency movements, 11 of the 12 economies studied had lower unit labor costs than the United States and 5 had greater productivity.[34] In any case, such studies further emphasize the importance of productivity as a factor in the competitiveness of the American labor market. They also highlight the anomaly that productivity increases tend to generate a decreasing demand for workers.

GLOBALIZATION AND ORGANIZED LABOR

Another notable consequence of the globalization of business has been the dilution of the ability of organized labor to deal effectively with the issues of economic and employment security for its constituents. In the past, the practices of collective bargaining and industrial unionism enabled labor unions to protect the interests of workers by effectively insulating wages from competitive market forces. In effect, as argued by one writer unsympathetic to the labor movement, "Economists have always understood that a labor union is merely a cartel. It is a group of sellers of labor services in collusion to eliminate competition among themselves and to try to quash competition from others."[35]

In the present environment, however, unions are often no longer in a position to function in this manner. "Instead," as one student of the labor movement has observed, "given the wage variability across locations that employers have to choose from for producing goods and services, it is the basic entrepreneurial decisions regarding competitive strategy, location, design of technology, organization scope and structure, relationships with suppliers and customers, and managerial style that shape the employment relationship and determine long-term worker welfare."[36]

During the peak period of union membership, unions were able to negotiate contracts that accorded union members a significant wage premium over nonunion workers. The extra labor costs were simply passed on to consumers. However, in the current environment, competitive forces preclude this from happening. Firms are unable to raise their prices and remain competitive in the market. As a consequence, for almost two decades unions have been losing their clout in garnering wage gains for their members. Between 1983 and 1997, the wage premium paid to private-sector nonagricultural workers declined from 40 percent to less than 30 percent.[37] In 1998, the wage premium declined to 27 percent, as private-sector union membership declined by 50,000.[38] Another 1998 study estimated that the wage premium was at a substantially lower figure, only about 15 percent.[39] In fact, union wage increases have not kept up with those achieved by many nonunion workers which, in 1996, rose more than a percentage point faster than hourly pay among union workers. As pointed out by Gary Burtless of the Brookings Institution: "Nonunion employers now set the pace in determining compensation patterns. They have required workers to share the cost of important fringe benefits, like pensions and health care. Union bargainers have been forced to follow suit."[40]

The diminishing ability of organized labor to influence the critical business decisions that shape the employment environment is one of the factors contributing to the current decline in union strength. In the mid-1950s about one worker out of three on non-farm payrolls was a member of a union. By the mid-1990s, however, less than one worker out of six held a union card.[41] In 1994, only 9.6 million, or 10.9 percent of all workers in the private sector were members of labor unions. An additional 7.1 million workers in the public sector (Federal, State, and local governments) representing 38.7 percent of all government employees were members of unions and employee associations.[42] By 1998, union membership in the private sector had declined to 9.5 percent and to 37.5 percent in the public sector.[43] As noted by one writer, "About 2 million new workers enter the job market every year, and the AFL-CIO should be signing up about 400,000 of those just to keep its membership rolls even. But in fact, the unions lost nearly that many members in 1995, and almost 100,000 in 1996."[44]

This decline in union membership, particularly in the private sector, is serving as a spur for unions to redefine their roles in the new configuration of the world of work. Once again, the European experience is instructive in this regard. According to Robert Minikin of Bankers Trust Co., labor unions across Europe are exhibiting "a pragmatic and cautious approach in negotiating new pay deals, despite the economic upswing." Suffice it to note, in this regard, that unit labor costs in Britain are declining at about 1.5 percent a year, and that 1994 unit labor costs in Germany were approximately 11 percent below the figure for the preceding year.[45]

As a consequence of these developments, unions are beginning to adopt a significantly different approach to collective bargaining than was their usual practice in the past. For example, in 1970, approximately 30 potential workdays out of every 1,000 were spent in idleness as a result of labor disputes. In 1996, only two out of every 1,000 workdays were lost to strikes.[46] According to Jimmy Smith, an official of the Communications Workers of America: "It's now more of a problem-solving process. Our objective is to make our companies the best in their industries because this is the only way to maintain jobs. We can now work together because management has the same goal."[47] The concern about preserving jobs has led some public service unions to urge their members to agree to "givebacks," that is, to defer or eliminate pay increases, overtime pay, and holiday pay as the price of avoiding downsizing in local government employment.[48]

Union leaders have been forced by circumstances to come to terms with the realities of the new world of work. This was stated forthrightly by George Becker, president of the United Steelworkers of America. "If it is inevitable that a place is going to go down and there is nothing that can be done to save it, if there is no way to compete or there is no market for the product—if that is going to happen, we are going to negotiate with the company."[49] As a consequence, with the new wave of downsizing that took place in 1998 and 1999, unions could be seen working with management to find ways of easing the transition of workers, rather than struggling to assure their retention.

In the past, union contracts were built around very specific job descriptions, which facilitated the union's accountability to and for its members. This meant, in effect, that any time an employee undertook work or responsibility outside the confines of the job description the union could ask for an appropriate wage adjustment. Today, however, unions increasingly are accepting the concept of "broadbanding," that is, the consolidation of jobs into a relatively wider salary band that permits workers to expand their job skills and to take on responsibilities in areas other than those specified in one's sharply defined job description. The net effect of this is to increase the flexibility and adaptability of the employee to meet the needs of the employer, and thereby to enhance job security by adding value to one's employment. According to Nancy Capezzuti, a human resources executive: "Broadbanding allows employees to create their own job security by acquiring new skills. . . . Because it enables people to be proficient in multiple areas, we don't have to send them home when there isn't enough work to keep them busy. Instead, we can send them to an area that has a shortage of employees."[50] It remains to be seen whether this reorientation of organized labor can have significant effect in offsetting the trends in the restructuring of business that is currently leading to a declining need for human labor.

GLOBALIZATION, POPULATION, AND EMPLOYMENT

One of the critical decisions faced by business today is reflected in the approach taken in dealing with some of the consequences of globalization. A *Business Week* review of the state of the economy put the issue in stark terms at the outset of 1998.

It seems incredible. The U.S. economy is chugging away vigorously in the seventh year of an economic expansion. U.S. stock markets are near all-time highs, corporate profits are strong, and the unemployment rate is the lowest in two decades. Yet the Christmas season—and the entire fourth quarter, for that matter—was marked by a wave of layoffs that will affect tens of thousands of workers. And many of the cuts are coming at companies that are still racking up strong earnings.

What's going on? Global competition has made it impossible for companies to raise prices and forced some to cut them. A strong U.S. dollar only makes the situation more difficult. So if earnings are to be maintained and improved, corporations have one alternative: cut costs. And that usually means putting employees out of work—albeit in an extremely healthy job market.[51]

In a number of product fields it is no longer practical or even desirable for companies to increase their levels of production because of the intense competition, both global and domestic, and the relative saturation of the market. As a consequence, contemporary firms often struggle to maintain their current share of the market, expanding production only when natural growth in demand takes place or when competitors drop out of the market for one reason or another. Where this is the case, the primary means for increasing return on investment becomes that of seeking further gains in productivity while effectively limiting production and pruning costs, especially expenditures on labor and employee benefits. As pointed out by one corporate consultant, there is an inexorable logic to this approach.

In a very low inflation environment, there isn't much opportunity to raise prices for corporations unless they provide something of high value. At the same time, technology has increased to the point that it has brought about what I call a commoditization of many basic business products and that commoditization has driven down . . . prices so much that the only way corporations can maintain their bottom line is to pare back on cost. This has been going on now for some time. It's going on today and will go on in the future. It is a by-product of the globalization of business.[52]

The clear implication of this is that the ongoing decoupling of labor from productivity may well result in significantly diminished high wage employment opportunities for a growing and aging labor force.

NOTES

1. William Wolman and Anne Colamosca, *The Judas Economy: The Triumph of Capital and the Betrayal of Work* (Reading, MA: Addison-Wesley Publishing, 1997), pp. 23–24.

2. Thomas R. Donahue quoted in *International Labor Standards and Global Economic Integration: Proceedings of a Symposium* (Washington, DC: U.S. Department of Labor, Bureau of International Labor Affairs, 1994), p. 47.

3. Stanley Aronowitz and William DiFazio, *The Jobless Future* (Minneapolis, MN: University of Minnesota Press, 1994), p. 9.

4. John A. Challenger, "There Is No Future for the Workplace," *The Futurist*, October 1998, p. 16.

5. Lance Morrow, "The Temping of America," *Time*, March 29, 1993.

6. "Subsidy for the Stock Exchange," Editorial, *New York Times*, November 30, 1998.

7. "The Next 25: What Today's Leading CEOs, Management Gurus, and Futurists See Coming For Your Company, Your Job, and Your Life Between 1995 and 2020," *Industry Week*, August 21, 1995, p. 49.

8. James Sterngold, "NAFTA Trade-Off: Some Jobs Lost, Others Gained," *New York Times*, October 9, 1995.

9. "Trade Fax" (Washington, DC: Economic Policy Institute), 1997.

10. Ben Wildavsky, "Not Happy After NAFTA," *U.S. News & World Report*, January 11, 1999, p. 49.

11. Jesse Rothstein and Robert E. Scott, "NAFTA and the States," issue brief no. 119 (Washington, DC: Economic Policy Institute, September 19, 1997); Rothstein and Scott, "NAFTA's Casualties," issue brief no. 120 (Washington, DC: Economic Policy Institute, September, 19, 1997).

12. Robert E. Scott, "NAFTA at Seven," briefing paper, Introduction (Washington DC: Economic Policy Institute, April 2001).

13. Geri Smith and Elisabeth Malkin, "Mexican Makeover: NAFTA Creates the World's Newest Industrial Power," *Business Week*, December 21, 1998, p. 50.

14. Wayne A. Cornelius, Letter to the Editor, "Nafta Costs Mexico More Job Losses Than U.S.," *New York Times*, October 17, 1995.

15. "Where the Jobs Go—and Why," *World Press Review*, December 1995, p. 31, citing the *Financial Times*, September 21, 1995.

16. *World Employment 1995* (Geneva: International Labour Office, 1995), p. 39.

17. Carlos Salas, "The Impact of NAFTA on Wages and Incomes in Mexico," Briefing Paper: "NAFTA at Seven" (Washington, DC: Economic Policy Institute, April 2001).

18. Maggie Farley and Evelyn Iritani, "China: The Ultimate Buyer's Market," *Los Angeles Times*, December 2, 1995.

19. Peter Drucker, "The Future That Has Already Happened," *The Futurist*, November 1998, p. 16.

20. Lester R. Brown, Gary Gardner, and Brian Halwell, "Impacts of Population Growth," *The Futurist*, February 1999, p. 39.

21. Wolman and Colamosca, *The Judas Economy*, p. 33.

22. K. Schwab and C. Smadja, "The New Rules of the Game in a World of Many Players," *Harvard Business Review*, November 1994.

23. "Spice Up Your Services," *Economist*, January 16, 1999, p. 59.

24. Peter Gumbel, "Western Europe Finds That It's Pricing Itself out of the Job Market," *Wall Street Journal*, December 9, 1993.

25. Nathaniel C. Cash, "Luxuries They Can't Afford," *New York Times*, September 13, 1995.

26. Amity Shlaes, "Does German Business Need Germany?" *Wall Street Journal*, October 24, 1995.

27. Craig R. Whitney, "Western European Companies Head East for Cheap Labor," *New York Times*, February 9, 1995.

28. "International Comparisons of Hourly Compensation Costs for Production Workers in Manufacturing, 1975–1994," report no. 893 (Washington, DC: U.S. Department of Labor, Bureau of Labor Statistics, May 1995), Table 2.

29. "A Wobbly Time for Japan's Workers," *Economist*, December 18, 1993, p. 31.

30. Sandra Sugawara, "Prices in Japan Are Dropping, but Consumers Aren't Buying," *Washington Post*, September 30, 1995.

31. Bernard Wysocki, Jr., "Foreigners Find U.S. A Good Place to Invest," *Wall Street Journal*, August 7, 1995.

32. "The Better Bet," *Economist*, January 14, 1995, p. 27.

33. Gene Koretz, "The Equalizer: Productivity," *Business Week*, September 11, 1995.

34. "International Comparisons of Manufacturing Productivity and Unit Labor Cost Trends, 1997," USDL 98–393 (Washington, DC: U.S Department of Labor, September 25, 1998).

35. Charles W. Baird, cited in Brad Lips, "Temps and the Labor Market: Why Unions Fear Staffing Companies," *Regulation*, Spring 1998, p. 37.

36. Thomas Kochan, "Trade Unionism and Industrial Relations," *Dialogues* (Industrial Relations Research Institute), vol. 1, issue 1, May 1993.

37. "Strike Headlines and Union Decline," *Fact & Fallacy* (Washington, DC: Employment Policy Foundation, September 1998), p. 3.

38. "Union Wage Premium Continues 15 Year Decline," *Economic Bytes* (Washington, DC: Employment Policy Foundation, March 16, 1999).

39. David G. Blanchflower, "Changes Over Time in Union Relative Wage Effects in Great Britain and the United States," working paper no. 6100 (Washington, DC: National Bureau of Economic Research, July 1, 1998).

40. Gary Burtless, "The Future of Organized Labor," *Christian Science Monitor*, August 26, 1997.

41. Ibid.

42. Charles J. Muhl, "Union Members in 1994," *Compensation & Working Conditions* (U.S. Department of Labor, February 1995), p. 14.

43. Steven Greenhouse, "Union Membership Rose in '98, but Union's Percentage of Work Force Fell," *New York Times*, January 26, 1999.

44. Sabra Chartrand, "Unions Try to Secure a Place in the Changing Work World," *New York Times*, February 23, 1997.

45. *Business Week*, December 5, 1994, p. 26.

46. Gary Burtless, "The Future of Organized Labor."

47. Jimmy Smith quoted by Shari Caudron, "The Changing Union Agenda," *Personnel Journal*, March 1995, p. 47.

48. Robert E. Pierre and David Montgomery, "Pr. George's Unions Urge Members To Give up Some Pay to Save Jobs," *Washington Post*, March 31, 1995.

49. George Becker quoted by Louis Uchitelle, "Downsizing Comes Back, but Outcry from Unions and Workers Is Muted," *New York Times*, December 7, 1998.

50. Caudron, "The Changing Union Agenda," p. 48.

51. David Greising, "It's the Best of Times—Or Is It?" *Business Week*, January 5, 1998.

52. Robert C. Kryvicky, "More for Less and the Impact on Older Workers" (address presented to AARP Textbook Authors Conference, Washington, DC, October 8, 1993).

5

DOWNSIZING AND ITS CONSEQUENCES

> We trained hard—but it seemed that every time we were beginning to form into teams, we would be reorganized. I was to learn later in life that we tend to meet any new situation by reorganizing; and what a wonderful method it can be for creating the illusion of progress while producing confusion, inefficiency and demoralization.
>
> —Petronius

In recent years, the goal of trimming production costs has been achieved primarily through occasionally dramatic reductions in the size of the corporate workforce. This recourse was resorted to only rather infrequently in the past. In today's employment environment, such downsizing or, as some corporate spokespersons prefer, "rightsizing," has become commonplace. The basic distinction between the two terms is merely a matter of perspective. If it happens to someone else, it's rightsizing; if it happens to you, it's downsizing. In either case, it seems clear that this trend is not going to run its course anytime in the near future.

Downsizing, the permanent employment reductions that result from the changes in structure or size of a firm, has occurred so frequently in the last decade that it has become widely acknowledged as a business necessity. Large corporations, which beginning in the 1930s developed no-layoff policies as a means of restraining unionization, have now almost without exception reversed and discarded such policies. Robert Samuelson, a well-known economics columnist, noted,

Corporate firings, once frowned upon, have grown respectable. Until recently, classier companies strove to avoid layoffs. It was a last resort. And their behavior influenced other firms. It set a standard necessary to attract the best workers. But as model companies (IBM, Sears) have been forced—by competition or massive losses—to abandon their ideal, it has become easier for all companies to do the same. . . . It was once thought that the protective cocoon of the successful corporation would gradually spread. More businesses would adopt the practices of the enlightened and prospering few. Instead, the reverse has happened.[1]

Although most downsizing to date has taken place in the private-sector, there is an emerging trend in the same direction in the public-sector as well. Even the traditionally secure employment bastions of governmental bureaucracies are proving to be increasingly vulnerable. This is occurring even though a substantial number of the jobs created during the recovery from the recession that ended in March 1991 were in the public sector. According to a 1991 survey by the International Personnel Management Association (IPMA), 23 states, 27 counties, and 89 municipalities had downsized. Similarly, a 1992 survey of 66 large urban counties conducted by the National Association of Counties revealed that 70 percent had reduced their workforces, a significant increase from the 40 percent of counties that did so the previous year.[2] Similarly, direct federal employment decreased from 2.19 million non-defense, non-postal workers in 1993 to 1.87 million workers as of September 1998.[3]

Many of these manpower reductions were the direct consequence of the outsourcing of work, contracting out for work previously performed by employees of the public agency. The IPMA reports that, between 1994 and 1996, the number of its public sector member organizations that rely on temporary workers or privatized services increased from 9 to 24 percent. Similarly, a 1996 study indicates that the share of public services being provided by contract workers increased dramatically between 1987 and 1995. For example, contractor handling of data processing rose from 16 to 31 percent, waste collection from 30 to 50 percent, and street repair from 19 to 37 percent.[4]

This trend is clearly beginning to take hold as federal, state, and local governments continue to seek to reduce their payrolls, although the approaches taken to downsizing vary somewhat from those usually taken in the private-sector. As noted in a 1992 report from the Council of State Governments, "most states have tried to avoid laying off their employees . . . downsizing is being accomplished largely through attrition, early retirement incentives, leaving vacant positions unfilled or other methods."[5] The net result, however, is the same—a shrinking number of available permanent jobs that provide decent wages and important employee benefits.

DOWNSIZING IN THE PRIVATE-SECTOR

Over the past several years, as already indicated, we have witnessed a trend among businesses to cope with the realities of globalization and competition by garnering the benefits of higher productivity and by slashing employment. It is important to bear in mind that this is occurring throughout the industrialized world. According to a 1995 survey of some 1,800 chief executive officers and other senior corporate officials and managers in Japan, North America, and Europe, 94 percent indicated that their companies had gone through some sort of restructuring during the preceding two years.[6]

However, while in the past it was primarily corporations with a pressing need to stem huge financial losses that resorted to downsizing, it has now become an acceptable approach to improving short-term profitability for companies that are actually doing quite well. According to Eric Rolfe Greenberg of the American Management Association, "downsizing has become a systematic, ongoing corporate activity carried out without regard to current economic performance."[7] For example, although Xerox had just recently succeeded in regaining its share of the world photocopying and document processing market, the company announced at the end of 1993 that it planned to eliminate about 10 percent of its workforce of 10,000 over the next three years. This was to be done notwithstanding the significant contribution of these workers to the corporation's success. In explaining the decision, Xerox's chief executive, Paul A. Allaire, stated, "To compete effectively, we must have a lean and flexible organization which can deliver the most cost-effective document-processing products and services."[8] However, this assertion seems to be quite inconsistent with the fact that if the company were unable to compete effectively it would not have regained its market share in the first place.

In late 1997, the chairman and chief executive of General Electric, Jack F. Welch, set in motion plans for a nearly $2 billion across-the-company restructuring, even though all of the company's divisions were doing very well, with double-digit returns. Informed observers suggested that what GE does will be watched closely and emulated by many other corporations. According to Gail D. Foster, chief economist at the Conference Board, GE's decision will serve as a harbinger of a new wave of downsizing and restructuring to come. "1998 is going to be like a day when it rains but the sun's out," she noted. "We are going to see layoffs and pretty good economic growth at the same time."[9] This prediction proved prescient.

Severe criticism of such practices has begun to come from within the business community itself. Alan Downs, a self-confessed "corporate executioner," argues that what we are witnessing is the direct consequence of "the creation and public acceptance of a *culture of narcissism* in business." In this culture, "profit as the singular standard by which a company is managed and measured has become the accepted norm. Under the culture of corporate narcissism, it is perfectly acceptable to lay off thousands of workers, slash health care benefits, economically devastate communities, and pay management astronomical salaries, all for an increase in profit."[10]

This is not to suggest that there is anything wrong with making a profit, which has always been a basic although not exclusive (as some economic theorists would have us believe) business imperative. The problem emerges when profit is perceived as a value that takes precedence over all other considerations. Downs insists that this perception is by no means essential to business success. "It is possible for a company to have a community and family consciousness and still be on the cutting edge of success. Many companies have bucked the tide of corporate narcissism and managed to make a nice chunk of profit too. Unfortunately, the majority of American companies aren't willing to take this path."[11]

Presumably, downsizing should demonstrate conclusively that it is a major contribution to corporate profitability. Somewhat surprisingly, the record on this is far from clear. It has been estimated that downsizing has produced an average short-term increase of 8 percent in stock values, even though at least one study suggests that the value of a significant number of those same stocks probably fell substantially later on. One analysis examined the financial history of 16 major firms that trimmed more than 10 percent of their workforce between 1982 and 1988. The study showed that within two years of their downsizing, the stocks of 10 of the 16 companies were trading below the stock market by 17 to 48 percent, and 12 of these companies were trading below comparable firms in the same industry.[12] Nonetheless, as noted by Larry Chimerine of the Economic Strategy Institute, "The pressure from Wall Street on companies to boost short-term earnings growth (by cutting jobs) is just relentless. That's not going to change."[13] Thus, in 1998, notwithstanding the global economy's "summer from hell," the U.S. economy grew by 3.3 percent, primarily because of heavy household spending spurred by high-employment rates and increased wages. However, simultaneously declining profits threatened to reverse the situation. By November 1998, a slowdown in the economy was being predicted. "Faced with weak profits and an unforgiving Wall Street, companies are making investment and hiring decisions that are already starting to slow economic growth."[14]

Martha Peak of the American Management Association observed in this regard, "Today, downsizing is deemed a prudent management option. As one CEO explained it to me, if your competitors have downsized, but you haven't, then Wall Street will view you as behind the times and overstaffed to boot. This is scary."[15] Thus, in late 1998, ostensibly in response to global competition, some large corporations such as Raytheon and 3M announced large cost-saving layoffs, presumably calculated to improve their standing on Wall Street. However, as pointed out by Jeffrey Garten of the Yale School of Management, "pink slips do nothing to improve a company's products and sales, and they can destroy morale and productivity."[16] Nonetheless, and despite the alleged tight labor market, planned layoffs by major corporations through April 1999 exceeded the pace of the previous year by 41 percent, or some 265,000 jobs.[17]

There are, however, glimmers of some corporate rethinking about the benefits of arbitrary downsizing. It seems that even the leading downsizing expert Stephen Roach has recanted and begun to caution against quick-fix downsizing. "Tactics of open-ended downsizing and real wage compression," he warns, "are ultimately recipes for industrial extinction."[18]

Another partial explanation of the downsizing fad, offered in private conversation by an executive of a major American corporation, is that in some instances downsizing may be a consequence of corporate officers and managers receiving a significant part of their remuneration in company stock and stock options. In such instances, it may be in the short-term interest of the manager-shareholders to use downsizing as a means of increasing short-term profit margins and therefore the value of their shares. A study of executive pay from 1980 to 1994 indicated that "for any given shift in company value, the two researchers found that changes in CEO pay due to stock and option revaluations are more than 50 times larger than changes resulting from salary and bonus."[19] How many downsizing decisions are made on the basis of such considerations is not known. However, to the extent that this is a factor in such decisions, it brings us very far from the traditional notion that one of the purposes of establishing corporations in the first place was to separate management from ownership, a notion that appears to have been discarded or forgotten. This was made clear by Vernon R. Loucks Jr., chairman and chief executive officer of Baxter International. "In corporate boardrooms and among investors, it is widely recognized that if managers—indeed all employees—would think like owners, they would consider the impact of their decisions and actions on the stock price and drive shareholder value up." As a result, a variety of steps were taken to tie management earnings more tightly to shareholder value by giving the company's senior managers "the opportunity to take out personal loans from a bank in order to purchase up to several times their total annual compensation in Baxter common stock."[20]

THE IMPACT OF DOWNSIZING

A tangible consequence of the downsizing trend is that the *Fortune 500* industrial companies employed 3.7 million fewer workers in 1992 than a decade earlier. This represents about a 25 percent reduction in their labor force, and many large employers are planning to continue to pursue this course for the foreseeable future. Overall, more than 6 million workers have lost permanent full-time jobs since 1987. And, according to the seventh annual American Management Association Survey on Downsizing, conducted two years after the end of the last recession, 47 percent of the 870 organizations surveyed reported downsizing between July 1992 and June 1993, with an average reduction in workforce per company of 10.4 percent. Moreover, in a significant departure from past trends, 54.6 percent of the jobs that were cut were supervisory, middle management, and professional/technical positions.[21] This is a major change from past employment turndowns, in which those affected were principally blue-collar workers who could expect to be recalled once inventories were depleted and production had to resume. By contrast, most white-collar terminations tend to be permanent. The implication of this continuing trend is that even if one does have a job, the likelihood of not having that job a year or two from now is increasing. There is thus a greater degree of job insecurity in the current employment environment, regardless of position or status within a firm than at any time in the post-World War II era.[22]

It is hardly surprising that the downsizing movement has imposed a good deal of pain on many workers and their families. What is less obvious is that the pain inflicted on the workforce has brought little if any gain to the employers who have doled it out. "There is no serious evidence that the downsizing movement has led to a material improvement in the speed with which the efficiency of the American corporation is increasing or in the rate of growth in productivity in the American economy as a whole."[23]

Restructuring and downsizing have had a disparately significant impact on older workers. For one thing, older workers tend to be found in large numbers in the larger and older companies, especially in those engaged in manufacturing, the sort of firms that have experienced the greatest organizational changes and reductions in workforce over the past decade. A survey sponsored by the Commonwealth Fund in 1991 revealed that "firms that had sold business units, laid off substantial numbers, offered early retirement, or reduced management staff are found to have higher proportions of workers age 50 or older. Of companies that had dismissed a substantial number of employees, for instance, the workforce of 28 percent of the companies had at least three out of ten workers age 50 and above, whereas only 13 percent of the other companies had such a concentration of older workers."[24]

According to a research paper by Henry Farber of Princeton University, between 1981 and 1983, 10 percent of men between the ages of 45 and 54 and 11 percent of those 55 to 64 lost their jobs. Ten years later, between 1991 and 1993, the job loss rates for these two groups increased to 14 and 17 percent respectively.[25] Moreover, although there is a paucity of reliable data available about the employment and distribution of older workers, it is known that such workers are heavily represented in the ranks of those middle managers and professionals who have experienced workforce dislocations.

In some instances, downsizing seems to be a barely disguised form of age discrimination, which one writer describes as "the dark underbelly of downsizing." A case in point is the downsizing of Pacific Telesis, which resulted in the firing of 1,469 employees, most of whom were just a few years short of entitlement to a full pension. It has been estimated that the company saved an average of $326,632 in pension obligations alone per firing, in addition to avoiding the costs of the lifetime health-insurance coverage guaranteed to those eligible for full retirement. What is particularly striking about this case is that at the same time that the downsizing took place the company hired about 1,700 contractors, who were not paid any benefits. Of the latter, some 20 percent were former employees who, in effect, were rehired to do their former jobs for significantly reduced total compensation.[26]

A second consideration reflecting the disparate impact of changes in the workplace on older workers is the degree of difficulty they frequently experience in finding new employment. In 1994, 23.6 percent of all displaced managers in the United States had been unemployed for more than six months, and in 1995 managers and professionals accounted for 11.3 percent of the unemployed, a significant increase from the 1989 level of 9.4 percent.[27] A 1990 survey indicated that, while 22 percent of displaced workers age 25 to 54 were unemployed at the time of the survey, 47 percent of displaced workers over age 55 were still without work.[28] For purposes of comparison, it might be noted that the impact of downsizing and unemployment on older workers is even greater in other industrialized countries. Thus, a 1995 study revealed that in Spain, 56 percent (2.09 million) of the unemployed had been without work for more than a year, and of these about 55 percent were over age 45.[29] One consequence of this difficulty in getting re-employed is the disproportionately large number of discouraged older workers who drop out of the labor force entirely, despairing of any likelihood of finding an appropriate job.

The effects of downsizing on older workers may also be seen in the data on job tenure, which are typically misused by those who wish to argue that all is well, notwithstanding massive corporate restructurings, because median job tenure has remained constant for several decades. The fact is that, although *overall* median job tenure may have remained constant at four years, this does not hold for the situation of middle-aged men. Analysis of their job tenure in the years between 1983 and 1996 indicates a sharp decline in median tenure from 15.3 to 10.5 years for those workers aged 55 to 64 over the thirteen year period. Men aged 45 to 54 also experienced a decline in job tenure from 12.8 to 10.1 years. Moreover, tenure for men with a single employer for more than ten years showed significant decreases from 1983 to 1996. It went from 51.1 percent to 41.7 for those age 40 to 44; from 57.8 to 50.8 percent for those 45 to 49; from 62.3 to 54.9 percent for those 50 to 54; from 66.2 to 55.7 percent for those 55 to 59; and 65.6 to 50.4 percent for those 60 to 64. During this same period, the job tenure of women age 55 to 64 increased slightly from 9.8 to 10 years, which may be considered to reflect a change in attitude of older women to early retirement.[30] Corporate outlays for severance pay also show that "it's veteran workers who get the ax." In the second quarter of 1998 median severance was 25 weeks' pay, whereas the median was only 13 weeks in 1996. The figures, according to outplacement specialist John Challenger, "suggest that companies are targeting veteran workers for their layoffs and buyouts."[31]

A study by economists William J. Baumol and Edward N. Wolff of New York University also suggests that both the disparate impact of downsizing on older workers and their protracted periods of joblessness can be directly related to the acceleration of technological change in the workplace. Because changing technologies tend to require higher skill requirements, and because training and retraining costs are increasing, there is a growing tendency on the part of employers to avoid hiring older workers, the training of whom is presumed to be cost-ineffective. In the authors' analysis, it is the growing investment in computer technology that is having the most serious effect on the employment of older workers. In short, as *Business Week* put it, "today's technologically charged economy appears to be leaving many workers by the wayside—a situation that Baumol and Wolff think will require government action in the years ahead."[32]

Although it is true that many workers of all ages affected by downsizing have found other employment, it is also a fact that they have experienced an overall decline in the level of wages earned in these new jobs. A January 1990 survey indicated that 40 percent of workers who had lost and then found full-time employment were earning less than they did in their previous jobs. Moreover, about 25 percent of these reemployed workers experienced at least a 20 percent loss in pay.[33] In 1998, notwithstanding the tightest labor market in three decades, 38 percent of re-employed full-timers experienced a drop in pay, and 21 percent of them a drop of more than 20 percent in pay. This led one writer to conclude that "with only two-thirds of those laid off in recent years back at full-time jobs and nearly 40% of all full-timers taking pay cuts, it's clear that many workers—particularly those over 45—continue to suffer considerable economic pain."[34]

A 1993 study of some 2,000 workers released by RJR Nabisco revealed that 72 percent had found new jobs, but at wages that averaged only 42 percent of their previous earnings.[35] An even more disturbing example of this problem is revealed in a 1995 study of inner city youth employed in the fast-food restaurant industry, where full-time jobs paid only $8,840 a year and were subject to fierce competition for employment from displaced older and better-educated men and women. One of the researchers found that many of the young people seeking work in the fast-food industry are actually competing for the same jobs with older members of their own families.[36]

Even in expanding knowledge-based fields such as financial services, many high-salaried executives displaced because of corporate restructuring have had similar experiences with regard to the relative depression of their earnings in new jobs. For example, a study of the banking industry indicates that, although all of the 1,150 downsized bankers studied were able to find new employment, 46 percent took cuts in salary of 10 percent or more. It is noteworthy that 61 percent of those between the ages of 50 and 59, and 46 percent of those between 40 and 49, were among the group that found it necessary to accept a substantial cut in pay.[37]

A related concern is the nature of the jobs that are being added to the economy, a large number of which drove the official unemployment rates down significantly from 1995 to the end of the century, and have led some observers to speak optimistically of the "upsizing of America."[38] Since 1980, there has been a significant shift in employment numbers from higher to lower wage industries, with virtually all net new jobs being created in relatively low pay service sectors such as health care, state and local government, retail sales, and building security and maintenance. Although 13.6 million jobs were created between 1979 and 1989, nearly 5 million of these provided incomes of less than $13,091 a year, the low-earnings threshold which was about 8 percent below the established poverty level for a family of four. And, perhaps somewhat surprisingly, the problem of declining relative wages is not limited to low or unskilled workers. It is also affecting executive, professional, and technical workers, as may be seen from an analysis of the 3.66 million net new jobs that were created between 1988 and 1993. Even though 2.8 million of these jobs were for executives and professionals, all but 150,000 were in relatively low paying industries such as health care and lodging. About one million of these jobs were in the lowest paid service occupations such as cleaning and food preparation.[39]

A 1995 study by economist Neal Rosenthal of the Department of Labor examined job placements during the decade between 1983 and 1993. It indicates that 60 percent of the 20.9 million net replacement job openings that were filled, as well as 54 percent of the 41.6 million total job openings during the period, were in occupations in the bottom half of the pay scale. Moreover, only one percent more of all jobs were in the high-paying top 25 percent of occupations in 1993 than was the case ten years earlier.[40]

Economist David Gordon looked at available data for the non-farm private-sector from the standpoint of real hourly earnings in 1993 dollars. He argued that wages for all workers only increased 1.5 percent between 1979 and 1993, the bottom 80 percent of the wage spectrum experiencing an actual loss of 3.4 percent while the wages of the top 20 percent increased by 10.04 percent.[41] One net result of all this is that the median real wage for full-time male workers actually declined from $34,048 in 1973 to $30,407 in 1993. In this regard, Lester Thurow observed: "At no other time have median wages of American men fallen for more than two decades. Never before have a majority of American workers suffered real wage reductions while the per capita domestic product was advancing."[42]

Viewing the problem from a different perspective, figures from a 1994 Census Bureau study indicate that while 18.9 percent of full-time workers had low-wage jobs in 1979, the number grew to 23.1 percent by 1989 and reached about 25.7 percent in mid-1992. Moreover, while 9.9 percent of the population between the ages 35 and 54 had low earned income in 1979, a number that grew to 13.3 percent in 1992, 12 percent of those aged 55 to 64 had low earned income in 1979, the number increasing to 16.5 percent in 1992. One highly significant consequence of this is that increasing numbers of workers, especially those unskilled in terms of the needs of the contemporary job market, are working for wages that are too low to lift them out of poverty. Thus, while 13.1 percent of all Americans fell below the poverty line in 1989, that figure edged up to 15.1 percent by 1993. In general, using the poverty line as the benchmark, "the average American was 8 percent worse off in 1993 than in 1989 while the poor were 14 percent worse off."[43]

A 1995 Upjohn Institute study observed that real wages for men with a high school education or less declined almost 30 percent over the previous two decades, at the same time that home prices rose by 20 percent and rental costs by 13 percent over the same period.[44] These data lend further support to economist Paul Krugman's assertion that "the U.S. has achieved low unemployment by a sort of devil's bargain, whose price is soaring inequality and growing poverty."[45] Moreover, there does not appear to be any realistic prospect that this trend will reverse course at any point in the foreseeable future. As a 1994 Urban Institute conference report noted, "Labor market changes are moving low-skilled workers into lower-wage positions with few chances for advancement. In general, demand for high-skilled workers is *growing* faster than supply, and demand for low-skilled workers is *falling* faster than supply . . . the low-skilled will be placed in an increasingly noncompetitive position."[46]

Another factor seriously affecting the development of additional employment opportunities is the apparent preference of many employers to meet their increased needs for labor by extending the work hours of their existing employees rather than through the creation of new jobs. Even though such overtime work for non-salaried employees involves the payment of premium rates, for many employers this is preferable to adding permanent staff and paying the additional expensive employee benefits associated with such new positions.

According to Labor Department data, in April 1993 nearly $900 million a week were being paid for overtime work, which rose to an average 4.3 hours a week per factory worker, the highest level since the Bureau of Labor Statistics began collecting such data in 1948. Because of this increase in overtime, the average workweek rose to 41.5 hours, the longest in 27 years. It was estimated that if the $900 million a week in overtime pay had been converted into new employment, it would have been enough to create some 1.3 million jobs paying an average factory wage of $11 an hour. This would have caused the unemployment rate to drop by a full percentage point.[47]

Moreover, it is noteworthy that a large number of employees who are legally entitled to premium pay do not receive any extra compensation for significant amounts of overtime work. The extent of employer violations of the law in this regard, as conservatively estimated by the Employment Policy Foundation, an *employer-supported* think tank, is such that workers would have received an additional $19 billion in wages if the rules had been observed.[48] This amount of unpaid overtime would also have been enough to create approximately one million new jobs paying an average of $20,000 a year.

IMPLICATIONS FOR THE FUTURE

It seems clear that the ongoing restructuring of American business is not merely a short-term response to current market pressures. It involves a fundamental reorganization of productive activity as the wealth producing industries become increasingly more technologically and managerially sophisticated and efficient, requiring fewer but more technically proficient workers. Moreover, as noted earlier, the performance of high-valued services such as computer programming is increasingly being shifted to lower cost high-technology labor markets abroad. The long-term implications of this trend for an aging workforce are quite serious.

Some analysts of business organizations foresee dramatic changes in the character and duration of work life as we now know it, at least as far as most high-salaried occupations are concerned. It should be borne in mind that average annual hours worked have declined steadily in the United States and other industrialized countries. In the early 1890s, the average work year was about 2,800 hours. A century later, the average work year was about 1,700 hours, and about 1,600 in the United States and Britain, even though it has remained common to speak in terms of a 2,000–hour work year, or 40 hours a week for 50 weeks. Business thinker Charles Handy suggests that the projected overall decrease in future demand for even highly competent workers will probably reduce today's typical work life between 70,000 to 100,000 hours (35 to 50 work years at 2,000 hours per year) to about 50,000 hours, or an effective work life of only 25 years.[49] Similarly, sociologist Manuel Castells predicts that the average working lifetime could be shortened to about 30 years (from ages 24 to 54) out of a typical lifetime of about 70 to 80 years.[50] Economist Paul Ormerod wrote in this regard that, on average, a person born in the West today can expect to spend, over his or her lifetime, considerably less than half the amount of time in paid employment than was the case a century ago.[51] It hardly needs to be pointed out that these projections do not fit well with the proposed solution to the Social Security and Medicare funding problem indicated at the very outset of this book, namely, keeping older persons in the workforce for longer periods.

If these predictions have any validity, and there is good reason to believe they do, age 50 would become the typical age of exit from the labor force for many workers. This would create a large number of structurally unemployed at a time when persons at that age can look forward to 30 or more years of vitality. It seems evident that, at the moment, the economic and social support mechanisms necessary to cope with the needs of such a relatively young but economically displaced population simply do not exist and do not even appear on the national public policy agenda.

NOTES

1. Robert J. Samuelson, "The New Insecurity," *Washington Post,* December 29, 1993.

2. Jonathan Walters, "The Downsizing Myth," *Governing,* May 1993, p. 34.

3. Stephen Barr, "A Much Bigger Federal Workforce," *Washington Post,* December 28, 1998.

4. G. Pascal Zachary, "More Public Workers Lose Well-Paying Jobs as Outsourcing Grows," *Wall Street Journal,* August 6, 1996.

5. "State Employee Layoffs: Final Results of a Joint Survey Project of the Council of State Governments' State Policy and Innovations Group and the National Association of State Personnel Executives" (Washington, DC: The Council of State Governments, February 1992), p. 2.

6. *The Argus,* no. 324 (September 1995), p. 2.

7. James L. Tyson, "'Ready-Fire-Aim' Layoff Strategy Backfires on Corporate America," *Christian Science Monitor,* February 6, 1995.

8. John Holusha, "A Profitable Xerox Plans to Cut Staff by 10,000," *New York Times,* December 9, 1993.

9. David Greising, "It's the Best of Times—Or Is It?" *Business Week* (January 5, 1998).

10. Alan Downs, *Corporate Executions* (New York: American Management Association, 1995), p. 26.

11. Ibid., p. 27.

12. Alan Downs, "The Truth About Layoffs," *Management Review* (October 1955), pp. 59–60.

13. Bill Montague, "Study Says Economic Growth Offsets Job Cuts," *USA Today,* October 23, 1995.

14. James C. Cooper, and Kathleen Madigan, "Don't Be Fooled by the Strong Data," *Business Week* (November 16, 1998), p. 39.

15. Martha H. Peak, "All Pain, No Gain," *Management Review* (July 1996), p. 1.

16. Jeffrey E. Garten, "Cutting Fat Won't Be Enough to Survive this Crisis," *Business Week* (November 9, 1998), p. 26.

17. Gene Koretz, "Quick to Hire and Quick to Fire," *Business Week* (May 31, 1999), p. 34.

18. Aileen Keenan, "Companies Discover the Downside of Downsizing," *The Age Online* (Australia), January 4, 1988.

19. Gene Koretz, "CEO Success Is Its Own Reward," *Business Week* (February 1, 1999), p. 26.

20. Vernon R. Loucks, Jr., "An Equity Cure for Managers," *Wall Street Journal,* September 26, 1955.

21. American Management Association, *Management Review* (December 1993), p. 6.

22. David Wessel, "Is it Jobless Growth, or Just Slow Growth," *Wall Street Journal,* November 1, 1993.

23. William Wolman, and Anne Colamosca, *The Judas Economy: The Triumph of Capital and the Betrayal of Work* (Reading, MA: Addison-Wesley Publishing, 1997), p. 58.

24. Michael Useem, "The Impact of American Business Restructuring on Older Workers," *Perspective on Aging* (October–December 1993), p. 12.

25. John Cassidy, "All Worked Up," *The New Yorker* (April 22, 1996), p. 53.

26. Anne Monroe, "Getting Rid of the Gray," *Mother Jones* (July/August 1996), p. 29.

27. Fred R. Bleakley, "Job Searches Still Last Months, or Years, for Many Middle-Aged Middle Managers," *Wall Street Journal,* September 18, 1995.

28. Michael Useem, "The Impact of American Business Restructuring on Older Workers," *Perspective on Aging* (October–December 1993), p. 13.

29. *The Argus,* no. 324 (September 1995), p. 2.

30. "Employee Tenure in the Mid-1990s," USDL 97–25 (Washington, DC: U.S. Department of Labor, Bureau Of Labor Statistics, January 30, 1997).

31. Mike McNamee, "First Hired, First Fired?" *Business Week* (August 17, 1998), p. 22.

32. Gene Koretz, "Solving a Labor-Market Puzzle," *Business Week* (April 26, 1999), p. 26.

33. Diane E. Hertz, "Worker Displacement Still Common in Late 1980s," *Monthly Labor Review* (May 1991), p. 7.

34. Gene Koretz, "Downsizing's Economic Spin and Its Impact on Older Workers," *Business Week* (December 28, 1998).

35. *Time,* November 22, 1993, p. 35.

36. Bob Herbert, "Going Nowhere Fast," *New York Times,* December 1, 1995.

37. "Career Transitions in the Banking Industry, 1990–1992" (Right Associates, July 1993).

38. Peter Lynch, "The Upsizing of America," *Wall Street Journal,* September 20, 1996.

39. Aaron Bernstein, "The U.S. is Still Cranking Out Lousy Jobs," *Business Week* (October 10, 1994), p. 122.

40. Gene Koretz, "A Trend Toward Quality Jobs?" *Business Week* (October 9, 1995), p. 30.

41. David M. Gordon, *Fat and Mean: The Corporate Squeeze of Working Americans and the Myth of Managerial "Downsizing"* (New York: Free Press, 1996), p. 25.

42. Lester C. Thurow, "Companies Merge; Families Break Up," *New York Times,* September 3, 1995.

43. Peter Passell, "Economic Scene," *New York Times,* March 28, 1995.

44. Jean Kimmel and Karen Smith Conway, "Who Moonlights and Why? Evidence from the SIPP," Staff Working Paper 95–40 (Kalamazoo, MI: W.E. Upjohn Institute for Employment Research), p. 1.

45. Cited by David Wessell, "Central Bankers Say: Look Elsewhere on Jobs," *Wall Street Journal*, August 29, 1994.

46. "Self-Sufficiency and the Low-Wage Labor Market: A Reality Check for Welfare Reform," Summary of Conference April 12–14, 1994 (Washington, DC: The Urban Institute), p. 15.

47. Louis Uchitelle, "Fewer Jobs Filled as Factories Rely on Overtime Pay," *New York Times*, May 16, 1993.

48. G. Pascal Zachary, "Many Firms Refuse to Pay for Overtime, Employees Complain," *Wall Street Journal*, June 24, 1996.

49. Charles Handy, *The Age of Unreason* (Boston: Harvard Business School Press, 1990), pp. 173–181.

50. Manuel Castells, *The Network Society* (Oxford: Blackwell, 1996), p. 443.

51. Paul Ormerod, *The Death of Economics* (New York: St. Martin's Press, 1994), p. 24.

6

THE DECLINE OF CORPORATE PATERNALISM

The American business man cannot consider his work done when he views the income balance in black at the end of an accounting period. It is necessary for him to trace the social incidence of the figures that appear in his statement and prove to the general public that his management has not only been profitable in the accounting sense but salutary in terms of popular benefits.
—Colby M. Chester

Until quite recently, it was commonly assumed that when one went to work for a large or medium-size company, it could be the equivalent of a long term career decision that involved an implicit employment contract, unwritten and for the most part unenforceable, between the employer and the employee. "This unwritten pact assumed a long-term attachment between worker and employer. It also had the critical effect of insulating workers from fluctuations in the economy that affected the value of their labor in the outside market."[1] Moreover, this implicit contract was clearly weighted in favor of the employee, in that the worker could arbitrarily terminate his employment at his discretion, whereas the employer was expected to remove an employee only when justified with good cause.

The contract, at least in theory, dealt with four issues: corporate culture, employee skill development, a productive work environment, and, as a paramount concern, the assurance of employment security. This meant, in effect, that firms would operate their businesses in a way that treated employees as key stakeholders in them along with customers and shareholders. It was expected that companies would assist in providing their employees with the specific skills necessary to do their jobs, and would provide them with a work environment and a system of compensation and rewards that promoted excellence. It was generally understood that concerns about the job security of their employees would be an important consideration in decisions concerning the future of the firm.[2] It was also understood that, in return for faithful and productive service on the part of the employee, the employer would provide the employee with career development and advancement opportunities. Finally, and perhaps most important for some, the company would also commit substantial resources to help assure the health and welfare of the firm's employees, and often of their families as well.

As in all freely negotiated contracts, each of the parties stood to gain from the arrangement. For the employer, especially in the case of a large firm, it provided a means for assuring an acceptable level of worker effort and productivity where management could not always monitor or measure performance effectively. Such a long-term implicit employment contract, which was conditioned on continued good and reliable performance, gave the employee a stake in not jeopardizing the relationship by poor performance or low productivity. It also permitted the employer to develop a compensation system based on a deferred payment of benefits to reward workers who met the test of constancy over time. In practice, this often meant the receipt of somewhat substandard wages early in one's career in anticipation of above standard earnings later on. It also often involved an employer's commitment to the payment of employee post-retirement benefits, the level of which increased in accordance with one's longevity with the firm. Under such an implicit contractual arrangement, "Workers found to be shirkers during their careers are dismissed and forced to forfeit their remaining deferred payments. In view of this threat, the prospect of deferred compensation in the not-too-distant future—seniority wages and benefits, as seen by younger workers; pensions, as seen by older workers—tends to improve work effort, industriousness, and commitment to the firm among workers of all ages. A deferred-payment compensation profile is thus equivalent to having workers post an implicit performance bond."[3] This arrangement proved attractive to workers who were planning to establish a long-term career with a firm and provided incentive for a level of performance that met the firm's needs.

Such implicit employment contracts were the product of a distinctive approach to business, and employer-employee relations, that has been called "welfare capitalism" or "corporate paternalism." Corporate paternalism initially arose in the nineteenth century as a response to the uncertainties faced by large numbers of workers and their families as a result of the growing shift of population from rural to urban areas in search of the opportunities promised by industrialization. This corporate response was engendered primarily as a reaction to the alternatives available for dealing with the problem. One was the formation of mutual benefit associations of workers that sometimes developed into trade unions. Another was the intervention of government with protective legislation and the attempt to deal with risks faced by workers with social insurance programs, an approach favored in Europe that produced the welfare state. In the United States, many employers preferred to undertake the protection of workers against the risks of unemployment, illness, and security in old age in the hope that it would inhibit the growth of unions and the involvement of government. Hence the emergence of the paternalism that has been part of the corporate culture, notwithstanding the major disruptions that took place during the Great Depression of the 1930s, for more than a century.

In 1980, Robert Samuelson wrote of the negative impact of corporate paternalism on the individual's autonomy. "Increasingly, corporations serve as mini-welfare organizations, doing the things that individuals once expected to do for themselves: saving for retirement; paying health costs and in some cases, tending children in day care centers.... As larger employers provide more security, they may become more enslaving. Accumulated fringe benefits make it more difficult to leave. As we assign more individual responsibilities to employers, we become more dependent."[4] What Samuelson failed to mention in this otherwise accurate assessment is that the employer's principle motivation in offering these benefits was to attract and retain desirable personnel. In other words, many large employers deliberately sought to create dependencies to bind their workers to them, and they were largely successful in doing so.

Under this paternalism, the employer undertook to make many of the critical decisions that affected the well-being, present and future, of the firm's employees. These concerned the career opportunities made available to them, the benefits they received, and the financial expectations they could entertain both during their careers and in retirement. All of these implicit commitments are now under continuing reassessment by employers, and in many instances traumatic changes in them have already taken place. As Robert Reich has noted: "The most important part of the contract is that if the worker is diligent and reliable, and if the company is making money, that worker keeps his or her job. The second principle is enjoying rising wages and benefits as a company's profits improve. This social contract is no longer with us."[5]

FROM CORPORATE PATERNALISM TO PARTNERSHIP

The notion of an employment career with a single firm is now widely viewed as an anachronism, an expectation that is out of step with the new realities of the contemporary labor economy. Few are the corporations who can predict with any confidence what products they will be making or what services they will be providing five to ten years down the road, and fewer still are the firms who have any clear idea of what their manpower requirements will be. As a result, the burdens of career planning and career management are being shifted increasingly from a shared responsibility with corporate human resource departments to employees alone. A 1991 Conference Board report noted that "a senior executive at Bank of America even takes issue with the term 'career.' The bank," he maintains, "*does not have careers*; it has *jobs* to be done that meet customers' needs and bring a return to the shareholders."[6]

The business emphasis on achieving manpower flexibility has changed the very meaning of vocation and the words we use to describe it. As Richard Sennett points out, in its English origins, "career" meant a road for carriages. As eventually applied to labor, it came to mean "a lifelong channel for one's economic pursuits." The traditional career path has now been blocked for many workers, who have been shifted to "jobs" instead. The word "job" in medieval English "meant a lump or piece of something which could be carted around. Flexibility today brings back this arcane sense of the job, as people do lumps of labor, pieces of work, over the course of a lifetime."[7]

This situation has given rise to a school of thought that argues for the development of a new covenant under which employees would be asked to share some of the risks of doing business. Employees would no longer expect or be promised employment security. Instead they would be offered "employability security," which Rosabeth Moss Kanter defines as "the knowledge that today's work will enhance a person's value in terms of future opportunities."[8] Employers would provide opportunities for their workers "to develop greatly enhanced employability in exchange for better productivity and some degree of commitment to company purpose and community for as long as the employee works there." It is the employee's responsibility to manage his or her own career, whatever that might mean in the unfolding new world of work. The company's responsibility is "to provide employees with the tools, the open environment, and the opportunities for assessing and developing their skills."[9]

Under this approach, each worker becomes personally responsible for being knowledgeable about market trends and anticipating the skills and behaviors that will meet the firm's future needs. However, as some analysts have pointed out, such expectations assume an environment of calculable risk rather than one of radical uncertainty, within which employers and workers can make optimum training, job search, and hiring decisions. The reality, in today's volatile economy, is that "most workers have no way to estimate the payoffs from myriad alternative training decisions and career paths, and few individual employers can readily forecast their skill needs very far ahead."[10]

Although this approach to career planning and management clearly encourages greater self-reliance on the part of the employee, it is a mixed blessing because the individual worker is even less able than the corporation to anticipate future labor market needs or what skills or professional expertise will be in demand. And, even where the firm has a reasonable sense of its own future direction, there is little evidence that management makes more than a perfunctory effort, if that, at conveying such information to its employees in time for them to do anything to prepare themselves for that eventuality. Given that appropriate vocational preparation, in some instances, may require years of study, the failure to guess right can have traumatic consequences for the individual. Indeed, many dislocated highly trained, educated, skilled, and experienced mid-life and older workers now find themselves unable to avail themselves of significant employment opportunities because of a mismatch between what they can offer and what the job market is seeking.

Similarly, employee benefit plans typically required few decisions to be made by the plan participants, who were frequently passive recipients of what was perceived as corporate largesse. In the mid-1970s, however, a significant shift in corporate employee compensation and benefits policies began to take effect. This change was manifested in a fundamental reorientation in corporate thinking that became increasingly widespread during the following decade and is now virtually pervasive in the business community. This reorientation of management philosophy is intimately related to the accelerating trends toward corporate restructuring and downsizing, and the increasing reliance on a non-traditional, on-demand workforce to satisfy fluctuating needs for labor.

It is important, however, not to overstate the problem, as big as it is. As Sanford Jacoby of the University of California, Los Angeles points out, "While absolute job security no longer exists, especially in blue-collar employment, not all jobs are in peril, nor is modern welfare capitalism a relic of the past. Despite laying off thousands of workers, large corporations continue to offer career employment. Successful companies still put enormous effort into transforming new recruits into company men and women, both in the way they think and the skills they possess."[11] While this is true of a number of large corporations, mostly among the Fortune 500 companies, that number appears to be continually diminishing. Moreover, as Jacoby notes, there is much more to the U.S. economy than these relatively few giant corporations, and many employers have never been particularly concerned "with the niceties of employee commitment." Indeed, for every company still practicing welfare capitalism, "there are dozens of employers unconcerned with any type of commitment to their employees: places where the pay is low, jobs temporary, and benefits shrinking or nonexistent." He therefore concludes: "Welfare capitalism is not about to disappear in the United States, but its future looks less bright now than at any time since its postwar modernization."[12]

Corporate concerns about relative declines in productivity and competitiveness have increasingly precipitated the adoption of what appear to be draconian measures to reduce expenditures that do not contribute directly to improving a firm's profitability. In addition to trimming the workforce as much as seems practical at any given point in time, whole levels of middle management and marginal functions have been eliminated. Corporate management now tends to view employee compensation and benefits as an area that affords further opportunities for eliminating or reducing what are increasingly being perceived as unwarranted expenditures. Employers are seeking to make their long-term expense projections and commitments more predictable while reducing the level of such expenditures as much as practicable.

According to one government survey, the percentage of employees receiving health coverage from their own employer declined from 65 percent of all wage and salary workers in 1988 to 61 percent in 1993. This decline occurred almost entirely among private-sector workers whose coverage under employer sponsored plans declined from 62 percent of these workers to 58 percent during the same period. Workers in the public sector experienced a drop of only one percentage point.[13] Some of the consequences of this decline in coverage may be seen from an analysis of its effect on married men between the prime working ages of 25 and 55 employed in permanent full-time positions. Between 1979 and 1992, the proportion of such prime working age married men who were covered by employer-provided health benefits dropped from 89 to 76.6 percent, with coverage declining about 1.4 percent each year since 1986. At the same time, because of rising health-care costs, family health coverage has become increasingly dependent upon group health benefits provided by the spouse's employer. However, as pointed out in a 1994 analysis, notwithstanding the availability of spousal benefits under such plans, 13.5 percent of full-time employed working husbands were without any group health benefit coverage in 1992. The author of the study concluded that, "regardless of the causes for the change in health benefit coverage, the declines are substantial enough to generate widespread public concern."[14]

An example of this tendency to reduce if not eliminate employee benefits whenever possible is the case of Bank of America which, in mid-1994, had some 95,000 employees, 20,000 of whom were not provided with any health insurance as an employee benefit. Most of these uninsured employees were tellers and bank clerks who worked less than 20 hours a week and earned less than $8 an hour. According to a senior vice president at the bank's headquarters in Los Angeles, "If there were a tighter labor market with fewer people looking for work, we might have to offer health insurance."[15] But, since there was an abundant supply of potential workers to fill these positions, at least in California, the executive argued that insuring the bank's low-wage employees would unnecessarily add costs that would hurt the corporation's profitability and reduce dividends to its shareholders.

As a consequence of management reconsideration of the long-standing notion of an implicit contract between employer and employee, significant changes have been taking place in corporate employee compensation and benefits policies. In effect, traditional corporate paternalism has been giving way to the new philosophy of employee empowerment, one manifestation of which are human resource policies designed to promote employee "self-management." What this means, as a practical matter, is that the burdens of career development and financial planning for the future economic security of a firm's employees are being shifted from its corporate human resources managers directly to the workers. Indicative of this change in management philosophy is the fact that an increasing number of companies no longer consider it necessary or appropriate to offer their employees permanent careers or even career development opportunities in return for faithful service.

The rationale behind this fundamental change in corporate culture is described in a Conference Board study of the subject. "From the employer's perspective, self-management is an economic necessity justified by events, many of which are beyond the organization's control. The once-prevalent culture of paternalism is not compatible with a restructuring society—the corporation cannot overlook excessive labor costs just because an employee has long service."[16] In effect, the era of the long-term implicit employment contract and the corporate culture it helped spawn appears to be coming to an end.

The change has been taking place most visibly in large organizations, which are rapidly moving away from a paternalistic management philosophy toward one that is characterized by the notions of employer-employee partnership, shared responsibility and, most especially, individual employee responsibility. Employees of these firms are no longer being told, in the words of Dallas Salisbury, "Focus on work and productivity and you will have a job, and we will take care of economic security for you." Instead, they are being advised: "Focus on work and productivity and you might have a job, and we will provide benefit opportunities for you so that you can become self-reliant."[17] The consequences of this basic cultural reorientation may be seen clearly in the changes in compensation and benefits policies that are increasingly being adopted by employers.

A principal consideration in determining an individual's level of pay has traditionally been length of service. That is, fixed compensation was awarded on the basis of an employee's relative seniority. Today, an increasing number of employers are adopting a variety of flexible compensation schemes that seek to link pay directly to performance and outcomes rather than to length of service. However, as noted by Jeffrey Pfeffer of Stanford University, "Individual merit pay and even piecework, although growing in popularity, have numerous problems, and the research evidence suggests that they are frequently ineffective."[18] For one thing, the measures used for determining merit are often rather arbitrary, especially in non-production kinds of work, and therefore tend to demoralize those who do not receive the increases and cannot be given a reasonable explanation of why. Moreover, the amounts most companies actually put aside for merit raises are often limited to a percentage of total salaries that is equal to or perhaps slightly above the current rate of inflation. What this means, in effect, is that whoever does not get a merit increase is penalized by a real loss in income. This makes the competition for raises a less-than-zero-sum game. Since there is a fixed budget for raises, every dollar given to one employee not only means that another does not get it, but that the latter, because of inflation, actually takes a real loss in income as a result. This makes it in one's interest to want those who are competing for a raise not to perform well. "As most executives will tell you, individual merit pay does virtually nothing to encourage teamwork and cooperation and, to the contrary, provides disincentives for helping coworkers."[19]

As a rule, both merit and longevity-based increases constituted permanent additions to an employee's base salary and therefore became largely unrelated to variations in employee performance over time. Today, a significant number of companies provide one-time lump-sum monetary awards for meritorious performance that do not affect the level of the employee's base pay. According to a 1992 survey of 2000 employers, 61 percent utilized such one-time performance-related awards. This represents a substantial increase over the 1991 figure of 57 percent and the 1989 figure of 44 percent of the employers surveyed.[20] This trend tends to reinforce the notion that an employee's compensation is itself primarily a matter of career self-management.

IMPLICATIONS FOR OLDER WORKERS

This change in corporate culture has particularly serious consequences for older workers whose current income levels were attained under compensation schemes that are no longer applicable. Older workers are particularly prone to salary capping, which makes a mockery of the notion of merit increases, as well as to the charge of being overpaid for work that commands lower wages when performed by younger workers. This in turn seems to lend superficial credence to negative stereotypes about the value of older workers.

Notwithstanding its benefits from a corporate perspective, the new approach to employee compensation has the potential for producing some troubling social and economic consequences that have already been experienced in other countries. It is not unusual in some societies for base salaries to be held at relatively low current levels in order to reduce the levels of post-retirement benefit obligations that are calculated on the basis of average salary over a given number of years. To compensate employees for such low salaries, a variety of employee benefits are provided to supplement current income. These may include cash bonuses, car and telephone allowances, fully paid vacations, and other benefits that firms finance out of current operating revenues, without incurring long term obligations. However, it is not unusual for the level of effective income of recipients of these non-salary benefits to drop precipitously upon their leaving the workforce. This often creates an increased need for public assistance to make ends meet during retirement because of the reduced levels of social insurance, pensions, and savings that are realized as a result of such compensation policies.

In 1994, 60.1 percent of full-time wage and salary employees age 18–64 participated in retirement plans through their employers. This number rose to 60.8 percent in 1999.[21] However, it is noteworthy that the number of employees with pension coverage has been growing more slowly than the labor force as a whole. This may be attributed to the rapid growth in the non-traditional workforce (discussed in the next chapter) and the displacement of workers from large companies to smaller firms that do not offer comparable employee benefit packages.

For the most part, employer-financed pensions represent deferred compensation benefits that employees rarely gave much thought to until they reached retirement age. Previously, most public and many private pensions were provided in accordance with defined benefit plans that were based wholly or partially on employer contributions. These plans provide for a guaranteed fixed benefit at retirement that is determined by a formula that usually includes factors such as age, salary history, and length of service. Because the benefit is guaranteed, the employer bore a fiduciary responsibility for the sound investment of such pension funds.

In recent years, however, there has been a significant and continuing shift from defined benefit plans to defined contribution plans. Under the latter type of plan, employees are typically permitted to make tax-deferred contributions, which may be matched by employers, to an investment fund from which they withdraw their funds upon leaving the employer. These pension funds are distributed to the employee in a lump sum, which can be "rolled over" into another tax-deferred plan, such as one provided by another employer, or into an individual retirement account. This clearly provides some advantages to employees. The defined contribution type of plan provides pension portability that is generally unavailable with defined benefit plans, and is therefore advantageous to employees who can, in effect, take their pensions with them when they change jobs, something that cannot be done at present under most defined-benefit plans. More-over, in many cases firms offer defined-contribution plans as supplements to their regular defined benefit plans. Nonetheless, there are also some sig-nificant disadvantages for those employees whose primary source of pen-sion income is expected to come from such defined-contribution plans.

From a corporate management perspective, the shift from defined-bene-fit to defined-contribution plans has permitted many companies to signifi-cantly reduce pension-related costs and obligations, thereby improving their financial solvency and viability projections in an increasingly compet-itive marketplace, both domestic and global. It has been estimated that cor-porate contributions to employee pensions declined by as much as 50 percent between 1985–1995.[22] As a result, the number of defined-benefit plans decreased from 175,000 in 1983 to 146,000 in 1988, while the percent-age of defined-contribution plans increased from 67 percent of the total number of plans in 1975 to 80 percent in 1988.[23]

This decline in the number of defined-benefit plans offered has contin-ued, although there are indications that a not insignificant number of com-panies are taking a second look at their pension plans with more than a few beginning to offer defined-benefit plans to employees once again. A 1995 survey of 1,183 companies revealed that 41 percent offered defined-benefit plans, as compared with 34 percent the previous year.[24] It has been sug-gested that this surprising upsurge may be due in part to the need for com-panies to attract high-quality management talent, and a defined-benefit pension is highly valued as an inducement to join a firm. At the same time, however, an increasing number of companies are opting out of providing any pension benefits at all. At least 40 percent of the businesses that termi-nated defined-benefit plans since 1990 have not replaced them with any kind of company supported pension benefit.[25]

Under the defined-contribution type of plan, the employer has the op-tion of making a fixed or matching contribution to an employee's retire-ment account, leaving the ultimate investment decision to the employee. The employer, whose fiduciary responsibility is minimal under such a plan, guarantees no specific retirement income to the employee. Indeed, there may not be much or any income at all if the employee's investment of the pension funds proves to have been unwise or disadvantageous. More-over, there is evidence that many employers use their matching contribu-tions to effectively force their employees to invest their 401(k) funds primarily, or completely in company stock, causing people to lose much or all of their pension savings in the event of a loss of stock value or bank-ruptcy. This has triggered a move in Congress to propose legislation that would impose the same 10 percent ceiling on any single defined contribu-tion plan investment that federal law now places on defined benefit plans. As Senator Barbara Boxer put it, "We're sending a warning to American workers that federal pension law fails to protect 401(k) plans as it protects traditional pension plans."[26] At the same time, an increasing number of employers make no matching contributions to the employee's pension plan at all, making the benefit to be received entirely dependent on the tax-deferred payroll contributions made by the employee. This places the burden of financial planning for retirement squarely on the shoulders of the individual worker.

While many employees may welcome the empowerment afforded by participation in defined contribution plans, there appear to be serious grounds for concern that large numbers of workers may be ill-served by this movement away from the more traditional defined benefit pension plan. As noted by the chairman of the Pension Benefit Guaranty Corporation's advisory committee, "It is a very unfair thing to saddle young people with 401(k) plans. It shifts the burden of retirement planning and retirement investing to those people who are least able to afford it. A lot of people are not putting money in because they have kids in school and health costs."[27] Indeed, as noted in a study by the Massachusetts Mutual Life Insurance Co., although the employee participation rate in 401(k) plans increased by 8 percent since 1990, total employee contributions declined by 12 percent over the same period.[28] It has been estimated that as many as one-third of workers with access to a 401(k) do not participate, and that of those who do, only 38 percent contribute the maximum amount permitted.[29]

In addition, a 1993 supplement to the Current Population Survey indicates that only 32 percent of lump sums distributed from defined-contribution plans that year went entirely into retirement or other savings and investments. It is noteworthy that some 60 percent of workers age 55 to 64 placed their lump sum distributions entirely into retirement or other savings, while the remaining 40 percent either spent all of their distributions or put their funds to other uses. However, less than half of workers age 45 to 54 who received lump sum distributions in 1993 put those funds back into savings or investments.[30]

In addition, many if not most workers do not have sufficient knowledge of or experience with capital markets to make sound investment decisions. There is abundant research evidence that most individuals tend to be highly conservative in their investment decisions. They generally tend to prefer low-risk and consequently low-return investments, notwithstanding that the value of those returns are seriously eroded by even lower inflation rates, reducing the long-term significance of such savings as a source of retirement income.

It has been suggested by some commentators that the solution to this problem is to educate employees to become better investors. However, this seems rather unrealistic. As benefit plan advisor Barry S. Slevin observed,

We advise trustees, who are generally more sophisticated than the participants, of the need to appoint a professional investment manager to invest plan assets, as opposed to having the trustees make investment decisions themselves. Most boards of trustees also retain an investment consultant to help them monitor the investment managers and make asset allocation decisions. In this context, how can it be assumed that participants can ever be educated sufficiently to become sophisticated investors whose returns will in any way approach those of investment managers supervised by trustees advised by an investment consultant?[31]

As a result, according to Carter Beese Jr., a commissioner of the Securities and Exchange Commission who specializes in defined-contribution plans: "A lot of participants in 401(k) plans are not doing a good job. They are not investing well and leagues of them may be retiring at subsistence levels from their 401(k) plans." He concluded that, "for many retirees, the money won't be there, and this will have a direct effect on most Americans' standard of living."[32]

It has also been suggested by some that most people wouldn't even use 401(k) plans if they were not able to cash them out whenever they chose, which helps account for the fact that the median amount in such accounts in 1995 was about $5,000.[33] Moreover, a 1995 survey of 267 large employers revealed that 20 percent of plan participants had outstanding loans against their savings balances.[34] This situation is likely to worsen if banks go ahead with a plan to attach credit cards to 401(k) plans, which would make it even easier for "otherwise reluctant savers to tap their otherwise illiquid funds."[35]

These far-reaching changes in corporate culture and policy may be viewed as ultimately beneficial and desirable from a social policy perspective because they clearly promote individual autonomy and self-determination, attributes highly valued in our society. At the same time, however, it should be recognized that the decline in corporate responsibility to employees creates a lacuna in the social arrangements that have prevailed in this country for more than half a century. Under these arrangements, the benefits usually provided by governments in other industrialized democracies have been tied to employers here. Failure to fill that void effectively can have traumatic impacts on the future well-being of workers of all ages who have not been adequately prepared for the career and financial self-management responsibilities that are being thrust upon them. To deal with this and a number of related concerns, it may prove desirable to reexamine the entire question of the general corporate responsibility to the societies within which businesses operate, and more specifically to the workers they employ.

NOTES

1. Barbara Rudolph, *Disconnected: How Six People from AT&T Discovered the New Meaning of Work in a Downsized Corporate America* (New York: Free Press, 1998), p. 3.

2. Barbara Ettorre, "Empty Promises," *Management Review* (July 1996), p. 18.

3. John W. Straka, "The Demand for Older Workers: The Neglected Side of a Labor Market," publication no. 13–11776 (15) (Washington, DC: Social Security Administration, June 1992), p. 12.

4. Robert J. Samuelson, "A Rebel With a Cause," *National Journal* (April 26, 1980), p. 690.

5. Barry Bearak, "Cat on Strike: The Waning Power of Unions," *Los Angeles Times*, May 14, 1995.

6. "Encouraging Employee Self-Management in Financial and Career Planning," report no. 976 (New York: The Conference Board, 1991), p. 27.

7. Richard Sennett, *The Corrosion of Character: The Personal Consequences of Work in the New Capitalism* (New York: W.W. Norton, 1998), p. 9.

8. Rosabeth Moss Kanter, "U.S. Competetiveness and the Aging Workforce: Toward Organizational and Institutional Change," in *Aging and Competition: Rebuilding the U.S. Workforce*, eds. James A. Auerbach and Joyce C. Welsh (Washington, DC: National Planning Association, 1994), p. 27.

9. Robert H. Waterman, Jr., Judith A. Waterman, and Betsy A. Collard, "Toward a Career-Resilient Workforce," *Harvard Business Review* (July–August 1994), p. 88.

10. Stephen Herzenberg, John Alic, and Howard Wial, "A New Deal for a New Economy," *Challenge* (March–April 1999), p. 113.

11. Sanford Jacoby, "Downsizing in the Past," *Challenge* (May–June 1998), p. 109.

12. Ibid., pp. 110–111.

13. "Pension and Health Benefits of American Workers: New Findings from the April 1993 Current Population Survey" (Washington, DC: U.S. Department of Labor, Social Security Administration, U.S. Small Business Administration, and the Pension Benefit Guaranty Corporation, 1994), p. 4.

14. Craig A. Olson, "Health Benefits Coverage Among Male Workers," *Monthly Labor Review* (March 1995), pp. 58, 61.

15. Cited by Louis Uchitelle, "Big Companies Use Little-Company Arguments to Resist Insuring Workers," *New York Times*, August 20, 1994.

16. "Encouraging Employee Self-Management in Financial and Career Planning," report no. 976 (New York: The Conference Board, 1991).

17. Dallas L. Salisbury, and Nora Super Jones, eds., *Retirement in the 21st Century . . . Ready or Not* (Washington, DC: Employee Benefit Research Institute, 1994), p. 5.

18. Jeffrey Pfeffer, *The Human Equation: Building Profits by Putting People First* (Boston: Harvard Business School Press, 1998), p. 196.

19. Ibid., p. 204.

20. Donna Brown Hogarty, "New Ways to Pay," *Management Review* (January 1944), p. 34.

21. "EBRI Retirement Income Research: 2001 Findings" (Washington, DC: Employee Benefit Research Institute, January 2001).

22. Karen Ferguson and Kate Blackwell, "Do-It-Yourself Plans Aren't Enough," *Los Angeles Times*, July 3, 1995. This is substantiated by the statement of the Committee for Economic Development: "Total private pension contributions declined in constant 1987 dollars from about $1,470 per worker in 1985 to about

$1,140 per worker in 1991. The employer component declined in real terms from about $1,039 in 1980 to about $506 per worker in 1991," in "Who Will pay For Your Retirement?" (New York: Committee for Economic Development, 1995), p. 5.

23. *Databook on Employee Benefits* (Washington, DC: Employee Benefits Research Institute, 1992), p. 115.

24. Marianne Taylor, "New Life for Traditional Pensions," *Chicago Tribune*, June 15, 1995.

25. Larry Reynolds, "Potential Pension Disaster," *Management Review* (November 1992), p. 25. The numbers given are a conservative extrapolation from those cited by Reynolds to reflect developments through 1993.

26. Robert A. Rosenblatt, "Congress Examines 401(k) Plans," *Los Angeles Times*, July 16, 1996.

27. David A. Vise, "A Pensionless Future?" *Washington Post*, May 13, 1993.

28. "Labor Letter," *Wall Street Journal*, November 11, 1993.

29. Byron D. Oliver, "Retirement Blues," *Management Review* (May 1996), p. 33.

30. Diane E. Hertz, "Work After Early Retirement: An Increasing Trend Among Men," *Monthly Labor Review* (April 1995), p. 17.

31. Barry S. Slevin, "Defined Contribution Plans for Multiemployer Funds," *Employee Benefits Journal*, 21, no. 2 (June 1996), p. 19.

32. Leslie Wayne, "Pension Changes Raising Concerns," *New York Times*, August 29, 1994.

33. Karen Ferguson, and Kate Blackwell, "Do-It-Yourself Plans Aren't Enough," *Los Angeles Times*, July 3, 1995.

34. Ellen E. Schultz, "More Workers Are Cracking Their Nest Eggs," *Wall Street Journal*, August 17, 1995.

35. "Cracking Open the Nest Egg," *Economist* (July 27, 1996).

7

RESTRUCTURING THE WORKFORCE

The existing empirical evidence does not support the view that, for the most part, firms adopt new labor force management practices strategically. Rather, what the available data do portray is unplanned, haphazard management of the employment relationship.

—Jeffrey Pfeffer

In a study of labor market patterns from the mid-nineteenth century to 1969, labor economist Dean Morse wrote that the modern labor force "consists of a large nucleus of full-time, full-year workers, generally, but not always employed by large-scale organizations. This nucleus possesses a considerable amount of 'status' and is protected by a host of private and public institutions. Surrounding it are groups of 'peripheral workers,' numbering many millions, who do not have the status and protection taken for granted by workers who from one year to the next are likely to have continuous full-time employment."[1]

In the nuclear labor force, most workers tended to work for a single employer for extended periods of time, and employee benefits policies and programs were designed with such workers in mind. Although there were always peripheral workers who did not fit this profile, there is very little data available concerning them. For the most part, they appear to have included blacks, women, and newly arrived immigrants from Europe and

Asia, people who struggled for employment on the fringes of the labor market. During the 1980s, however, the number of such peripheral workers—now including large numbers of people formerly employed in the nuclear labor force—began to grow substantially, a trend that may be expected to continue well into the twenty-first century. "When this shift of white and middle-class male and female skilled workers into the secondary workforce began to occur, we failed to recognize that this was but a new turn in a longstanding labor market trend. Our historical amnesia was, in part, fueled by the fact that these workers were now being referenced by a new term—contingent workers."[2]

Labor economist Audrey Freedman first coined the term "contingent worker" in 1985. It was used to describe "conditional and transitory employment arrangements as initiated by a need for labor—usually because a company has an increased demand for a particular service or a product or a technology, at a particular place, at a specific time."[3] Reliable estimates of the size, composition, and significance of the so-called contingent workforce were constrained both by the lack of adequate data and by the absence of a more precise and standardized definition of the classification. Some considered the definition to be too broad, because "virtually any work arrangement that might differ from the commonly perceived norm of a full-time wage and salary job would fall under the rubric of contingent work."[4] Many analysts became confused about exactly what was being described by the term and what was being studied.

To deal with this problem, in 1989 the Bureau of Labor Statistics developed its own definition of contingent work: "Contingent work is any job in which an individual does not have an explicit or implicit contract for long-term employment."[5] Nonetheless, the definition commonly used by many analysts considered those engaged in part-time, temporary, and contract employment as members of the contingent workforce. Moreover, some analysts broadened the category to include leased employees and those employed by firms that provide services to other companies.

In August 1995, the BLS issued a report that, although it acknowledged the prevailing diverse use of the term, redefined contingent workers as "those individuals who do not perceive themselves as having an explicit or implicit contract for ongoing employment."[6] This introduced a higher level of ambiguity into the classification that did not exist in the earlier definition because of its complete reliance on workers' perceptions. Similarly, contingent *jobs* are considered by BLS to be "jobs which are structured to last only a limited period of time."[7] In other words, BLS is now using the term "contingent," for all practical purposes, as a synonym for "short-term temporary." In the view of some analysts, this effectively reduces the utility of the BLS reports for understanding what is taking place in the changing employment environment. Those who fit the BLS characterization of contingent workers are estimated to number only between 2.2 and 4.9 percent of the labor force.

This new BLS definition has provided grist for the mill of those who prefer to downplay the significance of the number of those previously considered contingent workers, most of which are part-timers. Thus, Max Lyons of the Employment Policy Foundation writes, "it is unreasonable to consider most part-time workers contingent, since a large majority of part-time workers choose to work less than a full-time schedule, and they expect an ongoing employment relationship."[8] And, because the number of voluntary part-time workers, in accordance with the new definition, far outnumbered involuntary part-timers, who were estimated to constitute only about 4 percent of the labor force, Lyons titled his study, *Part-Time Work: Not a Problem Requiring a Solution*. Of course, 4 percent of the labor force represents about 5 million real people, and some would take umbrage at the rather cavalier notion that their involuntary underemployment is "not a problem requiring a solution." Moreover, as pointed out by Chris Tilly, "many people counted by the official statistics as voluntary part-time workers are in fact trapped in part-time hours by the unavailability of satisfactory child care or elder care."[9] This situation is especially prevalent among women who are also single heads of families.

In any case, as pointed out by some analysts, the principal distinction between standard full-time permanent employees, or core workers, and contingent workers is not the extent to which the latter perceive themselves as having limited continued employment prospects. It is the distinction between equity and opportunity that is of greatest significance. In a 1998 report, the BLS acknowledged that "contingent workers earned less and were less likely than noncontingent workers to have been included in employer-provided health insurance or pension plans."[10]

The San Francisco-based organization New Ways to Work argues that "Core workers have legal protections, fringe benefits and some hope of advancement in the future; too many contingent workers do not." The contingent workforce is estimated to number a maximum of 4.9 percent of the labor force, in accordance with the current BLS definition. However, it will be seen to be considerably larger (at least 21 percent) if we include those workers whom the BLS characterizes as having "alternative employment arrangements." The latter category includes those workers who identify themselves as independent contractors (6.7 percent), on-call workers (1.7 percent), those available for temporary work assignments (1 percent), contract firm employees (0.5 percent), and part-timers who do not fall within any of the other categories (11.4 percent).[11] Even this expanded number represents a rather conservative estimate if one goes beyond the self-identified categories noted above and considers the actual work experience of the population in any recent year. Moreover, it should always be borne in mind that these percentages represent about 25 million real people whose actual numbers increase every year with the growth of the labor force even when the percentages remain constant or even decline slightly.

To avoid confusion between these various definitions and uses of the term "contingent," in this study any form of employment that involves less than 35 hours of compensated work per week or less than 50 weeks of compensated work per year will be referred to generally as "nonstandard" employment.

GROWTH OF THE NONSTANDARD WORKFORCE

Taking these problems of definition into account, analysis of BLS data indicates that in 1996 between 34 and 42.2 million workers (depending on the methodology used to derive the numbers), or 25.2 to 31.3 percent of the labor force, did not conform with the standard model of full-time, permanent employment. To put this figure in some perspective, consider that the overall growth of the labor force between 1980 and 1996 was 26.1 percent, while the number of part-time workers increased by 35.6 percent, temporary workers by 500 percent, business service workers by 118.2 percent, and self-employed workers by 23.5 percent. It should be noted, however, that the overwhelming bulk of nonstandard workers are part-timers. Thus, the number of part-time workers is about 3 times as large as the number of the self-employed, 18 times as great as the number of temporary workers, and some 30 times as great as the number of business service or contract workers. The data indicates that between 1980 and 1996 the nonstandard workforce grew between 9.9 to 22 percentage points faster than employment for the entire economy. They also suggest that between 32 to 49 percent of the jobs created during the period were to be filled by non-permanent and non-full-time workers.[12]

Some of the implications of this may be seen clearly in the arena of manufacturing employment. Although the overall number of manufacturing jobs has been declining consistently, the share of blue-collar jobs increased from 9 percent in 1983 to 23 percent in 1993. This, it is suggested, "indicates that manufacturers have moved away from periodically hiring and laying off workers, and toward filling more of their variable employment needs with contingent workers on a routine basis."[13] Part-time workers represented some 19 percent of the manufacturing labor force in 1988, and more than 25 percent in 1995. They also made up 36 percent of workers in service occupations, the sector of the economy from which we expect the principal growth in jobs over the coming decades.

Another factor that needs to be taken into account is that available statistics on part-time employment typically refer to numbers of workers rather than numbers of jobs, and therefore tend to understate the extent of part-time employment. As a result, a person who holds two or more jobs, which add up to 35 or more hours per week, is counted as a full-time worker. Standard part-time employment data therefore do not take into consideration that, between 1970 and 1989, the number of women holding multiple jobs increased from 636,000 to 3,109,000, accounting for 33 percent of all women in the labor force.[14]

It is estimated that women currently constitute more than two-thirds of the temporary workforce and about two-thirds of those working part-time, and that their availability for such work has helped significantly to spur the growth of such nonstandard employment. The reason for this is the common but only partially true perception by employers that women in the workforce tend to be 'secondary' earners rather than breadwinners. Because of this perception, employers are likely to pay women less and to provide them with fewer opportunities for training and advancement. "Women will tend to work in jobs with lower pay and fewer benefits because these are the jobs that are open to them. Over time, the available jobs seem to have become increasingly contingent in nature, and women have been considered the ideal person to fill them."[15]

Only a few years ago, conservative estimates projected that the total number of nonstandard workers of all categories in the United States would reach about 35 percent of the workforce by the turn of the century. These estimates are proving to have been quite realistic, because the actual growth in the size of the nonstandard workforce has already surpassed such predictions. The BLS report on the actual work experience of the population in 1993 clearly indicated that the number of those engaged in other than full-time, year-round employment was already more than 39 percent. This figure continued to hold through 1995, but declined to 35.8 percent in 1997 and to 34.1 in 1999, presumably as a result of the upsurge in the economy.[16] It remains to be seen if this number will continue to decline in the years ahead. Given the long-range trends discussed elsewhere in this work, some business analysts have suggested that it was conceivable that nonstandard workers might account for as much as half of the workforce within the next two decades.[17]

The principal growth in the nonstandard workforce has taken place in part-time and temporary employment. Between March 1991 and July 1993, only 46.3 percent of the total number of jobs created was in private-sector, full-time, non-temporary employment, and another 26 percent represented increases in government jobs, mostly at the state and local levels. The remainder, 27.7 percent of the 1.9 million jobs created, were temporary positions. The temporary help industry's own figures claim that it put an average of 1,635,000 people to work daily throughout 1993, a 21.3 percent increase over the previous year's amount.[18] This development led Mitchell Fromstein, chief executive of Manpower, to say, "You may not like what you see, but the facts are that we are now the conduit to the workforce. They can talk all they want in Washington about how to create jobs. . . . But down here, this is the reality, this is the job market."[19] Indeed, in 1997, average daily employment in the industry rose to 2,535,220, producing a payroll of $37.4 billion and temporary help agency receipts of an unprecedented $50.3 billion.[20]

While it is true that the temporary help industry has become a major vehicle for access to the workforce, and has enabled many temporary workers to find permanent employment, it is by no means an unmixed blessing. Through an arduous struggle lasting almost a half-century, the temporary help industry has managed to still remain virtually unregulated, thereby ensuring its own phenomenal growth to the point where Manpower Inc. can justly claim to be the largest employer in the United States. However, there is more here than meets the eye.

As pointed out by George Gonos, in a penetrating analysis of the temporary help industry, the "temporary" aspect is misleading because it has never been the defining characteristic of the industry that distinguishes temporary help firms from temporary employment agencies. Whereas employment agencies place workers in temporary jobs for a one-time fee, temporary help firms become the employers of such workers, who are placed in temporary work assignments with clients. The distinction is highly significant.

The defining characteristic of a temporary help firm is that it creates an ongoing triangular relationship between the firm, its employees, and the clients for whom its employees actually work. The central purpose served by this arrangement, which Gonos calls the "temporary help formula," is that it effectively "severs the employer-employee relationship between workers and those user firms on whose premises they work and for whom they provide needed labor inputs. That is, this arrangement allows the THF's [temporary help firm's] client to utilize labor without taking on the specific social, legal, and contractual obligations that have increasingly been attached to employer status since the New Deal."[21]

However, as a practical matter, the temporary help firm is the worker's employer only in a nominal legal sense. The employee is only paid when on actual assignment with a client. It is the client that exercises direct control of the work performed; the work performed benefits the client, not the employer. These considerations suggest that, notwithstanding that the temporary help firm collects withholding taxes, carries worker's compensation insurance, and serves as paymaster, in all other respects it is not very different from an employment agency, except that it is virtually unregulated. Because of this arrangement and the increased use by business of such temporary help firms, employees who do not get picked up by the client for whom they actually work would seem to be denied the advancement opportunities that might exist if they were directly employed. Although there is very little useful information regarding the opportunity costs incurred by workers under this arrangement, it seems reasonable to assume that it is not, as already suggested, an unmixed blessing for them.

One of the unanticipated consequences of the extraordinary growth of the temporary employment market is that it has spawned the emergence of "permatemps." These are temporary employees who remain with a company for an extended, often multiyear, period. According to the BLS, some 29 percent of workers employed by temporary employment agencies are such "permatemps."[22] This situation, which is particularly acute in the information technology industry, has arisen as a consequence of the desire of companies to continue to employ temps in place of regular employees because of the greater flexibility and lower overall labor costs involved. The long-term consequence of hiring long-term temporary employees, in the words of one such permatemp, is that "we are breeding a generation of workers who view companies as the enemy."[23] One of the reasons for this is that temporary workers in the information technology industry are often asked to sign nondisclosure agreements and noncompete clauses that limit a worker's ability to obtain a full-time assignment with the company's competitors.

The legality of this permatemp employment arrangement has been placed in question, and in a high profile lawsuit filed against Microsoft in November 1998 it was claimed that many of the software giant's thousands of temporary workers were really common-law employees of the company. As such, they would be entitled, under the Employment Retirement Income Security Act of 1974 (ERISA), to certain benefits, such as the discount stock purchases, that are normally provided to regular employees. Referring to the law suit, the company's director of contingent staffing was quoted as saying, "If you really look at what's going on, it appears as if they're saying there's no good reason to have temporary workers at all." While this reaction may be rather overstated, the controversy calls into question the legitimacy of misusing temporary workers in order to deny them valuable employee benefits.[24] On May 12, 1999, a three-judge panel of the U.S. Court of Appeals ruled that workers who are on the payroll for more than a few months, whether permatemps or independent contractors, are in fact common-law employees and are therefore entitled to the same benefits as permanent employees.[25] The effects this ruling will have on the companies that use, and the workers who are employed as, permatemps and independent contractors are uncertain at this writing, but seem likely to have a notable impact on the structure of the workforce

During the period of March 1991 to July 1993, the number of people working part-time accounted for some 26 percent of total employment growth. Three-fourths of these were working in part-time jobs because no full-time positions were available for them. This raised the number of *involuntary* part-time workers to about 6.5 million, contributing significantly to the growing national pool of the structurally underemployed. Moreover, this happened at a time when the growth in the numbers of *voluntary* part-time workers was diminishing. Thus, involuntary part-time employment increased by 178 percent during the period 1970 to 1992, at the same time that voluntary part-time employment increased by only 53 percent.[26] Between 1990 and 1992, the actual number of voluntary part-time workers decreased by 370,000, while there was an increase of almost 1.3 million involuntary part-time workers.[27] According to a 1993 analysis of developments in the labor market: "These trends suggest that the rapid expansion of part-time work in the recovery reflects the success of employers in expanding part-time jobs even though employees are shifting their preferences toward full-time jobs."[28]

With the upturn in the economy over the past several years, these trends appear to have reversed direction, showing significant declines in involuntary part-time work. However, these latest figures must be used with some caution. It has been pointed out that the share of involuntary part-time workers, which grew steadily from 3.8 percent in 1979 to 5.5 percent in 1993, fell sharply, to 3.7 percent in 1995. However, it is not clear what portion of the decline might be due to a change in the government survey method used to measure work hours.[29] Moreover, the definition of "involuntary" is becoming increasingly murky. A 1995 study indicates that about 6 percent of male workers hold part-time jobs in addition to their usual full-time positions at any one time, and that a much larger percentage "moonlight" at some point in their work lives. It also suggests that as many as 40 percent of "moonlighters" do so because of insufficient income derived from their primary jobs.[30] From the perspective of these workers, are they voluntary or involuntary part-timers?

A new phenomenon has recently emerged in the form of a "voluntary-involuntary" part-time worker. This is someone who is employed on a part-time basis but who actually winds up working full-time for a reduced salary. A case in point is the 200 part-time administrative law judges in New York City who joined the City Employees Union in early 1999 to gain some bargaining leverage. Although considered part-time employees, some work 35 hours a week and often work nights doing the same work as full-time hearing officers at the Environmental Control Board, Taxi and Limousine Commission, and Department of Health.[31]

It has been suggested that it is primarily professional women who find themselves in this situation. Accepting a part-time assignment, in many instances so they might be free to attend to family-care matters, they find themselves under pressure to put in a full-time workweek in order to deal with the workload assigned to them. Bearing in mind that anyone who works 35 or more hours is considered by definition to be a full-time worker, no one really seems to know how many full-time part-timers there are in the workforce. However, according to the 1997 National Study of the Changing Workforce conducted by the Families and Work Institute, approximately one-third of the salaried part-timers surveyed indicated that they worked at least 35 hours a week.[32] This suggests that such voluntary-involuntary part-timers may already represent a sizeable percentage of the nonstandard workforce.

In addition to the large numbers of temporary and part-time workers, the nonstandard workforce also includes an increasing number of contract workers, in both the private and public sectors, who perform work previously done by full-time permanent employees. In February 1997, the BLS identified some 8.5 million people as "independent contractors, independent consultants, or freelance workers," about 26 percent of whom worked part-time.[33] Estimates by the IRS also indicate that as many as 3.4 million employees have been improperly classified as independent contractors by about 15 percent of all businesses.[34] A national commission examined the problem and concluded that employers have powerful economic incentives for such misclassifications. "The employer will not have to make contributions to Social Security, unemployment insurance, workers' compensation, and health insurance, will save the administrative expense of withholding, and will be relieved of responsibility to the worker under the labor and employment laws."[35]

Generally speaking, contract employees tend to earn substantially less than those performing comparable work as permanent employees. In some cases, a contractor will rehire the same employees who were released by the contracting organization to perform the identical work they did before for their previous employer. "In these cases, for the employees the job is the same; only the employer—and likely the pay and benefits—have changed. Workers rehired by contractors typically lose all seniority and receive inferior pay and benefits compared to what they earned in their previously held jobs."[36] Moreover, in some instances, contractors for services have imposed an even greater economic burden on the workers who actually provide the service. An egregious example of this is a Seattle building-cleaning contractor who won some accounts as the lowest cost bidder and then began selling floors of the office building accounts as "franchises" to recent immigrants who paid from $4,000 to $7,000 for the privilege of cleaning those offices. Since the workers were now classified as self-employed franchisees, the contractor was able to disclaim any responsibility for Social Security or unemployment compensation contributions or minimum wage and overtime violations of the Fair Labor Standards Act. The responsibility for compliance with these requirements was shifted entirely to the service workers, who were rather poorly prepared for the task.[37]

Nonetheless, it should be recognized that for many highly trained and skilled knowledge workers, nonstandard working arrangements are both desirable and preferred. The principal reason for this, as Peter Drucker points out, is that "knowledge workers, unlike manual workers in manufacturing, own the means of production: They carry that knowledge in their heads and can therefore take it with them." This gives both them and their prospective employers a great deal of flexibility in meeting their mutual needs. "As a result, in developed countries more and more of the critical workforce—and the most highly paid part of it—will increasingly consist of people who cannot be 'managed' in the traditional sense of the word. In many cases, they will not even be employees of the organizations for which they work, but rather contractors, experts, consultants, part-timers, joint-venture partners, and so on. An increasing number of these people will identify themselves by their own knowledge rather than by the organization that pays them."[38] Nonetheless, it must also be recognized that the overwhelming majority of American workers do not fall into the category of "knowledge workers," and that the work arrangements that may be desirable for the latter do not necessarily apply to them.

FACTORS CONTRIBUTING TO THE PROCESS

How do we account for this unprecedented growth in the nonstandard workforce? It seems that there are two principal factors driving the process. First, nonstandard work arrangements offer the flexibility required by many workers who previously had been effectively excluded from the standard labor force because of the time constraints imposed by family care responsibilities. Part-time work has enabled large numbers of women, who comprise two-thirds of all part-time workers, as well as a more modest number of retirees, to reenter or remain in the labor force.

With specific regard to older workers, John Challenger has argued that the explosion of nonstandard work arrangements has had very positive effects. It has "allowed many people to achieve a balance in their lives that is so much more healthy and beneficial spiritually and emotionally and physically than just hitting the wall at a certain age and going from being a hard-working, very involved worker to not doing anything, which was just devastating to many people."[39]

From the perspective of those seeking flexible work arrangements to meet current income and other needs, the growth of the nonstandard workforce is clearly a highly desirable development, even if it comes at the expense of the employee benefits typically received by full-time workers. In 1992, according to BLS data, approximately 70 percent of all part-time employees were voluntary nonstandard workers. Nonetheless, that means some 30 percent of part-time workers, or close to 6.5 million persons, would have preferred full-time work, but were unable to find it.[40]

A second, more powerful factor driving the expansion of the nonstandard workforce is its strategic use by employers, for whom flexibility has a rather different meaning than it does for workers. As Richard Belous puts it, "Flexibility, in terms of corporate human resource systems and labor markets in general, means that compensation, employment relationships, work assignments, modes of staffing, and career paths are highly responsive to economic variables and business strategies."[41]

One such business strategy is to create what has been called a "boundaryless workforce." In the boundaryless workplace, standard work arrangements are almost completely discarded. People work together without regard to location or time, and may not report to the same supervisor. They may work at home, at a customer's site, while travelling, or with people in other states or countries who they may rarely or perhaps never actually meet. Such boundaryless work practices are growing rapidly in the business world, and all reasonable expectations are that they will characterize an increasing segment of the workforce.[42]

A recent study of the perceptions of those involved in these boundaryless arrangements indicates that 31 percent of workers and managers over the age of 50 believe that boundaryless workers are less respected than their standard counterparts. However, only 10 percent of workers and managers ages 19 to 29 and 13 percent of workers and managers ages 30 to 39 held similar views.[43] These data lend themselves to two diametrically opposite conclusions. One is that, as older workers and managers leave the workforce and younger workers and managers replace them, satisfaction with boundaryless arrangements will increase. The second is that, as younger workers and managers grow older, their degree of satisfaction with boundaryless work arrangements will decrease as they encounter the age biases that are so common in today's workplace.

A second business strategy is to reduce the costs of labor by not providing nonstandard workers with the same level of wages and benefits usually offered to full-time permanent employees. The value of such employee benefits currently represents as much as 45 percent of total compensation for permanent full-time employees.[44] In general, but with some occasionally notable exceptions, temporary and part-time workers tend to earn substantially less than full-time workers do. An estimate based on BLS data indicates that the difference in median hourly earnings for part-time workers ranges from 45 percent for service workers to 54.6 percent for technical workers.[45]

Moreover, most temporary and part-time workers are effectively excluded from most company pension and health plans, as well as other standard employee benefits. A 1998 study of health benefits indicated that the share of private-sector workers with health insurance from their employment decreased from 71.9 percent to 64.5 percent between 1979 and 1997. The drop was attributed primarily to the decline in the numbers of "peripheral" workers, part-time and temporary, that were eligible for coverage under employee benefit plans. The author of an article describing this study concludes: "Employers are continuing to provide insurance for their long-term employees. At the same time, however, they are cutting back on coverage for their short-term and part-time employees—workers who make up a sizable part of the nation's labor force."[46] According to the Employee Benefit Research Institute, in 1997, between 61 and 66 percent of contingent workers [as defined by the BLS] had health insurance coverage, compared with 82 percent of those with standard work arrangements.[47]

A 1995 BLS survey, covering some 1.1 million workers on the payroll of temporary help firms employing 20 or more, indicated that the average earnings of these temporary workers was only 2 percent higher, without adjustment for inflation, than it had been in 1989.[48] Another survey of 479 employers of part-time workers indicated that the most common benefit given employees was paid holidays. However, although 83 percent of the employers surveyed offered paid holidays to their part-time employees working more than 30 hours a week, only 51 percent gave it to employees working less than 20 hours. A similar situation prevails with regard to paid vacations, with only 47 percent of the companies offering the benefit to those working fewer than 20 hours a week.[49] Moreover, as noted earlier, some employers have deliberately misclassified their employees as self-employed contractors to avoid paying both optional employee benefits and mandatory Social Security, unemployment insurance, and worker's compensation.

"In other words," as the authors of a law journal article put it, "the *job* market is more responsible than the labor market for creating the contingent [nonstandard] workforce."[50] This is clearly confirmed by the *Fortune* CEO Poll of the Fortune 500 company chief executives, conducted in November 1993. Although 25 percent of the 203 executives who participated in the survey thought that the continued growth of the nonstandard workforce was not good for the country, 44 percent stated that they relied more on nonstandard workers today than they had in the past. An equal percentage said they expected to employ "still more here-today, gone-tomorrow workers five years from now."[51] A 1995 study by the Conference Board indicated that the numbers of large international employers with nonstandard workers comprising 10 percent or more of their workforces was projected to grow to 35 percent by the end of the decade. This would represent a very substantial increase from the only 12 percent of such companies in 1990.[52]

As Lillian Gorman of Edison International put it, "What you see now is a continual set of staffing shifts influenced not only by the economy but by a company's need to respond to competitive and regulatory forces." As a practical matter, this means an ongoing radical transformation of the workforce and the terms and conditions of employment. "We want to be more sophisticated in the kinds of people we will need for the near-, mid- and long-term. We want people who want to work in flexible ways, so we can have the option of putting them back on the shelf when we don't need them."[53]

To achieve this kind of flexible workforce, increasing numbers of employers are adopting what has been described as a "core-ring" employment strategy. In this approach to workforce management, the company workforce is reduced to a relatively small core of full-time employees who sustain essential business functions and operations. Surrounding the core is an outer ring that is composed of nonstandard workers that are hired as necessary and discharged when no longer needed to supplement the core group. An alternate version of the strategy describes it as a "shamrock" organization, one that is composed of three elements: a core workforce, the contracting out of as many support functions as possible, and a nonstandard workforce to provide additional needed labor on demand.

This reconfiguration has also been described as a "flexible workforce." It is comprised of a shrinking core of permanent managers, planners, and support staff that is expected to amount to no more than 42 percent of the total U.S. workforce. This restructured core workforce is augmented with an "expanding periphery" consisting of professional and specialized skilled workers who perform services for the firm on a contract basis, directly or through a small intermediary firm. This component is expected to amount to about 38 percent of the workforce. Finally, there is "the fringe," which is essentially a spot market for low-skilled labor to be employed as needed, representing some 20 percent of the labor force.[54]

This approach to human resource management is sometimes referred to as "accordion management," since the ability to expand or contract a company's productive capacity will respond to immediate or short-term needs. Moreover, this workforce management approach is not limited to large employers, since it offers the same if not even greater benefits to small businesses, many of which are subcontractors to larger companies and require comparable flexibility in their own workforces.

For example, a small plastic container manufacturer located in Piedmont, S.C., began restructuring by first cutting its full-time workforce from 250 to 238. Then, as full-time employees left the company, they were replaced by nonstandard workers as needed, thereby assuring that the permanent full-time core staff remained fully utilized despite fluctuations in demand for the company's products. The temporary workers that were hired to meet upsurges in demand were paid $2 less per hour than the full-time employees performing the identical tasks and received no company-paid benefits.[55]

It should nonetheless be recognized that there is nothing really new about this workforce management strategy. It was previously employed extensively for decades in the defense and aerospace industries. Government contractors and subcontractors typically hired the appropriate numbers of technical and support workers necessary to fulfill their contract commitments, and discharged them as projects terminated and were not replaced by new equivalent contracts, or if the new contracts required a different mix of worker skills. Except for some occasionally massive cutbacks, particularly in aerospace companies, the loss of contracts by an employer did not necessarily entail any net reduction in the overall industry workforce because the industry as a whole was growing as defense budgets continued to increase. For employees, it was in effect a zero-sum game. The loss of a contract by Company A was compensated for by a new contract for Company B. This meant that there would be a shift in the workforce from one company to another. However, even though large numbers of employees in these industries were nonstandard workers in the sense that their employment with a particular company was only for the duration of a project or contract, their overall employment situation remained relatively stable. However, it was difficult for many such workers to become vested in company pension plans because of the frequent job turnover and the lack of defined benefit pension portability.

Today, the "core-ring" strategy is increasingly being applied across the entire spectrum of employers. Moreover, even though nonstandard workers have been employed historically to supplement and carry out tasks that are peripheral to the company's core activities, this has been changing as well. Such workers, especially "permatemps," are increasingly being used to perform core functions as the drive to reduce permanent overhead continues to gain momentum as companies increasingly view human resources more as a variable instead of a necessary fixed cost. As a result, the nonstandard workforce is growing dramatically as corporate managers continue to restructure and downsize, seeking to lower the costs of labor by significantly reducing expenditures on the employee benefits usually associated with full-time permanent employment. Since benefit programs were originally designed to reward employee loyalty and longevity in a company, many of those most adversely affected by this management strategy are likely to be mid-life and older workers who may find themselves without the health and other benefits previously taken for granted. As Robert Reich observed: "These workers are outside the standard system of worker-management relationships. As the contingent workforce grows—as many people find themselves working part-time for many different employers—the social contract is beginning to fray."[56]

SELF-EMPLOYMENT

The self-employed, a category that includes independent contractors, are becoming an increasingly significant component of the nonstandard workforce, as many workers seek to compensate for the loss of jobs or inadequate income by going into business for themselves. A 1996 study indicated that approximately 13 percent of all nonagricultural workers were self-employed in a primary or secondary job. The number of unincorporated self-employed grew by about one and a half percent a year between 1983 and 1994. By contrast, the number of incorporated self-employed increased an average of 3 percent annually between 1983 and 1988, and 5.9 percent from 1988 to 1994. It is noteworthy that the self-employed tend to be older than wage and salary workers are. Among the incorporated self-employed, 46 percent were age 45 to 64, whereas only 26 percent of full-time exclusively wage-and-salary workers were in this age bracket.[57] About 26 percent of those self-employed that are considered to be independent contractors work part-time (less than 35 hours a week) and about 30 percent work more than full-time (in excess of 48 hours a week).[58]

There is little data on the success rates of older workers who have turned to self-employment for their livelihood. However, there is data on younger people in self-employment that clearly indicate a high degree of volatility in this field of endeavor. A longitudinal study (1979 to 1990) of entrepreneurs under the age of 37, sponsored by the Small Business Administration, shows that a total of 28.5 percent of all men and 20.7 percent of all women in the labor force tried self-employment during the decade of the 1980s. However, high exit rates dramatically reduced the number of persons so engaged at any one time. Thus, in 1989, only 10.6 percent of men and 7.7 percent of women were actually self-employed. Moreover, only 1 in 5 male and 1 in 12 female entrepreneurs earned an income that exceeded the median wage in any year of the decade studied.[59] Although these data cannot be extrapolated for older entrants into self-employment, they do urge some caution in assuming significant success rates.

There have always been large numbers of people who have traditionally been self-employed, and such self-employment continues to provide a constructive and often highly lucrative outlet for those with marketable skills combined with an entrepreneurial spirit. In 1993, the annual median earnings of the incorporated self-employed reached $38,000, at a time when the annual median earnings of full-time wage and salary workers reached only $33,000. However, the recent growth in this category has not come from such standard incorporated self-employment occupations as medicine, law, and accounting. In fact, self-employment in medicine and law has declined significantly. Between 1931 and 1980 self-employment among doctors dwindled from 80 percent to about 50 percent. Similarly, the number of attorneys in private practice declined from more than 50 percent in 1950 to about 30 percent today. In both cases, the costs of specialized equipment and support services became so high that fewer independent practitioners could afford them.

The current accelerating growth in self-employment is being spurred by corporate downsizing and layoffs that have displaced large numbers of white-and blue-collar workers of all descriptions who turn to self-employment as the only available work option open to them. In 1993, such unincorporated self-employed workers registered annual median earnings of only $20,000.[60]

Because estimates of the numbers of the latter type of self-employed are based for the most part on self-definition, it is difficult to know how many workers are actually self-employed in the traditional sense of being a full-time independent contractor. There is good reason to believe that many of those currently identified as self-employed are merely attempting, more or less successfully, to eke out a living in this manner while continuing to seek regular employment. In effect, such workers constitute a reserve labor force that can be drawn upon as the need arises. As an official of the Bureau of Labor Statistics noted: "The self-employed are part of the labor reserve and you really don't get into labor shortages until you use up some of this reserve. It is not that they are not working; it is that they are a flexible labor asset, there to take care of bottlenecks and shortages."[61] This may also be part of the reason that wages were not driven up during the period of the tight labor market in the last years of the twentieth century.

The BLS estimated that, in 1993, about 12 million Americans, approximately 10 percent of the workforce, were self-employed, of which at least one third were involuntarily displaced workers. However, the Internal Revenue Service considered the numbers to be significantly higher—about 15 million, or roughly 13 percent of the workforce, excluding agricultural workers and the thousands who work in the underground economy and do not report income to the government. Some labor economists suggest that the numbers of the self-employed would be considerably higher if the high rate of turnover, that is, those who go into and out of business within a year, were taken into account.[62]

IMPLICATIONS

For many, the economic implications of such nonstandard employment are quite worrisome. Laura D'Andrea Tyson, a former chairman of the President's Council of Economic Advisers pointed out that, "job quality" is currently the greatest economic problem facing the country: "The issue is not job creation per se, it's the quality of jobs, it's living standards of Americans."[63] For instance, the BLS reported in 1997 that the median weekly income of "non-contingent" part-time workers was approximately 28 percent of that of full-time workers.[64] It is therefore not surprising that, in 1993, 14.8 percent of part-time workers had participated in public assistance programs for one or more months, and 4.8 percent for two full years, compared with 8.5 and 1.3 percent of full-time workers, respectively, who took advantage of such public assistance.[65] Moreover, substantially more families headed by part-time workers tend to fall below the poverty line than families headed by full-time workers. In 1988, some 21 percent of families headed by part-time workers had incomes below the poverty line, compared with only 5 percent of families headed by full-time workers. The net result has been a much higher demand for public assistance to families headed by part-time workers, about 12 percent of whom received public assistance in 1988, while only 2 percent of families headed by full-time workers received such help.

The situation was even more severe for single-parent families headed by part-time workers. Approximately 40 percent of such families had incomes below the poverty line, with 26 percent receiving public assistance. Moreover, 29 percent of these families lacked health insurance coverage from any source, and an equal number were forced to rely entirely on Medicaid for their health needs. Given that levels of future retirement income are based on current income, the economic security prospects for these future retirees seem rather dismal.

The numbers of part-time workers included under employer-sponsored pension plans are even fewer than those covered by some form of employer-provided health insurance benefits. Under the Employee Retirement Income Security Act (ERISA), employers who offer defined-benefit pension plans must extend coverage to employees working at least 1,000 hours per year. But less than half of current part-time workers qualify for such benefit protection. In 1991–1992, only about 15 percent of all part-time employees had employer-provided defined-benefit pension benefits compared with 47 percent of full-time employees. The situation was only slightly better for workers participating in defined-contribution plans: 12 percent of part-time workers participated in some type of plan compared to 35 percent of those working full-time.[66] Moreover, because of their relatively low wages and intermittent employment, many nonstandard workers can also expect to receive low Social Security benefits, which are based on average earnings over an assumed 40-year work life. As a result, there is good reason to believe that there will be an increasing number of nonstandard workers who will have to depend on some form of public assistance to augment their minimal Social Security benefits.

In addition to the dislocations and other negative impacts on the workforce, corporate management's promotion of nonstandard employment may prove ultimately counterproductive from a business as well as a social standpoint. As some analysts point out, in a world without economic borders, capital and production are highly mobile, whereas people generally are not. A highly skilled and motivated workforce may, therefore, prove to be a key national resource that may enable a country to maintain a competitive advantage in the global marketplace, notwithstanding the competition from lower cost overseas labor markets. Viewed from this perspective, the growth of the nonstandard workforce may be seen as a disinvestment in the nation's future, in effect, the squandering of a principal national asset.

NOTES

1. Dean Morse, *The Peripheral Worker* (New York: Columbia University Press, 1969), p. 68.

2. Kathleen Barker, and Kathleen Christensen, "Controversy and Challenges Raised by Contingent Work Arrangements," in *Contingent Work: American Employ-*

ment Relations in Transition, eds. Kathleen Barker and Kathleen Christensen (Ithaca, NY: Cornell University Press, 1998), p. 8.

3. Audrey Freedman, "The New Look in Wage Policy and Employee Relations," report no. 865 (New York: The Conference Board, 1985), p. 35.

4. Anne E. Polivka, "Contingent and Alternative Work Arrangements, Defined," *Monthly Labor Review* (October 1996), p. 3.

5. Anne E. Polivka, and Thomas Nardone, "On the Definition of 'Contingent Work,'" *Monthly Labor Review* (December 1989), pp. 9–16.

6. "Contingent and Alternative Employment Arrangements," report 900 (Washington, DC: U.S. Department of Labor, Bureau of Labor Statistics, August 1995), p. 1.

7. "New Data on Contingent and Alternative Employment Examined by BLS," USDL 95–318 (Washington, DC: U.S. Department of Labor, August 17, 1995).

8. Max R. Lyons, *Part-Time Work: Not a Problem Requiring a Solution* (Washington, DC: Employment Policy Foundation, 1997), p. 9.

9. Chris Tilly, *Half a Job: Bad and Good Times in a Changing Labor Market* (Philadelphia, PA: Temple University Press, 1996), p. 3.

10. Steven Hipple, "Contingent Work: Results from the Second Survey," *Monthly Labor Review* (November 1998), p. 33.

11. *Work Times*, 13, no. 3 (September 1995), p. 7. These figures remained almost the same two years later. See BLS report, "Contingent and Alternative Employment Arrangements," USDL 97–422 (Washington, DC: U.S. Department of Labor, February 1997).

12. Richard S. Belous, "The Rise of the Contingent Workforce: Growth of Temporary, Part-Time, and Subcontracted Employment," *Looking Ahead* (Washington, DC: National Policy Association, June 1997), pp. 6–7.

13. Jan Larson, "Temps Are Here to Stay," *American Demographics* (February 1996), p. 29.

14. "Part-Time Work: Characteristics of the Part-Time Workforce, Analysis of the March 1992 Current Population Survey," working paper P–55 (Washington, DC: Employee Benefit Research Institute), p. 13.

15. Roberta Spalter-Roth, and Heidi Hartmann, "Gauging the Consequences for Gender Relations, Pay Equity, and the Public Purse," in *Contingent Work: American Employment Relations in Transition*, eds. Kathleen Barker and Kathleen Christensen (Ithaca, NY: Cornell University Press, 1998), p. 70.

16. Bureau of Labor Statistics, "Work Experience of the Population in 1993," USDL 94–559; "in 1995," USDL 96–512; "in 1997," USDL 98–470; "in 1999," USDL 00–333 (Washington, DC: U.S. Department of Labor).

17. Jaclyn Fierman, "The Contingency Workforce," *Fortune* (January 24, 1994), p. 30.

18. Bruce Steinberg, "The Temporary Help Industry Annual Update," *Contemporary Times* (Spring 1994).

19. James Risen, "Temporary Manpower Industry Riding a Crest," *Los Angeles Times*, July 5, 1994.

20. "Temporary Help Reaches Record Levels in Strong Economy," press release (Alexandria, VA: National Association of Temporary and Staffing Services, April 24, 1998).

21. George Gonos, "The Interaction Between Market Incentives and Government Actions," in *Contingent Work: American Employment Relations in Transition*, eds. Kathleen Barker and Kathleen Christensen (Ithaca, NY: Cornell University Press, 1998), p. 173.

22. Aaron Bernstein, "When Is a Temp Not a Temp?" *Business Week*, December 7, 1998, p. 90.

23. Barb Cole-Gomolski, "Reliance on Temps Creates New Problems," *Computerworld* (August 31, 1998).

24. Ibid.

25. "Now, Temp Workers Are a Full-Time Headache," *Business Week* (May 31, 1999), p. 46.

26. *Handbook of Labor Statistics* (Washington, DC: U.S. Department of Labor, Bureau of Labor Statistics, August 1989), p 121; "Employment and Earnings" 211 (Washington, DC: U.S. Department of Labor, Bureau of Labor Statistics, January 1993).

27. "Employment and Earnings" 201 (Washington, DC: U.S. Department of Labor, Bureau of Labor Statistics, January 1991); "Employment and Earnings" 211 (Washington, DC: U.S. Department of Labor, Bureau of Labor Statistics, January 1993).

28. Lawrence Mishel and Jared Bernstein, "The Joyless Recovery: Deteriorating Wages and Job Quality in the 1990s," briefing paper (Washington, DC: Economic Policy Institute, September 1993), p. 16.

29. "The State of Working America 1996–1997," executive summary (Washington, DC: Economic Policy Institute, 1996).

30. Jean Kimmel, and Karen Smith Conway, "Who Moonlights and Why? Evidence from the SIPP," staff working paper 95–40 (Kalamazoo, MI: W.E. Upjohn Institute for Employment Research, 1995), p. 1.

31. AFL-CIO, *Work in Progress* (March 1, 1999).

32. Reed Abelson, "Part-Time Work for Some Adds Up to Full-Time Job," *The New York Times*, November 2, 1998.

33. Sharon Cohany, "Workers in Alternative Employment Arrangements: A Second Look," *Monthly Labor Review* (November 1998), p. 4.

34. *Pension & Benefits Reporter*, 21 (August 8, 1994), p. 1545. A Coopers & Lybrand study put the number somewhat higher at 4.1 million ("Projection of the Loss in Federal Tax Revenues Due to Misclassification of Workers," January 9, 1995).

35. "Report and Recommendations of the Commission on the Future of Worker-Management Relations," *Daily Labor Report*, no. 6 at S-50 (January 9, 1995).

36. Jonathan P. Hiatt, and Lynn Rhinehart, "The Growing Contingent Workforce: A Challenge for the Future," *The Labor Lawyer* 10, no. 143 (1994), p. 146.

37. Ibid.

38. Peter Drucker, "The Future That Has Already Happened," *The Futurist* (November 1998), p. 18.

39. Eric Hubler, "The New Faces of Retirement," *New York Times*, January 3, 1999.

40. *Monthly Labor Review* (October 1993), p. 98.

41. Belous, "The Rise of the Contingent Workforce," p. 4.

42. "The Boundaryless Workforce: Fundamental Changes in the Workplace" (Ceridian Employer Services, January 25, 1999).

43. "Research Reveals Opinions on Boundaryless Workforce Vary by Workers' Age, Position, Company Size" (Ceridian Employer Services, January 26, 1999).

44. "Into the Dark: Rough Ride Ahead for American Workers," *Training* (July 1993), p. 26.

45. Belous, "The Rise of the Contingent Workforce," p. 18.

46. Gene Koretz, "Employers Pare Health Benefits," *Business Week* (November 30, 1998), p. 30.

47. "Contingent Workers and Workers in Alternative Work Arrangements," issue brief no. 207, executive summary (Washington, DC: Employee Benefit Research Institute, March 1999).

48. "BLS Survey Shows Temp Workers' Pay Rising Slowly; Most Don't Get Benefits," *Daily Labor Report*, no. 173 (September 7, 1995).

49. "Your Money," *The Washington Post*, June 11, 1995.

50. Hiatt, Rhinehart, "The Growing Contingent Workforce," p. 148.

51. Jaclyn Fierman, "The Contingency Workforce," *Fortune* (January 24, 1994), p. 32.

52. "Work Week," *Wall Street Journal*, October 3, 1995.

53. Robert J. Grossman, "Short-Term Workers Raise Long-Term Issues," *HRMagazine* (April 1998), pp. 81–82.

54. *The Corporate Toolkit for the Nineties* (Institute for the Future), 4, no.2 (1993).

55. Julia Lawlor, "Cutbacks Fuel Contingent Workforce," *USA Today*, March 9, 1993.

56. Janice Castro, "Disposable Workers," *Time* (March 29, 1993), p. 44.

57. Frank A. Scott, Mark C. Berger, and Dan A. Black, "Changing Characteristics of the Self-Employed," research summary, RS no. 185 (Washington, DC: U.S. Small Business Admininstaration, April 1998).

58. "Independent Contractors—A Positive Alternative Work Arrangement," *Fact & Fallacy* (Washington, DC: Employment Policy Foundation, August 1998), p. 2.

59. Bradley R. Schiller, and Philip Crewson, "Entrepreneurial Origins: A Longitudinal Inquiry," research summary, RS no. 152 (Washington, DC: U.S. Small Business Administration, February 1995).

60. "Independent Contractors—A Positive Alternative Work Arrangement," *Fact & Fallacy* (Washington, DC: Employment Policy Foundation, August 1998), p. 2.

61. Louis Uchitelle, "More Are Forced Into Ranks of Self-Employed at Low Pay," *New York Times*, November 15, 1993.

62. Ibid.

63. James Risen, "Job Growth is Higher for Part-Timers, Report Says," *Los Angeles Times*, February 15, 1994.

64. Table 13, Median usual weekly earnings of full- and part-time contingent and non-contingent wage and salary workers and those with alternative and traditional work arrangements, in "Labor Force Statistics from the Current Population Survey" (Washington, DC: U.S. Department of Labor, Bureau of Labor Statistics, February 1997).

65. Jan Tan, "Who Gets Assistance?" *Current Population Reports*, P70–58 (Washington, DC: Bureau of the Census, July 1996).

66. "Employee Benefits in the United States, 1991–1992," *Compensation and Working Conditions* (Washington, DC: U.S. Department of Labor, Bureau of Labor Statistics, July 1994), p. 3.

8

DOWNWAGING THE WORKFORCE

Note to salary setters: Pay your people the least possible and you'll get from
them the same.
                                                                —Malcolm Forbes

The restructuring of American business and with it the restructuring of the
traditional workforce, and the enormous direct impact both are having on
the lives of American workers, have serious implications for the well-being
of American society as a whole. It has contributed mightily to an unprecedented degree of economic inequality in the country that is placing heavy
strain on the resiliency of its social structure. Hedrick Smith, an astute ob-
server of the American scene, wrote only a few years ago, "it remains an
open question how long rank-and-file workers who are falling behind economically will continue to tolerate growing disparities in earnings without
social protest."[1]

As Robert Reich noted, "Except for those who revere ideological precon-
ceptions over the evidence of their own eyes, the growth in inequality and
the precariousness of the middle class are stunningly obvious features of
the contemporary American landscape."[2] This statement is significant not
only because it comes from a highly respected thinker, but also because it
reflects and highlights a particular ideological perspective that is not uni-
versally shared, and because the "evidence" of one's eyes tends to be condi-

tioned by one's ideological predisposition. The point at issue is whether the elimination or significant reduction of economic inequality is socially and politically desirable, or to turn it around, should society strive for a greater degree of economic equality among its members. This question was addressed from a worldwide perspective by the 1997 United Nations Conference on Trade and Development in terms that merit citation at length.

History shows that in most societies there is at any moment in time a notion of a socially acceptable distribution of income, and hence of inequality, which is widely regarded as legitimate. It reflects a long history of class bargains and struggles over income distribution specific to each society. In other words, the degree of socially acceptable income inequality varies among societies. Although the notion of what is acceptable changes over time as the balance of power among different classes shifts, at any particular moment it sets a limit to the extent to which income distribution and inequality can be changed in either direction without causing serious socio-political dislocations. Thus, just as a sharp deterioration in income distribution often leads to serious socio-political instability and even to a social revolution, there are also socio-political limits to policies of progressive income distribution.[3]

Few will dispute that there has been a growth in economic inequality, but many will challenge the implication that this is a problem so severe that it must somehow be rectified by public policy. Indeed, why should we be concerned about economic inequality as long as the income base, and with it the general standard of living, is rising for all? After all, if I earn progressively more, what practical difference does it make to me that someone else is making even greater strides forward? Should we not applaud the fact that we are both doing better?

But, as pointed out by economist Robert H. Frank, "income level isn't everything. . . . Increased spending at the top causes real, unavoidable harm to families in the middle, even those whose incomes have risen slightly. It harms them by raising the cost of achieving goals that almost every family cherishes."[4] A case in point is public education. Few middle-income parents would be content with the knowledge that their children were attending second-rate public schools, and would therefore seek to buy homes in districts with first quality schools. The rub, however, is that school quality is closely related to the level of local property taxes, which are similarly linked to real estate prices. The problem arises because people with higher incomes tend to build larger houses that cost more and therefore pay higher taxes. So, if one wants to make sure that one's children go to good schools, it almost becomes necessary to buy a house in a neighborhood that requires a higher mortgage and that commands higher property taxes. The alternative too often is to simply accept a lower quality education for one's children. The availability of disproportionately higher levels of income at the top thus results in a trickle down pressure on those in the middle and below to spend beyond their means. This process helps explain in part the negative savings rate and the high average credit card debt borne by American families. The widening income gap, even when all boats rise to some extent, still has significant social and economic consequences for those whose relative incomes lag behind those at the top of the income ladder.

Now suppose that the economic situation we are facing is not one wherein there are very large gains for those at the top of the wage ladder and moderate gains for those on the lower rungs. Suppose instead that the real situation is one in which there are very substantial gains for the most highly paid workers, stagnant real wages for the average worker, and falling real wages for the low paid. Would this change our perception of what if anything should be done?

In the following discussion of wages and income we will examine the evidence of income inequality in the United States, explore its causes and, most important, consider its relation to the contemporary employment environment and implications for the future.

THE ECONOMIC STATE OF WORKING AMERICA

Reviewing the state of family income in 1995, Dean Baker and Lawrence Mishel of the Economic Policy Institute concluded: "Growing inequality has created a wedge between economic growth and rising living standards, leaving the vast majority of American families no better off in 1995 than in 1989."[5] There are two principal factors that have contributed to creating this income gap. First, the large number of business restructurings and downsizings for more than a decade, aside from creating a climate of general job insecurity, have had the effect of dampening overall wage growth. The result is that there has been a persistent redistribution of income from labor to profit as the economic return to capital reached historically high levels in recent years. Second, in a period of general wage stagnation, low- and middle-wage earners, with little bargaining power, have been forced to accept reductions in real wages as their earnings generally failed to keep pace with inflation. This reflects what has been called the low road to company profitability. The surprisingly large number of companies that take this road try to overcome their competition by lowering labor costs instead of improving the efficiency and quality of their production. The implications of this trend are cause for unease. As Bennett Harrison has suggested, "we should worry about the future prospects for a restoration of the historic American economic pattern of growth at high wages with declining inequality."[6]

The increasing income inequality that has resulted from these factors may be seen reflected in the indices calculated and published by the Census Bureau. The Census Bureau has been studying the distribution of family income since the late 1940s, drawing its data from the annual demographic supplement to the Current Population Survey (CPS). The most commonly used measure of income inequality is the so called Gini index, also known as the index of income concentration, which is one way of measuring how far a given distribution of income is from equality. The Gini index ranges from 0.0, a situation in which every family (household) has the same income, to 1.0, the situation when one family (household) has all the income. From 1947 to 1969, the Gini index indicated a decline in family income inequality of 7.4 percent, from .376 to .340. However, since 1969, income inequality has consistently increased, rising to .456 in 1998.[7]

Looking at income inequality from the standpoint of the share of aggregate household cash income, the share held by the highest income quintile, that is, the 20 percent of households with income above $62,841 in 1994, increased from 42.8 percent in 1968 to 49.1 percent in 1994. The middle 60 percent of households saw their share decline from 53 percent in 1968 to 47.3 percent in 1994, while households in the bottom quintile declined from 4.2 percent in 1968 to 3.6 percent in 1994. During this same period (1968 to 1994), the income share of households in the top 5 percent increased from 16.6 to 21.2 percent, and rose to 21.7 percent in 1997. Looked at still another way, the household income of the top 5 percent in 1968 was six times that of the lowest 20 percent, increasing to more than eight times as great by 1994 ($109,821 compared to $13,426).

Viewing income inequality from the perspective of average household income in each quintile, the average income of households in the top quintile grew by 44 percent, from $73,754 in 1968 (in 1994 dollars) to $105, 945 in 1994. For households in the bottom quintile, average income grew a mere 8 percent, from $7,202 to $7,762. The ratio of the average income of the top 20 percent to that of the bottom 20 percent increased from 10.2 in 1968 to 13.6 in 1994.[8]

It is widely assumed that the growth in income inequality has been offset to a significant degree by the receipt of non-cash benefits such as food stamps and employer contributions to health insurance. However, although such non-cash benefits do have an ameliorating effect on the extent of inequality between quintiles, it does not change the reality of increasing income inequality. It is true that an increasing proportion of total employee compensation had been coming in the form of employer-provided benefits such as health insurance and retirement contributions. The cost of these employee benefits increased from about 5 to almost 12 percent of compensation between 1968 and 1995. Nonetheless, few low-income households are recipients of such benefits, either because of high unemployment among low-wage earners or because their employers do not provide them. Although there are no comprehensive data showing the distribution of employer-provided benefits among households, it seems reasonable to assume that such benefits probably increase the effective income levels of non-poor households more than those with low incomes.

The Census Bureau calculates the Gini index in two ways, including and excluding health insurance supplements to wages and salaries, which represent about two-thirds of all employer-provided benefits. A comparative analysis of these indices by Brian Motley of the Federal Reserve Bank of San Francisco indicates that including these benefits increases the share of total income received by middle-income households, but has almost no effect on the share of low-income households and somewhat reduces that of upper-income households. It therefore widens slightly the gap between middle-and low-income households and narrows the differences between the middle-income and the rich. In other words, the net effect of including health insurance benefits in the calculation of the overall inequality measured by the Gini index is quite small.

The situation is rather different with regard to government-provided *cash* benefits, which have tended to reduce overall inequality significantly, principally because such benefits are awarded for the most part to lower income households. In 1994, these benefits reduced the Gini index of inequality by about 18 percent and increased the share of total income of the bottom quintile of households by 3.8 percent. By contrast, non-cash benefits, such as Medicare and food stamps, increase the share of income of households in the bottom quintile by less than a single percentage point. Motley concludes his analysis by asserting that, "judging by their impact on Gini ratios, changes in these programs appear not to have had much effect on the trend of inequality in the last fifteen years."[9]

In assessing why the observed changes in income inequality are taking place, the Census Bureau analysis cited earlier concludes: "The long-run increase in income inequality is related to changes in the Nation's labor market and its household composition. The wage distribution has become considerably more unequal with more highly skilled, trained, and educated workers at the top experiencing real wage gains and those at the bottom real wage losses."[10] It should come as no surprise that, for most families, overall income is critically related to wages. Generally speaking, middle income families, comprising the second to fourth income quintiles, receive little capital income (interest, dividends, capital gains) or cash assistance from government, and depend almost entirely on earned income for their economic well-being.

That there is a relationship between "household composition" and income inequality also seems rather clear. However, whether this is a cause-and-effect relationship is a matter of conjecture. According to data from the March 1997 Current Population Survey (CPS), the share of families with children under 18 years of age headed by a married couple declined from 89 percent in 1970 to 73 percent in 1996. Over the same period, the share of such families headed by a single parent increased from 11 to 27 percent. Relating these data to levels of family income, married-couple families made up 94 percent of the top income quintile, while single-parent families constituted more than half of the lowest quintile. Forty-eight percent of families headed by a married couple had incomes in the highest two quintiles, while 70 percent of single-head families were to be found in the lowest two quintiles. Moreover, 39 percent of families in the lowest quintile had no earners and 46 percent had only a single earner. This is in sharp contrast to the highest quintile, where 83 percent of families had two or more earners and only 3 percent had no earners. In addition, between 1969 and 1989, the average number of hours worked by wives of low income earners increased by 40 percent, whereas the hours worked by wives of high income earners soared upward by about 150 percent.[11]

Further exacerbating the inequality problem is the persistent wage gap between men and women that, according to a report from the AFL-CIO and the Institute for Women's Policy Research, costs the average working family more than $4,000 per year, or a total of some $200 billion annually.[12] This led Linda Chavez Thompson, Executive Vice President of the Umbrella Union, to state at a February 24, 1999 news conference: "For many families, equal pay could mean living above the poverty level, decent health care, a college education for the kids and a secure retirement."[13]

Kenneth Deavers of the Employment Policy Foundation provides some additional insight into the significance of the household composition data for lower income families. His 1996 analysis shows that only some 15 percent of families with incomes in the lowest quintile had two earners. This was, in part, because women headed over 40 percent of such families. Nearly 60 percent of these families had a family head that was not employed, and in those instances where the family head was employed, only 19 percent worked full-time for 50 weeks or more during the year. Moreover, almost 43 percent of family heads in these low-income families had less than a high school education.[14]

As suggested, the implications of these data, especially for public policy, is by no means clear because, as Herbert Stein argued, "they compare the incomes of people with unspecified and very different characteristics." To illustrate his point, Stein noted that in 1973 the median income of households headed by 15- to 24-year-olds was a little more than half that of those headed by persons age 45 to 54. "Surely," he argued, "that is inequality, in arithmetic. But in economics and in conscience it is not inequality. We expect 15- to 24-year-olds to earn less than 45- to 54-year-olds, and it doesn't bother us. This may not be a very interesting case, but it shows that what we are interested in is not inequality as such but inequality that violates our notions of a proper relationship among people."[15] Stein suggested that the discussion of income distribution would be clarified if at least four kinds of changes over time were taken into consideration: (1) changes in the degree of inequality among people with *similar* relevant characteristics; (2) changes in the degree of inequality among people with *different* relevant characteristics; (3) the degree of inequality among diverse groups that change over time, such as the poorest or richest quintile of the population; and (4) changes in the distribution of different kinds of people in the population.

Unless these distinctions are made, the statistics on household income can be quite misleading. Suppose, for example, that half of the bottom quintile in 1979 consisted of female-headed families with average incomes of $10,000, and the other half of male-headed families with average incomes of $20,000, so that the average for the quintile as a whole was $15,000. Then suppose that between 1979 and 1993 the real income of each family group showed an *increase* of 10 percent ($11,000 and $22,000, respectively), making the average for the quintile $16,500. Now suppose that over the same time frame the percentage of low-income families headed by females increased from 50 to 84 percent. In this case, the average income of the quintile will be $12,760, representing a *decrease* of approximately 15 percent. Similarly, Stein suggested that "if the average incomes of male and female doctors remain constant, the average income of the top fifth of all families will rise significantly if the doctors marry each other."[16]

Stein is undoubtedly correct in cautioning about the use and possible misuse of statistical data. Nonetheless, even taking into account his caveat, there is still abundant evidence of the continuing growth in income disparity that, as he put it, "violates our notions of a proper relationship among people."

In considering family income as a measure of inequality, some fundamental questions come to the fore. It seems clear that family composition is a major determinant of family income. But is it equally true that earnings similarly influence family structure? Do the economic and social problems associated with low income tend to undermine family stability, thereby contributing to the continuing growth of income inequality? The answers to these questions will fall on opposing sides of the contemporary ideological divide concerning the role of government and its intervention into the economy. One approach places primary responsibility for the situation associated with low income on individual choice, and would effectively limit the public role in ameliorating it to essentially superficial treatment of the problem. Opposing this approach are those who assign a significant responsibility both for creating or exacerbating the problem, and therefore for ameliorating it, to society. The fundamental public policy issue, however, is not who is at fault but rather whether it is in the public interest to allow it to continue to fester without remediation. And, if something is to be done with regard to low income, what is that something? It may be helpful in considering this issue to consider the character of wages and earnings in our society.

THE EARNINGS LADDER

According to the Census Bureau (1994), workers who earned less than $13,091 (in 1992 dollars) were considered to be low earners.[17] It is noteworthy that this figure was lower than the official poverty threshold of $14,228 for a four-person family with two children. In 1992, 16 percent of all year-round, full-time workers had low earnings. This represented a significant increase from the 12 percent who fell in this category in 1979. The distribution of low earners by age over the period was as follows:

Age	1992	1979	%Change
18–24	41.9%	22.9%	+19.0
25–34	15.7%	8.8%	+6.9
35–54	12.3%	9.9%	+2.4
55–64	16.1%	12.0%	+4.1

Clearly, the dramatic increase in low earnings of those aged 18–24 is necessarily a matter of societal concern, given the social volatility of this age group. However, the percentage of low earners in the 55–64 group (and presumably in the 65+ group as well) should also be of concern because of its implications for economic security in later life. Many, if not most, persons in the latter age group are ill positioned to undertake some of the steps necessary to improve their earning ability. Of these steps, that of increasing the level of one's education unquestionably appears to be the most significant.

Using 1992 data (including 1992 dollars), the earnings a person might be expected to accrue over a lifetime of work, defined as a 40-year work life between ages 25 to 64, were estimated for varying levels of education.

Not a high school of graduate	$609,000
High school graduate only	$821,000
Some college, no degree	$993,000
Associate degree	$1,062,000
Bachelor's degree	$1,421,000
Master's degree	$1,619,000
Doctorate	$2,142,000

These estimates of lifetime earnings assumed that 1992 earnings levels would remain constant throughout one's working life. In reality, of course, the value of the dollar changes continually. Moreover, it may be seen that, historically, the market value of workers with higher levels of education increased at a faster rate than that of those with lower levels of education.

Thus, comparing 1975 and 1992 figures, it can be seen that average annual earnings:

- Doubled for high school drop-outs (from $6,014 to $12,809)

- Increased about 2.5 times for high school graduates ($7,536 to $18,737)

- Nearly tripled for those with a Bachelor's degree ($11,574 to $32,629)

- Tripled for those with advanced degrees ($15,619 to $48,653)

The Census report also points out, however, that in 1992 the consumer price index was two-and-a-half times what it was in 1975. "This means that the earnings of high school dropouts did not even keep up with inflation, and high school graduates just barely managed to keep pace. Real wages rose only for persons with education beyond the high school level."[18] These earnings data are especially troubling in view of the fact that, according to government estimates, about 70 percent of the occupations expected to have the most job openings through 2006 will call for skills that do not require a college-level education.[19] Does this imply that we may expect a dramatic rise in employment opportunities for those without at least some college-level education? A brief review of the relevant actual employment data will be edifying.

Between 1992 and 1998, the U.S. population grew by 11.4 million. Employment increased by 11.6 million, unemployment decreased by 2.7 million, and the number of those outside the labor force increased by 2.5 million. The population of those who did not finish high school declined by 2.8 million, a decline mostly attributable to the demise of many in this category who were over 65 and out of the labor force. An analysis of these data yields the rather surprising result that the employment of high school dropouts *fell* by 95,000 during the 6-year period. This means "that *all* of the rise in the employment rate for that group was due to a shrinking population and none to rising employment. High school graduates gained just 784,000 jobs." Accordingly, throughout the period under consideration, a period of economic expansion, "less than 700,000 new jobs were created for the half of the population that has not attended college. The other half—those with at least some college education—obtained 10.9 million of the 11.6 million new jobs, a whopping 94 percent, contradicting the story that a tight labor market is forcing firms to reach down to hire the less skilled."[20]

Further compounding the problem is the fact that as the number of U.S.-born high school dropouts declined from 20 to 13 million between 1980 and 1994, the number of working-age immigrants without a high school diploma increased from 2.8 to 5.1 million. Two-thirds of these poorly educated workers have never attended high school at all, and 20 percent do not speak English. Nonetheless, presumably because of a relatively higher work ethic, their unemployment rates are significantly lower than is the case among poorly educated U.S. born workers. According to a study by economist Maria E. Enchautegui of the University of Puerto Rico, assuming that the trends in both legal and illegal immigration continue, such workers will soon constitute the majority of low-skilled labor in the country. They already comprise about 30 percent of workers without a high school diploma and represent about 75 percent of the low-skilled workforce in high immigration areas on the East and West coasts, and in Florida and Texas. However, the declining demand for low-skilled workers, coupled with the rapidly growing number of low-skilled immigrants, is driving down their wages, producing soaring poverty rates among working-age immigrants generally, from 14.7 percent to 21.3 percent between 1980 and 1994, and to 36 percent among the poorly educated.[21]

The failure of the tight labor market at the end of the decade to produce significant numbers of new jobs for the less educated bodes ill for any realistic expectations that income inequality will be reduced in the foreseeable future. Lawrence Katz has argued that structural changes in the labor market have played an important role in the rising income inequality and, in effect, that the market itself cannot resolve the problem through self-correction. "Tight labor markets need to be complemented with greater access to education for the disadvantaged, workforce preparation strategies that better enable those without college degrees and from poor backgrounds to take advantage of emerging opportunities, and with policies to supplement the earnings and possibly subsidize the employment of the less-skilled."[22]

Barring this, a reduction in income inequality is most likely to come at the expense of the many that in fact are heeding and taking action on the message that higher income comes with better education and training. This may happen, as one writer puts it, because "the supply of skilled workers is swelling, which will hold down wage growth at the top."[23] In other words, as matters currently stand, it appears that any reduction in income equality will come about by compression at the top of the earnings ladder rather than by raising the bottom at a relatively faster rate.

The analysis thus far has dealt with only one dimension of the problem, namely, the pay differentials between workers with different measured levels of education and skill. However, it is noteworthy that there is also a widening earnings distribution among workers with comparable skills and education. That is, there is frequently a marked pay difference among workers in the same occupation or among workers of the same age and education within an occupational category. As economists Robert Frank and Philip Cook point out: "Ability and know-how matter at every step along the way. But the distribution of earnings within a group of experienced dentists, psychologists, accountants, or technical salespeople is far more diffuse than suggested by the initial distribution of measurable ability, and reflects the vagaries of chance events along the career path."[24]

Within these peer groups, workers who were paid more to begin with also received larger wage increases than those who were paid less. Because of this, the 1979 ratio of earnings of the top 10 percent of college graduates to that of the lowest 10 percent was 3.46. By 1995 the ratio had increased by 22 percent to 4.22. This led Richard B. Freeman of Harvard University to observe that "the rise of inequality within narrowly defined groups throughout the job structure poses major problems for simple monocausal explanations for the rise in inequality."[25]

Let us now turn to a closer look at wages, wage structure, and the labor market in the United States.

HAVE REAL WAGES DECLINED FOR MOST AMERICANS?

It has been repeatedly asserted that real wages have declined for more than a decade for most American workers. Is this so? According to a 1996 report by the Council of Economic Advisers, the answer to the question would be negative because it found that "two-thirds of the net growth in full-time employment between February 1994 and February 1996 was found in job categories paying above-median wages."[26] Calculating the median wage across the economy in 1994 and comparing it to the median wage in those sectors of the economy where there was net job growth will yield this conclusion. Accordingly, the implication of this finding is that living standards are not declining because the majority of the new jobs being created in the recent economic upturn are paying higher than median wages, which amounted to $489 per week during the first quarter of 1996.

An example of such net job growth is the nearly one million new jobs in the relatively high-wage service-sector category of "professional specialty," which includes engineers, doctors, lawyers, and teachers. But, as pointed out by Jared Bernstein of the Economic Policy Institute, the real median earnings of full-time workers in this category actually fell by one percent between 1994 and 1995. This leads to the rather different conclusion that, "the fact that net job growth occurred in relatively high-paying sectors reveals nothing about the wage trends of workers in these sectors."[27]

In fact, according to some writers, analysis of data from the Bureau of Labor Statistics indicates that the real wages of the median worker (in 1994 dollars) declined 3.7 percent from 1979 to 1989, and an additional 3.1 percent from 1989 to 1994. Moreover, this analysis suggests that 70 percent of the workforce experienced lower hourly wages and total compensation than in either 1979 or 1989, with the hourly wages of the non-college-educated, some 75 percent of the workforce, falling consistently since 1979.[28] Another study, using 1997 dollars as the reference to account for inflation, examined the difference in average wages between the top and the lowest 10 percent of the wage ladder between 1982 and 1996. It found that, in 1982, those in the top 10 percent earned an average of $24.80 an hour, a figure approximately four times as great as the $6.28 earned by those in the bottom 10 percent. By 1996, the wage gap between the two groups had widened, with those at the top earning an average of $25.74 an hour, or some 4.72 times the $5.46 earned by the bottom 10 percent.[29]

Nonetheless, a study produced by the National Association of Manufacturers (NAM) argued that concern about falling wages is overstated because of the increases in average overall worker compensation.[30] That is, in looking at income from employment, it asserted, one must consider both wages as well as employer-provided benefits, and, in the view of the authors of the study, the growth of benefits tends to offset any decline in wages. However, another study based on BLS data indicates, again using 1997 dollars to account for inflation, that the total compensation in 1982 of the top 10 percent of earners was 4.56 times that of the bottom 10 percent. By 1996, the ratio had increased to 5.43 to 1, with those at the top realizing a total compensation increase of $1.73 an hour while those at the bottom lost $0.93 an hour. To make matters worse, growing numbers of workers at the bottom of the wage ladder have lost access, because of legal loopholes, to important employer-provided benefits, especially pension and health benefits.[31]

Moreover, a consideration of the methodology and conclusions of the NAM study raises the question of the utility and validity of using averages when such figures are becoming increasingly irrelevant to the typical worker, whose economic well-being is better represented by the median. Thus, taking into consideration both wages and benefits, the total compensation of the median worker can be shown to have declined by 5 percent from 1979 to 1994.[32] In other words, as Richard B. Freeman put it, "taking account of fringe benefits raises inequality in the earnings distribution and the extent to which inequality has increased."[33]

The distinction between the use of averages and medians in assessing the relative well-being of the workforce is obviously of great significance since the use of average real wages as the appropriate measure tends to obscure and distort the situation of the majority of wage earners. Daniel Sullivan of the Federal Reserve Bank of Chicago makes this clear in an essay on trends in real wage growth. "Since the early 1970s there has been a substantial increase in wage inequality," with the result that "the real wages of certain groups of less-skilled workers may have fallen even while average wages rose for the economy as a whole."[34] Laura D'Andrea Tyson, former economic adviser to the president, has reaffirmed this view. "The real compensation of the median worker was actually about 3% lower in 1997 than it was in 1989, even though growth was solid in 1996 and 1997. The real income of the median family fared somewhat better, regaining its 1989 level by 1997. But this came about because the median family in 1997 worked more hours, equivalent to about six full-time weeks."[35]

There is substantial evidence of a consistent decline in real median wages over the decade-and-a-half ending in 1996. Is there any indication of a fundamental change in the economy and the labor market since early 1996 that would lead us to conclude that things have now changed in a positive direction? After all, since mid-1996 the unemployment rate has gone down substantially to well below 5 percent and, as a result of both low inflation and relatively rapid wage growth, real wages in February 1998 showed an increase of 2.9 percent over the preceding year. However, as pointed out by some business analysts, the rise in wages had been outpacing productivity, which has averaged 1.9 percent annually for the previous two years. It therefore seems clear that businesses cannot continue to pay for increases in real wages which exceed their growth in productivity without seeing their profit margins squeezed ever more tightly while being unable, as a practical matter, to raise their prices sufficiently to compensate for declining profits. Accordingly, as these analysts put it, "As long as businesses lack pricing power, this cycle is self-limiting. That's because profits will get squeezed. Capital spending will suffer. Employment will slow, and the economy will cool down on its own. So if you're a worker, enjoy the good times while they last."[36]

Given the tight labor market experienced throughout the boom year of 1998, with the unemployment rate reaching the lowest levels in decades, it comes as something of a surprise that wages are not going up at a faster rate, as labor market theory would suggest. Unit labor costs in 1998 rose only 2 percent as productivity increased by 2.2, offsetting a good part of the 4.2 percent increase in wages and benefits. The answer seems to be that "companies are finding creative ways of holding down basic wage rates, such as reclassifying production workers as salaried employees or the increased use of one-time bonuses and other forms of variable pay."[37] Moreover, there is an expectation that, should wages begin to rise sharply, businesses will begin to invest more heavily in capital improvements, rather than in their workers, to improve productivity.

These analyses are especially applicable to blue-collar workers, who are most susceptible to what Robert Reich has aptly described as downwaging, even in this buoyant economic period. "Because wages and benefits paid to workers typically constitute about 70 percent of corporate outlays, the most direct route to higher profits for many companies has been to cut payrolls. But the preferred method of cutting has evolved in recent years. Companies have moved from 'downsizing' their operations to 'downwaging' them. After all, downsizing can only be taken so far, particularly in the vast and growing service sector of the U.S. economy. . . . Downwaging (along with its close relative, 'downbenefitting') can reduce labor costs still further, even if people have to be employed."[38]

One significant unintended and unanticipated consequence of downsizing and downwaging is the effect these trends are having on the health of older workers. A study headed by Peggy McDonough of Canada's York University examined U.S. survey data from 1972 to 1989 and correlated the death rates of persons aged 45 and over with their income levels. As in earlier studies, an inverse relationship between income and health risk was found. Other factors being equal, it concluded that those 45 and older with average household incomes of less than $20,000 (in 1993 dollars) over a five-year period were 2 to 3 times as likely to die in the following five years as those with average incomes that exceeded $70,000. At the same time, those in the middle income range of $20,000 to $70,000 had a 50 percent greater probability of dying during the next five years as those in the higher income group.

The study also produced some very interesting if not provocative findings with regard to health and income stability. They found that sharp drops in income of 50 percent or more in a five-year period had little effect on both the already high mortality rates of low-income earners and the relatively low rates of high-income earners. However, this was not the case for those in the middle-income group. A sharp decline in income in the prior five years was found to double their risk of death, raising it to the higher levels common among the lower income group. In other words, income instability, most often resulting from downsizing and significant downwaging, creates substantial health risks for middle income older workers.[39] Moreover, the fiscal implications of this for people who will become eligible for Medicare seem clear as well.

THE LABOR MARKET

Current discussions about employment and wages are all conducted within the context of the classic notion of the "labor market." The labor market is viewed simply as a particular form of the generic concept of a "market," defined by a pattern of relationships represented by supply and demand curves, that is, schedules of price and quantity, bids and offers, that apply to a transaction. Where there is a "market," certain relationships between supply and demand for any particular item are assumed to exist. For example, in a market for apples, within practical limits, the price of apples will determine the demand for them. When the price drops, the demand will rise, and conversely, when the price rises, demand will fall. This relationship generally holds true across the apple market, even though there is a wide variety of kinds of apples, because for the most part these different types of apples are reasonably close substitutes for one another.

This same pattern of relationships is generally held to prevail in all other markets as well, including the market for labor. This conventional assumption, however, as argued most forcefully by James K. Galbraith, does not hold under close examination. "The labor market—especially when considered as an aggregative entity covering an entire region or country—has *never* been a market in this sense. Each individual worker brings a complex package of characteristics, skills, job history, and reputation to each possible job match. While people do change jobs, after an early age most never change from one line of work to another. Jobs themselves are, perhaps, not so complex as the people who hold them, but they too are highly differentiated. Neither individuals nor jobs are close substitutes for one another."[40]

The implications of this argument are profound. It suggests that with regard to labor, there is no supply curve in the sense that one exists for commodities. For such a labor supply curve to exist, workers would have to be interchangeable, and the instances where such is the case are quite few, notwithstanding attempts by some employers earlier in this century, through the use of technology and work organization, to transform workers into interchangeable units of labor.

Moreover, to the extent that some sort of labor market does exist, it clearly does not respond in the same way as a commodity market to excess supply. That is, the price of labor (wages) will not necessarily drop when there is an oversupply (high unemployment). Thus, even when there is low demand for labor, workers who are employed will strongly resist a reduction in their wages, and even unemployed workers will hesitate to accept what they may consider exploitative wages until compelled to do so by sheer need. On the other hand, when the demand for labor is high, as at present, wages will not necessarily rise significantly in response to such demand. In other words, as Galbraith argues, there is no supply curve for labor, and without such a curve there is no labor market as such. Accordingly, "one is forced to look outside the classical confines of the labor market to find the determination of employment and of wages."[41]

In place of the concept of a labor market, Galbraith would substitute the concept of "job structure," which he asserts, "is a historically, socially, and politically specific set of status and pay relationships in the economy, within and between firms, within and across industries."[42] The implications of this alternate concept are far-reaching. For one thing, it would sever the public policy link between unemployment and the control of inflation. This link is critically dependent upon the concept of a labor market and a supply curve for labor, which predicts that as unemployment drops wages will rise, thereby setting in place the conditions for an increase in inflation. This view has led, as a practical matter, to a national *unemployment* policy, artificially constraining economic growth in order to maintain unemployment at a level that is believed necessary to keep inflation in check.

Although the concept of "job structure" as the principal determinant of wages is not yet fully developed, it does help explain, albeit intuitively, numerous anomalies in the world of work. It helps explain why, for example, chief executives will receive extraordinary salary increases and bonuses that are disproportionate to their direct contribution to corporate earnings, and why teachers are often paid dismal salaries for work that is crucial to the well-being of society. It also helps us begin to understand the factors that are driving the growing polarization of American society into widely separated economic classes, an understanding that is essential if steps are to be taken to keep the social fabric from coming apart at its seams.

One consequence of the prevailing notion of a classical labor market is that it provides a dubious conceptual basis for the explanation of the long-standing decline in median real wages. Thus it is widely argued that the cause of the problem is "skill mismatch." That is, as a result of continuing technological changes there has been a fundamental shift in the demand for skills in the labor market, which has led to the collapse of job opportunities for many unskilled or low-skilled workers. It will be recalled that, in the textbook labor market, relative wages are necessarily a reflection of relative skills and, with a decline in demand for low skills, the unemployment or downwaging of the less skilled results. Thus, Laura D'Andrea Tyson observes: "By far the most important determinant of the growing inequality in labor incomes has been the increasing demand for workers with a high level of skills, particularly those with a college or graduate degree."[43]

There appears to be significant supportive evidence for this thesis. A 1993 Census Bureau paper reports that: "Drawing upon a data base of over 10,000 U.S. manufacturing plants, researchers found that technology-intensive plants pay significantly higher production-worker wages than plants that adopt few or no advanced technologies."[44] The average hourly wages paid by those plants ranged from $8.63 at plants that did not make use of such technologies to $11.84 at plants that incorporated six or more such technologies. The report also indicated that it is primarily large plants, those employing 20,000 or more workers, which use the most advanced technology and pay the highest wages. However, the use of such technology with the accompanying higher wages was also found in many smaller manufacturing plants that employed less than 100 production workers.

These findings suggest that employers are pursuing a high-technology, high-wage strategy, which in turn has led to a public policy focus on skill upgrading and retraining as the key to resolving the emerging wage crisis, and the broadening income inequality that is of concern to so many people. However, as pointed out by Lawrence Mishel, "To believe the technology story, we must also believe that a technological revolution is dramatically affecting our wage and employment structures but somehow fails to raise productivity growth enough to improve living standards."[45] Moreover, if technology is the culprit in this mystery, it would have to be introducing new technologies at a faster pace than in recent decades in order for the skills mismatch explanation to hold. However, there is little if any evidence that such is the case. As was argued several years ago by David R. Howell, "a review of the statistical evidence casts considerable doubt on the skill-mismatch hypothesis. There is little direct evidence that the rate of skill upgrading was substantially greater in the 1980s than in earlier decades or that technological change was the main source of the skill upgrading that we can measure. Nor is there evidence that changes in the mix of skills can explain much of the recent growth in either earnings inequality or the share of low-wage jobs."[46]

An alternate approach to the problem, one that also requires setting aside the notion of a labor market functioning accordance to the presuppositions of microeconomics, seems to afford an explanation that is more in accord with the facts. First of all, beginning in the late 1970s, there was a substantial and relatively rapid increase in competitive pressures resulting from globalization and deregulation, accompanied by an ideological shift away from corporate paternalism and toward the commoditization of labor. In this new environment, both business strategies and government policies effectively undermined traditional wage-setting vehicles such as collective bargaining and internal job and wage structure norms. As a result, low-skilled workers were no longer buffered from the shocks of an increasingly volatile labor market.

A second factor contributing to the problem was a significant increase in the number of workers competing for low-skill jobs, many of whom were overqualified for the jobs they were seeking. According to Howell, a number of factors contributed to the "crowding at the hiring gate." Employment opportunities at the median wage, most notably high-wage blue-collar and moderately skilled white-collar jobs, diminished rapidly. "Fewer good job opportunities, rising numbers of displaced workers and sharply rising numbers of low-skill immigrant workers fed the pool of workers competing for moderate and low-skill jobs paying low wages. Blue-collar labor markets also became more competitive than at any time since the early 1930s because of the decline in union membership and the growing capacity of firms to relocate to and buy supplies from low-wage areas. The result was a collapse in the wage paid for low-skill work." In other words, "the main restructuring trend among nonsupervisory male workers . . . was not a massive shift away from lower skill jobs. Indeed, the share of low-skill jobs was remarkably stable from 1983 into the 1990s. Rather, the real shift was away from higher wage jobs."[47]

In the new employment environment, with the possible exception of the manufacturing sector, which employs only about 12 percent of the workforce, employers generally adopted what has been called a "low-road" human resource management approach, the primary aim of which is to reduce current labor costs. That is, contrary to the "skill-mismatch" thesis, most employers did not pursue the assumed high-technology, high-skills path, with the anomalous result that where workers were compelled to upgrade and learn the new skills demanded by more advanced production technologies, their higher productivity did not produce higher wages for them. Accordingly, if Howell's analysis is correct, "the erosion in wages is mainly the result of an asymmetry in bargaining power, reflecting low-wage strategies by employers, a failure of government to help maintain traditional labor market institutions, and increased wage competition in the external labor market. Growing shares of workers with low wages reflect neither major skill shifts nor the use of new technologies. There is nothing inevitable or 'natural' about the growing earnings problems of the two-thirds of the workforce without college degrees."[48]

IMPLICATIONS

Given this analysis, it seems clear that the problems of downwaging and growing income inequality are unlikely to be resolved through the unhampered operation of assumed labor market forces. Indeed, as observed by Richard Freeman, "A major reason for this high inequality in earnings is that the United States relies extensively on market forces to determine pay, whereas most countries rely also on institutions such as collective bargaining and minimum wage regulations. Distributions of wages set by institutions invariably are more compressed than distributions of wages set by markets. Institutions reduce firms' leeway to pay wage rates that differ from the national average and reduce supervisors' leeway to vary pay among workers in a given job."[49] This is not to suggest that there is an easy public policy solution to the problem, only that doing nothing does not make a great deal of sense since that approach has contributed mightily to creating the problem in the first place.

Nonetheless, the still prevailing economic wisdom in the United States is that it would be both unwise and counterproductive to interfere in any significant way with the natural operation of the labor market. Unfortunately, this approach to the problem does not offer much hope of positive change for the many millions of workers, and their families, in the lower reaches of the earnings ladder, and especially for those at or near the official poverty level. In this regard, Rebecca Blank of Northwestern University wrote: "The recent welfare reforms emphasize that the labor market is the only way out of poverty, even as falling wages make full-time work less and less useful as an escape from poverty. Although the long-term consequences of such policy changes, when combined with the trends in wages, are unknown, they do have the potential to lead to increases in poverty and class conflict."[50]

NOTES

1. Hedrick Smith, *Rethinking America: Innovative Strategies and Partnerships in Business and Education* (New York: Avon Books, 1996), p. 412.

2. Robert Reich, Letter to the Editor, *Washington Times*, December 4, 1995.

3. "Income Distribution, Capital Accumulation, and Growth," A report on the United Nations Conference on Trade and Development, *Challenge*, March–April 1998, p. 64.

4. Robert H. Frank, "The Victimless Income Gap?" *New York Times*, April 12, 1999.

5. Dean Baker and Lawrence Mishel, "Profits Up, Wages Down: Worker Losses Yield Big Gains for Business" (Washington, DC: Economic Policy Institute, 1995).

6. Bennett Harrison, *Lean and Mean:The Changing Landscape of Corporate Power in the Age of Flexibility* (New York: Guilford Press, 1997), p. 213.

7. Robert J. Bressler, "The Dilemma of Income Inequality," *USA Today* (Magazine, May 2000). Cited from www.FindArticles.com.

8. Daniel Weinberg, "A Brief Look at Postwar U.S. Income Inequality," *Current Population Reports*, P60–191 (Washington, DC: U.S. Bureau of the Census, June 1996). It should be noted that the method of data collection was changed in 1992, creating some uncertainty about the accuracy of comparisons with earlier years. However, there is every reason to believe that any discrepancies are minor.

9. Brian Motley, "Inequality in the United States," *FRBSF Economic Letter*, no. 97–03 (January 31, 1997).

10. Daniel Weinberg, "A Brief Look at Postwar U.S. Income Inequality," *Current Population Reports*, P60–191 (Washington, DC: U.S. Bureau of the Census, June 1996), p. 3.

11."E-Mail Trends in Labor and Employment" (Washington, DC: Employment Policy Foundation, October 29, 1997).

12. AFL-CIO, *Work in Progress*, March 1, 1999.

13. Ibid.

14. Kenneth L. Deavers, "The Shrinking Middle Class: More American Families Gain Than Fall Behind," *Fact and Fallacy*, 2, no. 1 (Washington, DC: Employment Policy Foundation, January 1996).

15. Herbert Stein, "The Income Inequality Debate," *Wall Street Journal*, May 2, 1996.

16. Ibid.

17."The Earnings Ladder: Who's at the Bottom? Who's at the Top?" statistical brief SB/94 (Washington, DC: U.S. Bureau of the Census, June 1994).

18. Ibid.

19. Marc Adams, "The Stream of Labor Slows to a Trickle," *HRMagazine* (October 1998), p. 88.

20. Marc-Andre Pigeon, and L. Randall Wray, "Did the Clinton Rising Tide Raise All Boats," *Policy Brief Highlights* no. 45a (Anandale-on-Hudson, NY: The Jerome Levy Economics Institute, September 1998).

21. Gene Koretz, "Immigrants' Economic Woes," *Business Week* (June 7, 1999).

22. Stuart E. Weiner, and Stephen A. Monto, "Income Inequality: A Summary of the Bank's 1998 Symposium," *Economic Review* (Federal Reserve Bank of Kansas City, Fourth Quarter, 1998), p. 3.

23. Christopher Farrell, "Strong Growth Will Shrink the Wage Gap," *Business Week* (March 15, 1999), p. 58.

24. Robert H. Frank, and Philip J. Cook, *The Winner-Take-All Society: How More and More Americans Compete for Ever Fewer and Bigger Prizes* (New York: Free Press, 1995), pp. 93–94.

25. Richard B. Freeman, *When Earnings Diverge: Causes, Consequences, and Cures for the New Inequality in the U.S.* (Washington, DC: National Policy Association, 1997), p. 11.

26."Job Creation and Employment Opportunities: The United States Labor Market, 1993–1996" (Washington, DC: Council of Economic Advisers, 1996).

27. Jared Bernstein, "Anxiety Over Wages Still Justified" (Washington, DC: Economic Policy Institute, 1996).

28. Ibid.

29."Wages and Benefits Dwindle for Unskilled U.S. Workers," *Argus*, no. 360 (September 1998), p. 7.

30."Improving the Economic Condition of the American Worker" (Washington, DC: National Association of Manufacturers, 1996).

31."Wages and Benefits Dwindle for Unskilled U.S. Workers," p. 7.

32. Bernstein, "Anxiety Over Wages Still Justified."

33. Richard B. Freeman, *When Earnings Diverge: Causes, Consequences, and Cures for the New Inequality in the U.S.* (Washington, DC: National Policy Association, 1997), p. 13.

34. Daniel Sullivan, "Trends in Real Wage Growth," *Chicago Fed Letter*, no. 115 (March 1997, note 3).

35. Laura D'Andrea Tyson, "Why the Wage Gap Just Keeps Getting Bigger," *Business Week* (December 14, 1998), p. 22.

36. James C. Cooper, and Kathleen Madigan, "U.S.: Heady Times for Workers, Hard Times for Companies?" *Business Week* (March 23, 1998).

37. James C. Cooper, and Kathleen Madigan, "Earnings Growth Caught in a Vise," *Business Week* (February 22, 1999), p. 28.

38. Robert B. Reich, "UPS and the Down-waging of Blue-Collar America" (The Electronic Policy Network, 1997).

39. Gene Koretz, "Income Swings Can Be Deadly," *Business Week* (March 2, 1998).

40. James K. Galbraith, "Dangerous Metaphor: The Fiction of the Labor Market," public policy brief no. 36 (Anandale-on-Hudson, NY: Jerome Levy Economics Institute of Bard College, 1997), pp. 11–12.

41. Ibid., p. 13.

42. Ibid., p. 15.

43. Laura D'Andrea Tyson, "Why the Wage Gap Just Keeps Getting Bigger," *Business Week* (December 14, 1998), p. 22.

44."Higher Wages Accompany Advanced Technology," Statistical Brief SB/93–14 (Washington, DC: U.S. Bureau of the Census, August 1993).

45. Lawrence Mishel, "Rising Tides, Sinking Wages," *The American Prospect*, no. 23 (Fall 1995).

46. David. R. Howell, "The Skills Myth," *The American Prospect*, no.18 (Summer 1994).

47. Ibid.

48. Ibid.

49. Richard B. Freeman, *When Earnings Diverge: Causes, Consequences, and Cures for the New Inequality in the U.S.* (Washington, DC: National Policy Association, 1997), p. 14.

50. Rebecca M. Blank, "Is There a Trade-off Between Unemployment and Inequality?" public policy brief no. 33 (Anandale-on-Hudson, NY: Jerome Levy Economics Institute of Bard College, 1997) p. 21.

9

THE QUESTION OF THE MINIMUM WAGE

A fair day's-wage for a fair day's-work: it is as just a demand as governed men ever made of governing. It is the everlasting right of man.
—Thomas Carlyle

One of the perennially controversial public policy attempts to deal with the problem of downwaging at the lower end of the wage ladder, where the economic and social consequences are the greatest, is the periodic adjustment of the minimum wage to reflect the rise in the cost of living. It is hoped thereby to constrain the growth of poverty in the country. This is controversial because there is a substantial basis in economic theory for the argument that society is best served by a policy of free trade, in which the exchange of goods and services is governed, with as few exceptions as practicable, by the rules of supply and demand. The case for free trade in labor is based on the presumptions that the parties to an exchange are competent to look after their own best interests, and that they will in fact do this if not interfered with. From this perspective, any outside intervention aimed at limiting the range of bargains that individuals are free to negotiate can only reduce the gains that would otherwise be realized from trade.

Minimum wage laws may be seen as interventions in the labor market in the form of price controls which, in general terms, are considered to limit the volume of transactions and distort the quality of goods or services ex-

changed in the marketplace. Clearly, such interventions can alter the distribution of the benefits from labor transactions to favor those at the bottom of
the earnings ladder. However, it may be argued from an economic standpoint that there are more efficient methods of redistributing income to protect the interests of the less fortunate members of society than the
disruption of the normal operations of a free trade labor market.

This argument, of course, is based on the traditional microeconomic assumption that there is in fact a "labor market," in the same sense that there
are markets for commodities, the operation of which may be described by a
supply-and-demand curve. However, one may argue, as James Galbraith
and others have done, that there is no supply-and-demand curve for labor
and therefore there also is no "labor market" in the traditional sense. According to this view, wages and wage levels are determined by "job structure" and not by supply and demand. The free trade argument against
minimum wages, based on conventional economic theory, would therefore
lose much of its force.

Moreover, even assuming the existence of a "labor market," the argument in favor of the free trade approach to the setting of wages would be
more credible if the imposition of a minimum wage was the only such intervention by government in an otherwise free market. However, this is very
far from the reality of the tens of billions of dollars of public money expended annually on agricultural price supports and other forms of direct
intervention in the economy, much of which has become known as "corporate welfare." It is therefore somewhat disingenuous to rail against the minimum wage as though it alone upsets the fine balance of the otherwise free
market. As in the case of other interventions in the market economy, economic theory is not, and perhaps should not be, the principal determinant
of governmental action. Other considerations of public interest usually
play a greater role in determining such questions of public policy. Accordingly, if one is to make a serious case for or against the minimum wage, it
must be done on the basis of whether it serves the public interest, and not
whether it conforms to a particular construction of economic theory.

THE ORIGINS OF THE MINIMUM WAGE

On June 25, 1938, after a year of occasionally acrimonious debate in the
Congress, President Franklin D. Roosevelt signed into law a piece of land-
mark legislation, The Fair Labor Standards Act of 1938 (FLSA). The act represented the culmination of an effort initiated by the president several years
earlier to mitigate some of the traumatic effects of the Great Depression. In
1933, he succeeded in putting through the National Industrial Recovery
Act (NRA), some of the most important provisions of which were deemed
unconstitutional by the Supreme Court on May 27, 1935. Under the NRA,
Roosevelt promulgated a President's Reemployment Agreement "to raise

wages, create employment, and thus restore business." More than 2.3 million such agreements, covering 16.3 million employees, were signed by employers who agreed to establish a workweek of between 35 and 40 hours and a minimum wage of $12 to $15 a week. At the same time, some industries developed employment codes of their own, the first and most important of which was the Cotton Textile Code, which provided for a 40–hour workweek and a minimum wage of $13 a week in the North and $12 in the South. However, many of the gains achieved in minimum wage legislation were lost when the Supreme Court struck down as unconstitutional the New York State minimum wage law in 1936.

The new Fair Labor Standards Act of 1938, as it was finally enacted, applied only to workers engaged in interstate commerce and the production of goods for such commerce. The minimum wage provisions of the act thus affected about 11 million workers, about one fifth of the total work force at the time. The maximum standard workweek was established at 44 hours, with a minimum hourly wage set at 25 cents. The rationale for the minimum wage, in part, was to prevent a repetition of the deflationary wage spiral that occurred earlier in the decade, as workers bid down wages in their search for gainful employment. In a "fireside chat" broadcast the night before signing the bill into law, President Roosevelt cautioned: "Do not let any calamity-howling executive with an income of $1,000 a day . . . tell you . . . that a wage of $11 a week is going to have a disastrous effect on all American industry."[1]

THE RELATIVE VALUE OF THE MINIMUM WAGE

Since 1938, the minimum wage has been adjusted upward numerous times from its original 25 cents an hour to $5.15 in September 1997, and amendments to the FSLA have extended its protections to most workers. What has this meant in real terms relative to the state of the economy and the cost of living? The following table shows the actual minimum wage (Nominal Dollars) and the relative value of the minimum wage in 1996 dollars adjusted for inflation using the consumer price index (Bureau of Labor Statistics). The years in which the minimum wage was raised are shown in bold.

Year	Nominal Dollars	1996 Dollars
1954	$0.75	$4.37
1955	0.75	4.39
1956	**1.00**	**5.77**
1957	1.00	5.58
1958	1.00	5.43
1959	1.00	5.39
1960	1.00	5.30

Year	Nominal Dollars	1996 Dollars
1961	**1.15**	**6.03**
1962	1.15	5.97
1963	**1.25**	**6.41**
1964	1.25	6.33
1965	1.25	6.23
1966	1.25	6.05
1967	**1.40**	**6.58**
1968	**1.60**	**7.21**
1969	1.60	6.84
1970	1.60	6.47
1971	1.60	6.20
1972	1.60	6.01
1973	1.60	5.65
1974	**2.00**	**6.37**
1975	**2.10**	**6.12**
1976	**2.30**	**6.34**
1977	2.30	5.95
1978	**2.65**	**6.38**
1979	**2.90**	**6.27**
1980	**3.10**	**5.90**
1981	**3.35**	**5.78**
1982	3.35	5.45
1983	3.35	5.28
1984	3.35	5.06
1985	3.35	4.88
1986	3.35	4.80
1987	3.35	4.63
1988	3.35	4.44
1989	3.35	4.24
1990	**3.80**	**4.56**
1991	**4.25**	**4.90**
1992	4.25	4.75
1993	4.24	4.61
1994	4.25	4.50
1995	4.25	4.38
1996	**4.75**	4.75

These data show that the minimum wage had its maximum relative value in 1968. It will also be seen that since 1968 the relative value of the minimum wage has generally continued to decline, despite seven increases between that year and 1996, hitting its lowest relative value in more than forty years in 1989, and returning to the second lowest 1954 level in 1995.

Considering that this analysis is based on a history of the relative value of the minimum wage in terms of 1996 dollars, we do not seem to have come very far, in relative terms, from the $0.25 per hour minimum that caused so much hand wringing in 1938. Even considering the most recent increase to $5.15 an hour, we are still talking about an annualized income that barely exceeds the average 1996 poverty threshold of $10,233 for a two-person family.

Moreover, the minimum wage should be considered in terms of its relationship to productivity, which is held to be the principal determinant of the standard of living. From the 1940s to the 1960s, increases in the minimum wage kept pace with the growth in productivity. However, for the last three decades, despite some increases, the minimum wage declined both in real terms and in relation to productivity. Indeed, "the minimum wage would have to rise to nearly $7 per hour to restore its real value to the 1968 level, and to more than $10.50—roughly the median wage in the U.S. service-sector—to restore its 1968 level relative to productivity."[2]

From this perspective, the proposal of the Clinton Administration to increase the minimum wage by $0.50 in January 1999 and then by another $0.50 the following year, establishing the wage floor at $6.15 in the year 2000, was rather modest. According to Jared Bernstein of the Economic Policy Institute, "using the Congressional Budget Office's inflation projections, $6.15 in the year 2000 translates into $5.72 in 1997 dollars." In effect, then, the increase that is the subject of much heated debate would only be about $0.60 higher than the current minimum wage of $5.15 if it were fully implemented in 1998.[3]

As a way out of the impasse, Robert Reich suggests that if we are serious about trying to deal with the issue of assisting low-income earners, we should stop the periodic political battles over increases in the minimum wage and simply index the minimum wage to inflation. "We could decide once and for all what the purchasing power of the minimum wage ought to be, and then let it move in tandem with prices. If inflation is flat, as now, the minimum wage would stay put. If inflation took off, so would the minimum wage."[4] This is certainly not a new argument—advocates have been making a case for it for two decades, but it gained new impetus in late 1998. On November 3 of that year the state of Washington made economic history by passing a law that automatically adjusts the state minimum wage for inflation every year.[5]

Opponents of this approach argue, however, that lifting up the wages of workers at the bottom of the pay ladder faster than those in the middle ranges could price some minimum wage workers out of the labor market. There is some risk of this occurring, particularly in some very low margin businesses where an increase in labor costs might impinge too heavily on profitability. On the other hand, advocates of the approach suggest that the negative effects are not very probable and that in any case it is better to run the risk than to periodically go through a wrenching debate about raising the minimum wage.

WHO BENEFITS FROM THE MINIMUM WAGE?

Approaching the question from the standpoint of family income, it is possible to draw very different conclusions, depending on what one wishes to find in the data. Thus, it is a common presumption of advocates for a higher minimum wage that the primary beneficiaries of such increases are low-income families. And, an analysis by Jared Bernstein indicates, with regard to the 1996 increases in the minimum wage: "Families in the lowest fifth, who have only 5.1% of total income, will benefit most from the increase, reaping 39.5% of the gains. Well over half the gains (57.4%) go to families in the bottom 40%. Workers from the highest fifth benefit the least (12.6%), suggesting that the increase is well targeted to lower income families."[6]

By contrast, opponents of an increase in the minimum wage argue that the increase is poorly targeted to lower income families. The Employment Policies Institute found that more than 70 percent of the 1996 minimum wage gains went to families and individuals in the upper four income quintiles (those earning more than $15,777 per year). Moreover, those in the upper three income quintiles (earning more than $29,424 per year) received more than half of the overall minimum wage gains. The Institute concluded that "less than 18 percent of minimum wage gains went to families and individuals living below the federally defined level of poverty, which in 1996 was $12,516 for a family of three."[7] These data led the Employment Policy Foundation to conclude that, "compared to the Earned Income Tax Credit or refunding a portion of the FICA tax to low-income workers, the minimum wage is not an effective policy to improve the economic well-being of the working poor."[8]

At issue here is not the raw data itself, but the interpretations given to the data through the use of different categories to present one's conclusions. Thus, the Economic Policy Institute paper broadly defines the bottom two quintiles as low income, whereas the Employment Policies Institute prefers to reckon the second lowest quintile as within the "upper four income quintiles." This seems, by implication, to be identifying low income with the poverty level for a family of three. Both analyses agree (within about 10 percent) that approximately half of the gains from the minimum wage increase went to the bottom two quintiles, but disagree as to whether the increase is therefore well or poorly targeted. The fundamental question, then, is what we mean by well targeted.

Let's assume for the purposes of this discussion that it is impracticable to means test the applicability of the minimum wage to make sure that only the deserving receive it. Should it then be acceptable from a public policy perspective for the upper three quintiles to garner half of the overall gain from a minimum wage increase in order to assure that the bottom two quintiles receive the other half of the much needed benefits of such an increase? It would seem that both logic and common sense would answer in the affirmative, because the potential loss to the bottom two quintiles is relatively much greater than the gains to be realized by the top three. If the real issue is targeting, then one might consider that the unwarranted gains achieved by the untargeted could be offset by increases in marginal tax rates, something that is probably anathema to the majority of opponents of the minimum wage.

Thomas Palley has argued that the minimum wage is good for both the working poor and middle class families. For the working poor it establishes a wage floor that inhibits excessive wage competition at the lower end of the wage scale. "It is good for middle-class families because many such families have two workers, one of whom is often a minimum-wage worker. By helping middle-class families, a minimum-wage increase can therefore serve as a surrogate middle-class tax cut and deliver far more than can any affordable tax cut."[9]

DOES ANYONE LOSE FROM MINIMUM WAGE INCREASES?

Opponents of the minimum wage commonly assert that one of the unintended consequences of minimum wage increases seems to be that "the number of families that fall into poverty because of job loss is greater than the number of families that rise out of poverty because of the minimum wage."[10] They argue, in effect, that most of the costs of increases in the minimum wage are borne by unskilled workers who lose their jobs, or by new entrants to the labor force who cannot get jobs. This happens, it is suggested, because minimum wages reduce the demand for unskilled or inexperienced workers and raise the demand for substitute resources, including skilled workers. Interestingly, it is this consideration that appears to make trade unions, whose members are paid significantly more than the legally prescribed minimum, supporters of minimum wage increases. A high minimum wage reduces the demand for unskilled or inexperienced workers and raises the demand for skilled workers, who are often unionized. Moreover, increased labor costs encourage employers to switch to newer, more efficient technologies. Opponents also suggest that losses in current employment may also have future costs as individuals who are denied valuable work experience are likely to suffer a reduction in future productivity and therefore employability. Finally, time out of work can also produce deterioration in one's previously acquired work skills. A Heritage Foundation analysis concludes: "The minimum wage is an uncompassionate tax by which some low-wage workers increase their earnings while others lose their opportunity to earn anything at all. Raising it will effectively prohibit people from working unless their skills are worth more than $5.15 per hour."[11]

The counter-argument of proponents of minimum wage increases is simply that it is by no means certain that raising the minimum wage in practice, rather than according to economic theory, will produce layoffs. A case in point is the nursing home industry, where low pay and difficult working conditions result in an annual average turnover rate of more than 100 percent among nurses' aides. Given that hiring and training an aide costs about $4,000, a typical nursing home spends an amount equal to a third of its annual wage bill on turnover costs.[12] There seems to be little doubt that higher wages would improve retention, and that much of the increased wage costs would be offset by the cut in turnover costs. Moreover, viewing the problem from a societal perspective, "lower turnover would raise performance in these classically interpretive jobs. Each resident in a nursing home has different needs (and some have considerable difficulty in communicating them), so that familiarity improves efficiency and quality."[13]

The effects of an increase in minimum wages are most often and easily assessed by observing the situation of teen-aged workers, the number of which appears to be a matter of dispute. According to the Economic Policy Institute, teenagers account for about 26 percent of all minimum wage workers.[14] However, other economists assert that the number is over 36 percent.[15] Mark Wilson of the Heritage Foundation suggests that, of the 4.2 million who worked at or below the minimum wage in March 1997, roughly half, or 44.2, percent were teenagers or young adults aged 21 or less. Sixty-six percent of these young workers lived in families with incomes at least twice the official poverty rate, the average family income being about $54,000.[16]

Opponents of any further minimum wage increases argue that teenagers suffer most from the effects of the minimum wage on employment. According to one writer, "the damage done to teenagers is twofold. First, they lose income immediately. Second, because minimum-wage legislation has rendered them unemployable, teenagers cannot gain the experience and skills that would make them employable at higher wages later. If there were no floor price on labor, teenagers could offer to work for a lower price until they gained the training, experience, and skills they needed to command a higher wage."[17]

What effect has the most recent increase in the minimum wage had on teenage employment? Based on an analysis of national employment data from the Bureau of Labor Statistics' Current Population Survey, the Employment Policies Institute concluded that the increase in minimum wage that went into effect on October 1, 1996 resulted in the subsequent destruction of 128,000 teen jobs over the following eleven months. By inference, as many as 380,000 entry-level jobs were lost overall.[18] It must be noted, however, that the number of teen-age jobs destroyed does not represent the number of actual existing teen jobs that were lost. Actual teen employment declined by 21,000 jobs, the remaining 107,000 jobs represent the increased number of such jobs that would have been expected to materialize during the same period had there not been an increase in the minimum wage.[19]

The data on current teenage unemployment is sparse. However, a 1996 analysis by the National Center for Policy Analysis concluded that there is a clear and significant direct relationship between increases in the real value of the minimum wage and teenage unemployment. "Teenage unemployment rates fell from the 22–23 percent range in early 1983 to less than 15 percent by the beginning of 1990, at the same time that the real minimum wage was falling from about $5.15 to under $4.00 (in late-1994 dollars). The minimum wage rose in two steps in 1990–91 and teenage unemployment rose with it."[20] Kenneth A. Couch drew a similar conclusion in a 1999 analysis. "My calculations indicate that we would expect the loss of 145,000 to 436,000 teenage jobs from raising the minimum wage from $5.15 to $6.15. From a base of 15.5 million teens in the U.S. in May of 1998 with slightly over 7 million employed, reductions of this magnitude are certainly meaningful, representing 2% to 6% of employment of that group."[21]

Opponents of an increase in the minimum wage also assert that raising the wage floor has also had significant undesirable effects on the socio-economic status of teenagers, basing this on a number of studies over the past decade. One study found that, although the net employment effect of raising the minimum wage is rather small, a higher minimum wage tends to decrease school enrollment and increase the proportion of idle teenagers—those neither employed nor in school.[22] Mark Wilson explains this phenomenon by noting that "neoclassical economic theory predicts that a higher minimum wage increases the relative demand for higher-skill (enrolled) teenagers and induces some of them to leave school for employment. As employers substitute toward these higher-skilled teenagers, lower-skilled, out-of-school teenagers at or near the old minimum wage are displaced from the labor market."[23] Thus, according to Heritage Foundation calculations, in response to the 1996 minimum wage increase, overall teenage school enrollment declined by half a percentage point, with the enrollment rate dropping 1.9 percent for teenage girls and 5.6 percent for Hispanics. At the same time, overall teenage idleness increased by 1.4 percent, with the proportion of idle Hispanic teens increasing by 6 percent.[24]

Assuming that the preponderance of evidence does show negative outcomes for the employability of teens, does this also hold for adults, particularly in view of the concern about increasing the longevity of older workers in the workforce?

WILL A MINIMUM WAGE INCREASE HAVE A NEGATIVE EFFECT ON EMPLOYMENT?[25]

One set of arguments against increasing the minimum wage focuses on the issue of productivity. Economic theory typically correlates wage increases with increases in productivity—if one produces more per hour, part of the benefit from such increased productivity can be returned to the worker in the form of higher wages. However, if wages are increased without a concomitant increase in productivity, the firm will be under pressure to reduce the level of employment. Hence the dour predictions of high increases in unemployment that were expected to result from the last minimum wage increase, predictions that failed to materialize.

One explanation of this is that minimum wages do not cover all sectors of the economy, and that some individuals displaced from covered sectors take jobs in uncovered sectors at a reduced wage rate. The opportunity to find work in occupations that aren't covered by the minimum wage therefore lessens the adverse impact of the minimum wage increase on overall levels of employment.[26] Economists making this argument suggest that some of the efficiency costs of the minimum wage will therefore take the form of an inefficient allocation of labor across different sectors of the economy.

In any case, there is now substantial evidence that *moderate* increases in the minimum wage have little if any measurable effect on overall employment. Nonetheless, virtually all economists agree that there is a point above which minimum wage increases will result in increased unemployment, but there is little agreement regarding just what that point is.

Opponents of a minimum wage increase also argue that even if there are no significant job losses that may be directly attributed to it, workers may suffer in other ways. It is asserted that while high minimum wages are likely to reduce productivity *growth*, the current *level* of productivity may be forced to increase. That is, many firms will be able to pay higher legally prescribed wages, without reducing employment, only by adjusting their operations to increase the amount of effort per hour of labor input. For example, a manufacturer may be able to compensate for increased costs of labor by making an assembly line run faster, in effect forcing employees to work harder for their pay.

Some opponents of the minimum wage argue that an increase will in effect overstock the labor market. That is, until workers become discouraged from their inability to find employment at the high minimum wage, that legally prescribed minimum will increase the supply of individuals willing to work. This suggests that the economy is incapable of creating sufficient jobs at the minimum wage to accommodate all those who will be enticed into the labor force by the prospect of higher minimum wage income. The resulting queue of individuals searching for a job unsuccessfully will necessarily increase unemployment.

Some advocates for the minimum wage argue for a new understanding of the labor market that adds the issue of bargaining power to that of free trade. This approach takes as its point of departure the notion that the amount firms are willing to pay depends in part on the productivity of workers. However, this only establishes an upper limit to wages, it does not indicate how much of their productivity workers will actually get to keep. The latter depends primarily on the leverage the workers can bring to bear. Can they successfully threaten to leave and take employment elsewhere, or is the firm in a stronger position to threaten employed workers with layoffs or possible replacement by other less-demanding workers? "In such a world," Palley argues, "a modest minimum wage is not a distortion that causes unemployment. Instead, it is an institutional mechanism that enhances the bargaining power of low-wage workers. By setting a legal wage floor, it helps workers obtain higher wages than they could get on their own."[27] In effect, it eliminates much wage competition among low-wage earners and prevents firms from exploiting the limited wage-bargaining power that they have.

There is, however, another aspect of the issue that also merits consideration. It should be recognized that the 1966 amendments to the Fair Labor Standards Act effectively extended minimum wage coverage to large numbers of low wage employees who were not previously covered. This included almost all employees in retail, restaurant, hotel, laundry, food processing, agriculture and domestic services, industries in which there is heavy concentration of entry level workers. Thus, as noted by Carlos E. Bonilla of the Employment Policies Institute: "Whereas the minimum wage was formerly a minimum *manufacturing* wage it has now become a minimum *service sector* wage. Productivity growth in service occupations has always grown much more slowly than in manufacturing."[28] This suggests that the across-the-board approach to the minimum wage is anomalous, compelling economically unjustifiable costs to service sector employers, given that the increases in wages are not related to commensurate increases in productivity. As one writer put it: "It remains an inescapable fact of economic life that *no legislature can make a person worth a certain amount simply by making it illegal for employers to pay him any less. . . .* Legislators ought to ask themselves this question: Is it conceivable that someone out there in the labor market, because of age, handicap or lack of experience, may not be worth as much as $5.15 per hour?"[29]

THE MINIMUM WAGE AS A PUBLIC POLICY ISSUE

Another way of looking at a mandated minimum wage is as what some economists refer to as an "off-budget tax transfer." Preston J. Miller, a vice president of the Federal Reserve Bank of Minneapolis, describes this tax transfer notion as follows: Let's suppose, he wrote in 1995 before the last minimum wage increase was put in effect, that the government sought to implement a $5 minimum wage through the federal budget. It would assign a government agent to collect taxes each month from employers and distribute the proceeds to low-wage workers. At each firm the agent would ask for a record of all employee hours that were worked for less than $5 per hour and the wages that were actually paid. The employer's tax bill would then be calculated as the sum of the hours worked for less than $5 each, multiplied by the difference between the wage actually paid and the $5 minimum. The agent would collect the taxes from the employer and then give each employee who earned less than $5 per hour the difference between the $5 minimum and the wage each below minimum worker actually received, multiplied by the number of hours worked that month. "This hypothetical tax-transfer scheme is identical to a minimum wage policy. The major difference is that the minimum wage mandate removes the government middle-man and moves the policy from on-budget to off-budget for the government."[30]

By making the minimum wage an off-budget mandate, the government avoids having to deal with a number of critical public policy issues such as justifying reductions in the Earned Income Tax Credit for low-income families at the same time that it mandates that the minimum wage must be raised. On the other hand, as Miller notes, "if the minimum wage were put on-budget, policymakers could weigh in a consistent manner the desirability of a minimum wage change relative to changes in other tax and transfer policies."[31]

There can be little doubt that the minimum wage is in effect an income redistribution scheme, using business instead of government as the redistribution mechanism. From a political standpoint this approach helps foster the popular illusion of diminished government involvement in the free market economy. The reality, however, is that recent changes in corporate culture reflect a growing dissatisfaction with the idea of using employers as instruments of government policy. Ironically, business people are increasingly becoming advocates of more direct government involvement in dealing with a number of social welfare issues, among which the minimum wage is but one. This would eliminate the economic distortions introduced into the marketplace when employers are forced or pressured into assuming the public burden. Indeed, this approach is fully consistent with the decline of corporate paternalism discussed earlier.

CONCLUSION

From the available evidence, it would appear that one could make a substantial economic case against an increase in the minimum wage. However, it is by no means a conclusive one, notwithstanding the overblown predictions of economic harm touted by opponents. One can also make a reasonable case that though it is virtually impossible to target the increase in such a way that only earners from low-income families benefit from it, it is still worth enacting because of the large number of people who will benefit from it.

Because there is significant disagreement among economists about the desirability and economic consequences of an increase in the minimum wage, a decision on whether or not to raise the minimum wage clearly cannot be made on the basis of economic analysis alone. It is unavoidably a question of public policy, only one aspect of which concerns its possible economic effects. The decision must also reflect a sense of national values. Of course someone has to pay the cost. But this is true of every public good, whether it be national defense or protecting business from unfair competition. Do we as a nation really want to help low-income earners and families participate more fully in the general wellbeing? If we do, then adopting either or a combination of the approaches that were discussed above would seem to be a reasonable way to go. Why not make the minimum wage an on-budget item, as suggested by Preston Miller, and why not index it to inflation, as proposed by Robert Reich? At heart, this is fundamentally a political and not an economic question.

The public policy dilemma is aptly pointed out by the Employment Policy Foundation. "Wage mandates do nothing to solve the underlying problem faced by workers with relatively low levels of skill and educational attainment. The solution is to increase the human capital and market value of low-wage workers through education and training. Of course, that takes money, time, and effort, while decreeing a higher minimum wage appears to be cheap, quick, and easy."[32]

NOTES

1. Franklin D. Roosevelt, *Public Papers and Addresses*, vol. 7 (New York: Random House, 1937), p. 392.

2. Stephen Herzenberg, John Alic, and Howard Wial, "A New Deal for a New Economy," *Challenge*, March-April 1999, p. 115.

3. Jared Bernstein, "Another Modest Minimum Wage Increase" (Washington, DC: Economic Policy Institute, February 1998).

4. Robert B. Reich, "A Better Way to Raise the Minimum Wage" (The Electronic Policy Network, February 23, 1998).

5. Aaron Bernstein, "Peg the Minimum Wage—For Good," *Business Week* (November 23, 1998), p. 63.

6. Jared Bernstein, "America's Well-Targeted Raise" (Washington, DC: Economic Policy Institute, September 1997).

7. "Job Loss in a Booming Economy" (Washington, DC: Employment Policies Institute, January 1998), p. 4.

8. "Increasing the Minimum Wage Costs Jobs and Increases Poverty," *Economic Bytes* (Washington, DC: Employment Policy Foundation, May 10, 1999).

9. Thomas Palley, "Building Prosperity from the Bottom Up," *Challenge* (September-October 1998), p. 60.

10. "Job Loss in a Booming Economy," p. 5.

11. "The Labor Home Page Issue Briefs–Minimum Wage" (Washington, DC: Heritage Foundation, n.d.).

12. Susan C. Eaton, "Pennsylvania's Nursing Homes: Promoting Quality Care And Quality Jobs" (Harrisburg, PA: Keystone Research Center, 1997), p. 41.

13. Herzenberg, Alic, and Wial, "A New Deal for a New Economy," p. 116.

14. Lawrence Mishel, Jared Bernstein, and Edith Russell, "Who Wins with a Higher Minimum Wage," briefing paper (Washington, DC: Economic Policy Institute, 1995).

15. Donald Deere, Kevin M. Murphy, and Finis Welch, "Sense and Nonsense on the Minimum Wage," *Regulation* (1996).

16. D. Mark Wilson, "Increasing the Mandated Minimum Wage: Who Pays the Price?" backgrounder no. 1162 (Washington, DC: Heritage Foundation, March 5, 1998).

17. Matthew B. Kibbe, "The Minimum Wage: Washington's Perennial Myth," *Policy Analysis*, no. 106 (May 23, 1988).

18. "Job Loss in a Booming Economy," p. 2.

19. Ibid., p. 3.

20. "The Effects of the Minimum Wage on Teenage Employment" (Washington, DC: National Center for Policy Analysis, 1996).

21. Kenneth A. Couch, "Distribution and Employment Impacts of Raising the Minimum Wage," *Economic Letter*, no. 99–6 (Federal Reserve Bank of San Francisco, February 19, 1999).

22. David Neumark, and William Wascher, "The Effects of Minimum Wages on Teenage Employment and Enrollment: Evidence from Matched CPS Surveys," *Research in Labor Economics* (1996).

23. Wilson, "Increasing the Mandated Minimum Wage," note 35.

24. Ibid.

25. For a discussion of this issue from an economic research perspective, see Marvin H. Kosters, ed., *The Effects of the Minimum Wage on Employment* (Washington, DC: AEI Press, 1996).

26. Yale Brozen, "Minimum Wage Rates and Household Workers," *Journal of Law and Economics* (October 1962).

27. Palley, "Building Prosperity from the Bottom Up," pp. 64–65.

28. Carlos E. Bonilla, "The Minimum Wage," presentation at a Joint Economic Committee (February 15, 1995).

29. Lawrence W. Reed, "Minimum Wage Hurts Jobless by Making Work Illegal, *Viewpoint on Public Issues*, no. 97–SRI (Midland, MI: Mackinac Center for Public Policy, February 24, 1997).

30. Preston J. Miller, "The New Economics of a Minimum Wage Hike," *Fedgazette* (Federal Reserve Bank of Minneapolis, October 1995).

31. Ibid.

32. *Economic Bytes* (Washington, DC: Employment Policy Foundation, January 12, 1999).

10

CORPORATE RESPONSIBILITY REVISITED

Corporation: An ingenious device for obtaining individual profit without individual responsibility.

—Ambrose Bierce

There is a widespread tendency to believe that most if not all labor market issues will eventually be resolved through the ultimately beneficent operation of impersonal and autonomous "market forces." This notion has been characterized by Pierre Bourdieu of the College de France as "the neoliberal utopia of a pure and perfect market." The purveyors of this conception generally tend "to favor severing the economy from social realities and thereby constructing, in reality, an economic system conforming to its description in pure theory, that is, a sort of logical machine that presents itself as a chain of constraints regulating economic agents."[1]

This theoretical construction has been promoted with fervor for some time by businessmen, politicians, business-oriented economists, management consultants, financial advisers, market analysts, and a large segment of the public, and has become part of the conventional wisdom of our time. Thus, one author writes in a popular magazine, "In a capitalist system, where resources, including people, are allocated in response to market forces, job creation and job destruction are inevitable consequences of economic development."[2]

This sort of widespread and unquestioning belief in what amounts to a form of economic determinism has had serious consequences for our society. Because of it, relatively little serious attention has been given in recent years to the potential of public policy to assist in harnessing or redirecting such so-called "market forces" to mitigate the sometimes negative effects of the changes taking place in the current employment environment. Public policy can do this because, in fact, there are no autonomous "market forces" at work in the economy, only the deliberate and not infrequently arbitrary choices of individual decision-makers. Contrary to popular economic myth, there is no "unseen hand" forcing a profitable company to downsize its workforce, only a conscious determination by one or more individuals with decision-making authority to further increase shareholder value at the expense of other stakeholders.

One of the principal factors that have contributed to this approach to corporate government has been the phenomenal growth of speculative financial markets in the United States. In 1968, the total value of trading on the New York Stock Exchange was 26.6 times as great as the national GDP. That is, $26.60 worth of shares was traded for every new dollar of goods and services produced. By the end of 1996, $878.10 worth of shares was traded for every dollar of new goods and services. This represented an extraordinary increase of 3,200 percent over the period for trading on the New York Stock Exchange alone. This explosion of speculative trading has placed corporate managers under a constant pressure to impress the stock market with their companies' quarterly earnings. As a result, their focus has shifted from expanding the production of new goods and services to protecting and enhancing the value of assets being traded on Wall Street.[3]

Referring to this "tyranny of improving shareholder value," David Fagiano, President and CEO of the American Management Association, wrote,

This idea has gained such credence that senior managers everywhere in the United States claim that their most important role is to improve shareholder value. Suddenly senior management is in the wealth creation business instead of the business of creating companies, building market share, strengthening brands, developing skilled workers and competing effectively. . . . Not too long ago the legacy senior management wanted to create was to leave the organization stronger than they found it. I'm afraid that if we keep going in our current direction, the legacy will be a few wealthy people and institutions—and a landscape littered with dismantled companies, as well as a nation of consultants looking for someone to talk to other than themselves.[4]

In this same general regard, it is noteworthy that a *Business Week* national poll conducted by Louis Harris & Associates during February 23–26, 1996 found that 95 percent of the public agreed with the following assertion: "U.S. corporations should have more than one purpose. They also owe something to their workers and the communities in which they operate, and they should sometimes sacrifice some profit for the sake of making things better for their workers and communities."[5]

Herbert Stein, a former chairman of the President's Council of Economic Advisers, challenged the idea of a corporate responsibility to stakeholders other than shareholders. Writing from an economist's standpoint, he argued: "It is not out of any special love for shareholders that economists say that it is the business of business to maximize profits. Maximizing profits is the guide for attaining a certain kind of efficiency in the use of the economy's resources. It means that a corporation tries to use the labor and capital available to it to maximize the excess of the value of their product over the value the same resources would produce if used elsewhere—the value in each case being measured by markets. We don't know any other way of using a nation's resources efficiently."[6] However, as Peter Drucker pointed out, it is an exercise in futility to argue that a business has only one responsibility, namely, maximizing profits. "Economic performance is the *first* responsibility of business. A business that does not show a profit at least equal to its cost of capital is socially irresponsible . . . Economic performance is the basis; without it, a business cannot discharge any other responsibilities, cannot be a good employer, a good citizen, a good neighbor. But economic performance is not the sole responsibility of a business. . . . An organization has full responsibility for its impact on community and society."[7]

Moreover, the notion articulated by Stein that it is the "business of business to maximize profits" is at best a dubious proposition, bearing only a tenuous relationship to the real world of business where optimization of profits is often the greater imperative. But, even if one is prepared to accept the argument that it is the "business of business to maximize profits," it is fallacious to simply equate a corporation with "business." Corporations are chartered by governments for a variety of purposes, none of which relates to the maximization of profit. Indeed, some corporations are specifically intended to be non-profit. All are intended by the terms of their charters to serve the public interest, an issue to which we will return below.

In practice, corporate decision-makers respond not to ostensibly autonomous market forces but to business circumstances and financial and operational constraints, which may in all likelihood be the consequences of decisions previously made by others in similar positions of authority. These circumstances and constraints may tend to condition a corporate executive's choices but do not necessarily predetermine them. Moreover, it should be recognized that in most cases it is corporate management alone that determines the course that the firm is to pursue, notwithstanding the conventional apologetics about management being pressured to make certain hard decisions in response to the demands of their boards of directors and stockholders.

With regard to the influence of corporate boards of directors, Myles L. Mace of the Harvard Business School found after extensive research that, "approval by boards in most companies is perfunctory, automatic, and routine. Presidents and their subordinates, deeply involved in analysis and decision making prior to presentation to the board, believe in the correctness of their recommendations and almost without exception they are unchallenged by the members of the board. Rarely do boards go contrary to the wishes of the president."[8] This should not be surprising since the company president or CEO, who is in most cases also chairman of the board, generally handpicks corporate directors with the expectation of their support of his or her decisions. Where this expectation is disappointed, directors tend to get forced out and replaced. Moreover, many directors, "including those who serve on the committees that set CEO pay—often have significant personal, financial and business ties to top executives that defy any common sense notions of 'independence.' Maybe that's why CEO pay is going through the roof."[9] The ratio of CEO to worker pay, which was 44 to 1 in 1965, increased to an unprecedented 326 to 1 by 1998.[10] Although there have been some encouraging developments recently in corporate governance, with some boards of major companies playing a more autonomous role in decision-making, it is not at all clear that this reflects a trend that will soon dominate the business world.[11]

Similarly, the notion that it is the stockholders who control or determine corporate decision making is more myth than reality, notwithstanding some highly publicized but rare instances of successful stockholder interventions. As pointed out long ago by Adolf A. Berle: "Essentially, the stockholders, though politely called 'owners,' are passive. They have the right to receive only. The condition of their being is that they do not interfere in management."[12] This point has been reemphasized recently in an Economic Policy Institute report on corporate responsibility: "Shareholders do not 'own' companies. Rather, they have an equity stake.... The laws that set up corporations separate the ownership of equity claims (shares of stock) from the ownership of property. Owners of a few shares of stock in a company are not entitled to the ordinary rights of property ownership—the rights to possess, use, dispose of, exclude others, manage, and control the company."[13] Should stockholders, even major institutional investors, decide to attempt to impose their will on corporate management, they face an uphill battle against overwhelming odds. For one thing, most individual stockholders do not take the trouble to attend stockholder meetings and prefer to assign their proxies to management. If a group of stockholders elects to challenge management in a proxy fight, it can become a very expensive exercise, because the contesting stockholders will have to pay the costs of soliciting proxies, and may have to do so several times, with little prospect of success. One early study of the problem concluded: "During the eighteen years for which data are available, 1956–73, management has won 99.9 percent of all proxy solicitations in ten out of eighteen years."[14]

Another piece of conventional wisdom asserts that large institutional investors, particularly pension funds, are able to bring great pressure to bear on corporate management to increase stock share value. This has led some commentators to make the rather specious argument that it is the beneficiaries of pension plans, older workers, who reap advantage from the downsizings that contribute to higher stock values, even though older workers themselves may be primary targets in such restructurings. However, a 1996 analysis of 197 large corporations and of 13 activist pension funds reported that, "activism has no appreciable effect on firm performance." Nonetheless, "institutions engage in activism as a means of enhancing their public image as monitors of firm management," even though, as one of the study's authors put it, "there is no evidence that their activity can be seen in the bottom line."[15]

One of the principal reasons why stock ownership generally confers little power is because it is only when capital is being raised through a stock offering that the shareholder has a real and direct relationship to the firm, which is not the case when stocks are traded in the market. As explained in a particularly lucid manner by Ralph Estes of American University,

Corporate stock transactions are sort of like used car sales. Ford is affected when it sells new cars. Later, when these cars are traded, maybe a number of times, in the used car market, Ford is not involved. The company does not receive a dime, and it is hardly affected by the prices its cars bring in the used car market. So too with Ford stock: after a stock issue is first sold (and for most outstanding stock that would have been years ago), all the stock market transactions we hear about have no direct effect on Ford. And if Ford never issues new stock again—which is more than a possibility—then the market price of its stock can go sky high or sink to the cellar without changing a dollar on Ford's balance sheet.[16]

In fact, established companies rarely issue new stock nowadays to raise capital, preferring to reinvest profits or to borrow what they need. If anything, the trend in recent years has been for such companies to buy back a percentage of their outstanding stock, further reducing any potential shareholder influence. In February 1998, the *Economist* reported in this regard that General Motors was planning to spend as much as $4 billion to buy back another ten percent of its shares, the third such recent purchase that would bring about a 20 percent reduction in outstanding GM shares.[17] However, it does serve corporate interests to suggest, disingenuously for the most part, that management is under pressure from shareholders, especially large institutional investors such as pension funds, to take decisions that may impact adversely on other stakeholders, particularly employees and the communities in which they live.

But if the stockholders, individual as well as institutional, generally have so little power over corporate management, what is it that drives the latter to place increasing share value as its principal imperative, overriding all other stakeholder considerations? It appears that there is in fact one relatively small group of shareholders/stakeholders who do exercise enormous power over corporate decision-making—the corporate executives themselves. As observed by John Kenneth Galbraith: "The management, though its ownership is normally negligible, is solidly in control of the enterprise. By all visible evidence it possesses the power. Yet there has been great reluctance to admit to a significant and enduring shift of power from the owners of capital. Some observers have sought to maintain the myth of stockholder power. As in foreign policy and bad marriages it is hoped that incantation may save what reality denies."[18]

Accordingly, one should not dismiss the significance for corporate decision making of the fact that many corporate executives increasingly receive much of their compensation in company stock or stock purchase options, in effect making them owner-managers with a strong vested interest in the share value of that stock. According to a report from the Institute for Policy Studies, "The CEOs of the 22 top job-cutting firms in 1995 held a combined total of over 22 million stock options in their firms. As stock prices rose on the day of the announced layoffs, the value of the CEO's stock options rose a combined total of $37 million."[19] Given this current reality, there is a certain sardonic truth to the assertion that corporate executives are compelled to respond to the demands of stockholders for increased share value.

Finally, it should be recalled that one of the most essential features of a corporation, that which distinguishes it from a partnership, is the immunity granted to its stockholders for liabilities incurred by the corporation, an immunity which is predicated on the separation of ownership and professional management. Contemporary executive compensation practices are effectively making this concept obsolete and therefore should raise some serious questions about whether corporate structures that blur the distinction between owners and managers, who are presumably disinterested professionals, continue to serve the public interest and merit the benefits accorded them by contemporary public law.

As economist Joseph Stiglitz pointed out, this situation raises serious questions about the presumed efficiency and effectiveness of the market economy. "If managers have the means and incentives to act in their own interests, if their own interests do not perfectly coincide with those of shareholders, and if diverse ownership provides no (or inadequate) incentives for monitoring managers, then how can large firms function? If firm value maximization is the key to the success of a market economy, and if, instead, firms maximize managerial returns, then what assurance do we have of the efficiency of the market economy?"[20]

Public policy interventions have the ability to modify, and in some instances to radically change, the operating environment of business and thereby facilitate a different set of responses to economic issues. In other words, the essential purpose of public policy is to constrain or facilitate decision-making in a manner that best serves the broader public interest. Investment and economic growth tend to take place under conditions in which the investor can receive an adequate return and, as editorialized by the *Economist* with specific reference to the third world, "establishing those conditions is the task of economic policy." In this regard, the editorialist asserts that "market-friendly" policies tend to work best.[21] The key point, however, is the recognition of the importance of public policy in determining the conditions under which the operation of the market best serves the general interest.

At this point, objections will be raised by some who will insist that government has no legitimate role to play in corporate business decisions, which are best left to the private-sector. A more extreme version of this view asserts that corporations should be entirely self-regulated and therefore immune from public policy intervention or government interference. In either case, it is a rather curious notion, given the intimate roles that government and public policies play in the very existence of the corporation. After all, there are no natural corporations, only those that are chartered by government in the public interest, and nurtured, protected, and often subsidized by government at public expense. In fact, the corporation is a creature of public law created solely for public purposes. Nonetheless, once established the corporation tends to take on a life of its own, often arrogating the right to do as it pleases without regard for the public good or ill, irrespective of the intentions and purposes for which it was permitted to come into existence. This reflects a public policy anomaly that was pointed out by Lord Eustace Percy as long ago as 1944. "The human association which in fact produces and distributes wealth, the association of workmen, managers, technicians and directors, is not an association recognized by the law. The association which the law does recognize—the association of shareholders, creditors and directors—is incapable of production or distribution and is not expected by the law to perform these functions. We have to give law to the real association and to withdraw meaningless privilege from the imaginary one."[22]

There is no little irony in the fact that corporation heads, believing themselves vulnerable to the widespread wave of corporate mergers and takeovers that began more than a decade ago, lobbied the legislatures of the states in which they are incorporated for protection from corporate raiders. As a result of their efforts, by 1994 more than half of the states enacted "constituency statutes" that specifically authorized corporate directors *not* to make their decisions solely on the basis of shareholder interests, but to take into account the broader public interest. For example, the Indiana Code contains such a "constituency" provision in its "Standards of Conduct for Directors," which enumerates the standards of conduct that avert personal liability. One of these standards specifies: "A director may, in considering the best interests of a corporation, consider the effects of any action on *shareholders, employees, suppliers, and customers of the corporation, and communities* in which offices or other facilities of the corporation are located, and any other factors the director considers pertinent" (emphasis added).[23] Although such "constituency statutes" are currently permissive rather than prescriptive, they nonetheless clearly reflect the public interest origins of incorporation and could be amended to mandate greater attention to stakeholder interests.

THE SHIFT TOWARD A NEW RESPONSIBILITY

It is noteworthy that there is a small but growing number of corporate executives who are prepared to acknowledge publicly that business has a clear responsibility for recognizing and responding to stakeholder concerns and interests. An outstanding example of this is John Browne, chief executive of British Petroleum, one of the most profitable corporations in the world. In his view, the corporation has a clear and unequivocal responsibility to the communities in which it operates, and he has gone to unusual lengths to ensure that this corporate philosophy is put into effect around the world. Moreover, as Browne puts it: "These efforts have nothing to do with charity and everything to do with our long-term self-interest. I see no trade-off between the short term and the long. Twenty years is just 80 quarters. And our shareholders want performance today, and tomorrow, and the day after."[24]

There is also some evidence that a growing number of business executives are discovering that there is an emerging relationship between corporate profit and social responsibility. Challenged by an unrelenting media, many corporations have learned that the consuming public is increasingly unwilling to reward what it sees as irresponsible corporate behavior, whether environmental or social. Others have learned that responsible behavior toward workers can result in significantly improved productivity or reduced costs of employee turnover. A case in point is the hotel industry's annual 100 percent turnover rate of low-wage workers. By instituting a 24-hour multilingual hotline staffed by trained social workers whom hotel employees could call for assistance and referrals to aid agencies, Marriott International cut the turnover rate of its approximately 150,000 low-wage workers to 35% over a five-year period. Although operation of the hotline cost the company more than $1 million annually, it saved more than $3 million in recruiting, training and other costs. Another example is that of Malden Mills, which lost its factory in Lowell, Massachusetts to, fire in 1995. Owner Aaron Feuerstein nonetheless continued to pay his workers' wages and benefits until a new factory was built. This demonstration of compassion and loyalty to his workers was amply rewarded in the new plant, where worker productivity improved by a reported 25 percent and a two-thirds drop in quality defects was seen.[25]

This emerging sense of corporate responsibility is also clearly reflected in the efforts of the international business executives who participated in the deliberations at the Caux Round Table that produced a set of proposed "Principles for Business" in 1994. The first of these principles deals with "The Responsibilities of Business: Beyond Shareholders Toward Stakeholders," frontally challenging the culture of corporate narcissism discussed earlier. The principle states,

The value of a business to society is the wealth and employment it creates and the marketable products and services it provides to consumers at a reasonable price commensurate with quality. To create such value, a business must maintain its own economic health and viability, but survival is not a sufficient goal. Businesses have a role to play in improving the lives of all their customers, employees, and shareholders by sharing with them the wealth they have created. . . . As responsible citizens of the local, national, regional, and global communities in which they operate, businesses share a part in shaping the future of those communities.

With specific reference to employees, the Principles state in part: "We therefore have a responsibility to provide jobs and compensation that improve workers' living conditions." It also called upon corporations to "be sensitive to serious unemployment problems frequently associated with business decisions, and work with governments, employee groups, other agencies and each other in addressing these dislocations."[26]

Were these principles to be adopted and acted upon by a substantial part of the business community, many of the most serious concerns about the changes taking place in the labor economy could be readily resolved. This was the case in an earlier era when corporations tended to view themselves as responsible to stakeholders and not only to shareholders, and there is no objective reason why it should not be so again. After all, as argued by the authors of an Economic Policy Institute paper, "like shareholders, employees make investments in a firm and take risks. Unlike most shareholders, however, employees' livelihoods can be severely threatened by poor investment decisions and bad management." It is in fact much easier for investors to sell their shares when they conclude that a company is poorly managed than it is for workers to change jobs. For one thing, as discussed earlier, in most cases, experienced older employees have great difficulty in finding other jobs at their previous wages. "Decisions in which they have had no part have essentially wiped out their investments in skills and knowledge. This is not only unfair, it is an inefficient use of society's resources."[27]

Unfortunately, it is not presently the case that significant corporate attention is being paid to stakeholder interests, nor is it likely to be the case anytime in the foreseeable future given the prevailing trends in corporate governance. It therefore appears rather unlikely that the necessary and appropriate solutions to the problems facing the American labor force will be forthcoming from the employer community, although positive developments in this regard would be warmly welcomed. In the meantime, other more interventionist approaches may be necessary if the situation of workers and the communities in which they live is to improve in significant ways.

It is noteworthy that there is a slowly emerging public anger at what is widely perceived to be corporate irresponsibility, and that this may well be transformed into a demand for appropriate public policies to rectify or at least ameliorate the situation. One recent study suggests that, notwithstanding a high degree of public anger at government generally, many people are so fed up with what they consider irresponsible corporate behavior that they are willing to risk further government intervention. This survey, conducted for the Preamble Center for Public Policy, indicates that "seven in ten people (69%) favor government action to promote more responsible corporate behavior and to penalize bad corporate citizenship. Large majorities favor a host of specific policy approaches, many of which are already part of the political debate."[28] Among the latter are 'living wage' laws, the proposed New Jersey legislation designed to penalize corporate downsizers, and Minnesota's law requiring corporations that get tax breaks for job creation, but do not create new jobs, to pay back the money.

There are a number of alternative and prospectively viable public policy approaches to dealing with the issue of increasing aggregate well-compensated work opportunities that have been suggested by a variety of business and economics writers and analysts. None of these approaches offers what could even remotely be construed as a panacea to the problems engendered by the current employment environment. Moreover, all of these ideas are highly controversial. Indeed, if the measures proposed were not so controversial, they most likely would already have been adopted as public policy. Nonetheless, there is reason to believe that some or perhaps all of these approaches, not singly but in combination, could prove to be effective in alleviating the mounting pressures on the contemporary American labor force, especially mid-life and older workers. Notwithstanding the decline in popular sentiment for governmental solutions to societal problems, there may be no effective alternative to creative public policy intervention in the employment environment. As Ray Marshall put it: "public policies can create the conditions that make it possible and necessary for companies to concentrate on improving productivity and quality instead of following a natural tendency to compete primarily by direct cost reductions, usually by lowering wages."[29] The challenge will be to keep any proposed inter-

vention as non-intrusive as possible in order to facilitate general acceptance by the spectrum of stakeholders in the American political economy.

Once the corporate world begins to acknowledge the responsibilities of
corporate citizenship, numerous opportunities for public-private partnerships and collaboration may be expected to emerge. One of the more innovative and promising contemporary approaches toward a public-
private-sector collaboration was that suggested by Sidney Harman, chairman of Harman International Industries Inc., and a former under-secretary
of commerce. Harman envisioned a cooperative venture between public
and corporate policy to produce employment opportunities during periods of business transition that he has dubbed "off-line employment."

The central idea of "off-line employment" is to create an internal buffer-
ing mechanism to help avoid worker layoffs during periods of slack demand for a firm's products. An example of this approach was that taken at
one point by Harman from his own $665 million consumer electronics com-
pany that employed some 1,500 production workers. To keep his workers,
who would otherwise be idle and subject to layoff, on the job, Harman reversed the tendency to outsource everything possible and brought some of
that work back into the company to be performed by those at-risk workers.
He also used slow production periods as opportunities to provide additional training for his workers, and planned to open outlet stores for his
products where temporarily idled workers could be employed.

His primary goal in this was the re-creation of a culture of long-term employment. As Harman put it: "My thinking was stimulated because I was
fighting against the use of temps. Temps are bad for the economy; they're
unfair and set up a second class of employee. If people have confidence in
their job security, productivity increases." Moreover, he argued, "when demand picks up again, I don't have to train a whole new batch of people."[30]

In this scheme, the task of public policy would be to help create additional job buffers both for individual companies and society as a whole.
Government could create a bank of public service jobs and retraining slots
that would be available to assist companies that wished to pursue the
"off-line employment" approach. Temporarily idled employees could be
placed in such job slots, with the companies continuing to pay employee
benefits, so that the long-term connection between the firm and its employees remains intact.

Harman has also suggested that the current national unemploy-
ment-insurance program could materially assist this approach if it were
converted from one that compensates people for not working into a program that subsidizes public service employment and the upgrading of
marketable skills. Some initial steps in this direction have already been
taken, but much more remains to be done before the impact on employment opportunities can become significant.

What is most significant at this point is that these ideas clearly suggest that there is ample room and opportunity for government and pri-vate-sector employers to work collaboratively in responding affirma-tively to stakeholder interests in the economy. However, for such collaboration to be effective, it would appear that a national employment policy might be necessary to provide the appropriate policy mechanisms to support the effort.

NOTES

1. Pierre Bourdieu, "The Essence of Neoliberalism," *Le Monde Diplomatique*, December 1998.

2. John Cassidy, "All Worked Up," *The New Yorker*, April 22, 1996, p. 52.

3. Robert Pollin and Stephanie Luce, *The Living Wage: Building a Fair Economy* (New York: The New Press, 1998), pp. 175–176.

4. David Fagiano, "The Legacy of Downsizing," *Management Review* (June 1996), p. 5.

5. *Business Week* (March 11, 1996), p. 65.

6. Herbert Stein, "Corporate America, Mind Your Own Business," *Wall Street Journal*, July 15, 1996.

7. Peter F. Drucker, *Post-Capitalist Society* (New York: HarperCollins, 1993), pp. 101–102.

8. Myles L. Mace, *Directors: Myth and Reality* (Boston: Harvard Business School Press, 1986), p. 186.

9. "Too Close for Comfort," *Executive Pay Watch* (Washington, DC: AFL-CIO, 1998).

10. "Runaway CEO Pay," *Executive Pay Watch* (Washington, DC: AFL-CIO, 1998).

11. "The Best & Worst Boards," *Business Week*, November 25, 1966.

12. Adolph A. Berle, Jr., *Power Without Property* (New York: Harcourt, Brace & World, 1959), p. 74.

13. Eileen Appelbaum, Peter Berg, and Dean Baker, "The Economic Case for Corporate Responsibility to Workers" (Washington, DC: Economic Policy Institute, 1996).

14. Ralph Nader, Mark Green, and Joel Seligman, *Taming the Giant Corporation* (New York: W.W. Norton, 1976), p. 81.

15. Jay Matthews, "Study Disputes Effect of Activist Pension Funds on Corporate Performance," *Washington Post*, August 4, 1996.

16. Ralph Estes, *Tyranny of the Bottom Line: Why Corporations Make Good People Do Bad Things* (San Francisco, CA: Berrett-Koehler Publishers, 1996), p. 50.

17. *Economist* (Internet edition, February 14, 1998).

18. John Kenneth Galbraith, *The New Industrial State* (Boston: Houghton Mifflin, 1985), p. 52.

19. Sarah Anderson, and John Cavanaugh, "CEOs Win, Workers Lose: How Wall Street Rewards Job Destroyers" (Washington, DC: Institute for Policy Studies, April 1996).

20. Joseph Stiglitz, "Quis Custodiet Ipsos Custodes?" *Challenge* (November–December 1999), p. 36.

21. "The Mystery of Growth," *Economist* (May 25, 1996), pp. 15–16.

22. Charles Handy, *Beyond Certainty: The Changing Worlds of Organizations* (Boston: Harvard Business School Press, 1996), p. 73.

23. *Burns Indiana Statutes Annotated*, Title 23, Article 1, Chapter 35–1–d.

24. Jeffrey E. Garten, "Globalism Doesn't Have to Be Cruel," *Business Week* (Internet edition, February 4, 1998).

25. Bennett Daviss, "Profits from Principle," *Futurist* (March 1999), p. 27.

26. Published as an advertising supplement in *Business Ethics* (May/June 1995).

27. Eileen Appelbaum, Peter Berg, and Dean Baker, "The Economic Case for Corporate Responsibility to Workers" (Washington, DC: Economic Policy Institute, 1996).

28. Ethel Klein, and Guy Molyneux, "Corporate Irresponsibility: There Ought to be Some Laws" (Washington, DC: Preamble Center for Public Policy, July 29, 1996), p. 2.

29. Ray Marshall, "A New Social Contract," in *Aging and Competition: Rebuilding the U.S. Workforce*, eds. James A. Auerbach and Joyce C. Welsh (Washington, DC: National Planning Association, 1994), p. 216.

30. Cited by Robert Kuttner, "Talking Marriage and Thinking One-Night Stand," *Business Week* (October 18, 1995).

11

NATIONAL EMPLOYMENT POLICIES

People who are hungry and out of a job are the stuff of which dictatorships are made.
—Franklin D. Roosevelt

Since the beginning of the last century, there has been a continuing shift of employment from the manufacturing to the services sector of the economy, where most new jobs are being created. At first glance, it would appear that history is repeating itself, since up to about the middle of the nineteenth century the American labor economy was based primarily on agricultural employment. Then, as industrialization began to make significant inroads, technological advances in the agricultural sector began to realize unprecedented levels of productivity, requiring fewer and fewer workers to produce continually increasing quantities of agricultural products. As agriculture became the most technologically advanced sector of the economy, with the relatively highest productivity, its need for workers continued to decline until reaching its current level of between 2 and 3 percent of the labor force.

Although the work dislocations that resulted were significant and often painful, most displaced agricultural workers were able to find employment in the newly burgeoning industrial and expanding services sectors. Typically, it was estimated that each manufacturing job produced ten other related industrial or service jobs. Then, as productivity increases in the manufacturing sector began to be realized through technological advances and improved industrial processes and organization, a development similar to what happened with agriculture took place. As both productivity and production increased at a far faster rate than the need for labor, the industrial component of the labor force began to shrink, ultimately reaching its current level of about 16 percent of the total.

Once again, displaced workers began to be absorbed by the rapidly growing services and the emerging knowledge sectors of the economy, bringing us to the current situation, which seems to be an unprecedented point in our economic history. Dramatic productivity increases are beginning to take place in these sectors as well, as a result of the application of new, highly sophisticated technologies and the export of jobs to lower cost labor markets. This will almost inevitably result in a diminished need for domestic workers, something that is already happening in some service and knowledge industries. The problem, however, is that there is no other sector of the market economy, either current or projected, that has the capacity to absorb the surplus workers being produced through the resulting labor force dislocations. In effect, the overall demand for labor is being reduced at a faster rate than new technologies are creating additional and increasingly more complex jobs. The net result is decreasing well-compensated work opportunities for an increasing percentage of the labor force.

It has been suggested that an appropriately designed national employment policy could contribute significantly to reducing the scale and scope of this labor market dilemma. One component of such an employment policy that could serve to ameliorate the problem, at least until some unforeseen remedying development takes place, might be increased public-sector job creation. In effect, this would make society itself the employer of last resort. It is important to note, however, that although this approach was employed with reasonable success during the Great Depression of the 1930s, the results of more contemporary efforts at combining employment and job-training programs are widely considered less favorably. Nonetheless, a substantial increase in public sector employment could serve as a means of relieving the economic pressures on a growing number of dislocated and underemployed workers.

Is such job creation an appropriate role for government? This question has been a matter of serious public discussion for more than sixty years. It first rose to prominence during the Great Depression with the growing awareness that "whatever the theoretical causes or cures of depressions, the federal government was the only institution with sufficient power to do anything substantial—and at a practical level—about the economic collapse. The experience of the great depression forced the federal government to extend its functions and responsibilities."[1] In response to the challenge, President Franklin D. Roosevelt appointed a cabinet-level Committee on Economic Security in 1934. The committee came up with two basic recommendations, one targeted at the economic security needs of those members of society who were not expected to support themselves through work, the second focusing on those who were expected to be self-supporting through employment. The first was addressed through a series of ongoing income transfer programs authorized under the Social Security Act of 1935. The second was dealt with through the Emergency Relief Appropriations Act of 1935, which set in place large-scale public employment programs that were designed to relieve the massive unemployment in the country.

Of particular importance to the question of the appropriateness of government intervention in the labor market, the Committee on Economic Security stated: "The first objective in a program of economic security must be maximum employment. As the major contribution of the Federal Government in providing a safeguard against unemployment we suggest employment assurance—the stimulation of private employment and the provision of public employment for those able-bodied workers whom industry cannot employ at a given time." Significantly, the committee saw the proper role of government in job creation as extending beyond periods of national crisis. "In periods of depression public employment should be regarded as a principal line of defense. Even in prosperous times it may be necessary, on a smaller scale, when 'pockets' develop in which there is much unemployment. Public employment is not the final answer to the problem of stranded communities, declining industries, and impoverished farm families, but it is a necessary supplement to more fundamental measures for the solution of such problems."[2]

President Roosevelt gave the issue prominence in his 1944 State of the Union message to Congress. Reflecting in part on both the experience of the depression here and abroad and the world war in which the country was engaged at the time, he declared: "We have come to a clear realization of the fact that true individual freedom cannot exist without economic security and independence. 'Necessitous men are not free men.' People who are hungry and out of a job are the stuff of which dictatorships are made." He then called upon Congress to enact a "second Bill of Rights under which a new basis of security and prosperity can be established for all—regardless of station, race or creed." The first two of those proposed rights were, "the right to a useful and remunerative job," and "the right to earn enough to provide adequate food and clothing and recreation." This position was reaffirmed and advanced further that same year by his political rival, Governor Thomas E. Dewey, the Republican presidential candidate. Dewey asserted that, "if at any time there are not sufficient jobs in private enterprise to go around, the government can and must create job opportunities, because there must be jobs for all in this country of ours."[3] This bipartisan approach had the broad support of public opinion at the time. In a *Fortune* magazine poll conducted in 1944, almost 68 percent of respondents supported the proposition that the government should guarantee employment for anyone wishing to work.[4]

In December 1944, a Senate subcommittee, under the leadership of Vice-President Elect Harry S Truman and Senator James E. Murray, who introduced the bill, issued a report that proposed a "Full Employment Act of 1945." The Murray bill declared: "Every American able to work and willing to work has the right to a useful and remunerative job in the industries or shops or farms or mines of the Nation." The senators concluded: "It is the responsibility of the Government to guarantee that right by assuring continuing full employment."[5]

However, bipartisan political support for the notion of a "right to a useful and remunerative job," which was relatively high when the idea was proposed in late 1944 while the war was still in progress, soon dissipated once hostilities came to an end. The result was the compromise Employment Act of 1946, which omitted consideration of any such "right." As discussed in the report of the Conference Committee convened to reconcile the differing positions of the Senate and the House of Representatives:

The Senate bill declared that it is the responsibility of the Federal Government to maintain full employment and to assure at all times sufficient opportunities for employment to enable all Americans able and willing to work to exercise their right to continued full employment.

The House substitute declared that it is the continuing policy of the United States to promote employment, production, and purchasing power under the system of free competitive enterprise, and that the function of the Government is to promote and not to assure or guarantee employment. It is the theory of the House substitute that employment is not the sole responsibility of the Government and that industry, agriculture, and labor have their responsibility.

Moreover, to remove any ambiguity about the question, the conference report asserted: "The term 'full employment' is rejected, and the term 'maximum employment' is the objective to be promoted."[6] The difference between the two formulations, of course, is highly significant: full employment sets an absolute goal whereas maximum employment is a relative goal, that is, the most employment that is achievable under a given set of circumstances. Full employment is the antithesis of structural unemployment. By contrast, the goal of achieving maximum employment can be compatible with high levels of unemployment and underemployment.

It is noteworthy that the asserted theory of the House, to the effect that employment is a shared responsibility of government and the private-sector, was diluted even further in the actual Declaration of Policy included in the final version of the Employment Act of 1946. The policy enacted into law asserts that it is the responsibility of the Federal Government, with the assistance and cooperation of the private-sector and state and local governments, to use its capabilities and resources to create and maintain "conditions under which there will be afforded useful employment opportunities." Then, almost as an afterthought, it added, "and to promote maximum employment, production, and purchasing power."

It would take another three decades before a new attempt was made to fashion a national employment policy predicated on a legally enforceable right to work. In June 1974, Congressman Augustus Hawkins introduced a bill that would have created such a right, with Hubert Humphrey introducing an identical bill in the Senate. A central feature of the Humphrey-Hawkins proposal distinguished it from the earlier Murray bill, which was based on the notion that a growth-oriented fiscal policy would create the business conditions for full employment. This central feature was its provision, echoing the view of the 1935 Committee on Economic Security, that the federal government itself should serve as the employer of last resort for those who were unable to find jobs in the regular labor market.

Although the version of the Humphrey-Hawkins bill that was finally enacted some four years later was entitled, "Full Employment and Balanced Growth Act of 1978," the employment provisions it contained lacked any real force and were basically ignored by subsequent national administrations, Democratic and Republican alike. The aim of the original bill, which was to create an enforceable right to employment for all those who wished to work, was diluted significantly. It now established as a national goal, "the fulfillment of the right to full opportunities for useful paid employment at fair rates of compensation of all individuals able, willing, and seeking to work." However, the Congress also insisted that the effort to expand jobs to the full employment level had to be done in a manner "consistent with balanced growth," giving highest priority to "expansion of conventional private jobs through improved use of general economic and structural policies." The final section of the act's Declaration of Policy gives unequivocal emphasis to this approach. "The Congress further declares that it is the purpose of the Full Employment and Balanced Growth Act of 1978 to rely principally on the private-sector for expansion of economic activity and creation of new jobs for a growing labor force."

It seems rather clear that there has been little consensus among those in the public policy community regarding the desirability of an enforceable national employment policy. Without such a consensus, little of any real consequence can be expected with regard to a national policy that can deal effectively with the serious dislocations taking place in the contemporary labor economy. Philip Harvey, who suggests that it is not so much wrong-headed as self-interested, has aptly summarized the nature of the opposition to such a national employment policy.

Business leaders are not likely to admit it publicly, but they do not perceive full employment to be in their interest and will generally oppose measures designed to achieve it. It is also not surprising that the business community would oppose proposals to expand the government's role as a direct provider of goods and services. . . . Another source of opposition to employment assurance proposals can be found in the biases of neoclassical economic theory. Conservative economists are generally not prepared to admit that active management of the economy is needed to achieve full employment, and their liberal counterparts are generally not prepared to countenance measures for achieving full employment that extend beyond macroeconomic manipulation. Neither group believes that direct job creation by the government is either necessary or desirable to achieve full employment.[7]

Nonetheless, the fact that opposition to a national employment policy has diluted or crippled previous attempts to deal with a problem of increasing concern does not in itself constitute a valid argument for complacency. Neither the private labor market nor neo-classical economic theory seem to be capable of dealing constructively with the growing problem and it may be time to reconsider the question of a national employment policy as a matter of urgent public interest. Moreover, the Full Employment and Balanced Growth Act of 1978, despite its deficiencies, did establish an important principle. It recognized "the right to full opportunities for useful paid employment at fair rates of compensation of all individuals able, willing, and seeking to work." Perhaps it is time for the principal stakeholders in the economy, business, workers, and government, to begin once again to explore how best to give effect to that currently ignored right.

Could such an effort succeed today, given its history of relative failure? To the extent that the national economy is increasingly consumer-based, it is surely in the interest of business for the country to have a strong consumer base with significant disposable income. Matthew Forstater points out that "the fact that public sector plus private-sector spending now provides a level of employment that leaves well over 6 million workers involuntarily unemployed is de facto evidence that aggregate demand is below the level required for full employment. If aggregate demand were higher, the population would be spending more and creating more jobs for the unemployed."[8] And, if the private-sector cannot create a sufficient number of well-paying jobs to maintain that consumer base, its own self interest should argue in favor of a national employment policy that will do what it cannot. As pointed out by Hyman Minsky more than a decade ago:

The policy problem is to develop a strategy for full employment that does not lead to instability, inflation, and unemployment. The main instrument of such a policy is the creation of an infinitely elastic demand for labor at a floor or minimum wage that does not depend upon long-run and short-run profit expectations of business. Since only government can divorce the offering of employment from the profitability of hiring workers, the infinitely elastic demand for labor must be created by government.[9]

This would be achieved through the introduction by government of a public service job opportunity program that would be financed through highly beneficial deficit spending. The concept of such an employment program is elegantly simple. The government would develop a plan, let's say, to repair and enhance the national infrastructure. It would then announce a wage at which it is prepared to hire and would then hire all who are willing to accept employment at the announced wage. In this manner, anyone who is willing and able to work, but cannot find a job in the private-sector, will have an opportunity for a job at a decent wage. Moreover, the program would offer real jobs that have performance standards that workers would be expected to meet. Workers not measuring up to those standards would be subject to dismissal and forced to rely on the social safety net to meet their critical needs.

For as long as additional government deficit spending for the program continues to increase employment, it is reasonable to conclude that the aggregate demand for jobs must still be below the full employment level. However, once the point is reached at which all voluntary unemployment is eliminated, government spending for the program will be held at the amount necessary to maintain the full employment level that it achieved. The program would not be inflationary because, as Minsky pointed out, the government is free to fix wages arbitrarily and does not have to respond to the same wage pressures as the free labor market. Because the government is not established to make a profit, it can base its decisions about products, production methods, and hiring on the public administration principle of maximizing benefit rather than on the business administration principle of maximizing profit. It can implement the program to achieve broader social values and economic goals without being limited by the cost constraints faced by businesses in a competitive market.

Finally, the program would effectively replace the current reserve labor pool of the unemployed with a pool of available workers that are currently employed, workers that can be drawn upon by business to meet its cyclical or growth needs. L. Randall Wray discusses this notion in his extensive elaboration of the suggested job opportunity program idea, which he calls the Employer of Last Resort (ELR) program. "In a sense, the government will act as a 'market-maker,' creating a market in labour by standing ready to 'buy' unemployed labour at a fixed price, or 'sell' (provide it to non-ELR employers) at a mark-up over the BPSW [basic public sector wage]. . . . What we are proposing to do is to 'make a market in labour' by establishing a 'buffer stock of labor.' This is the 'trick' that allows us to obtain full employment and stable prices."[10]

A complementary approach, proposed by Herzenberg, Alic, and Wial, would use public policy to "foster multi-employer institutions to take responsibility for training, worker-job matching and career development, and work-related communication across firm boundaries."[11] Such multi-employer institutions might receive government planning grants or seed money to get established. It seems clear that state and local governments have the ability, under the authority of the 1998 Workforce Investment Act, to work with businesses to build workforce development institutions that will serve the public interest.

In the words of Andrew Levison, penned two decades ago, "The conclusion is clear. Genuine full employment is a realistic social goal that America can achieve. There is no inevitable tradeoff that prevents it; the necessary reforms can be achieved in the context of America's economic institutions, and the crucial elements of a full employment policy are supported by a majority of the American people." He suggested further that, although there is no simple way to describe what a full employment policy might be like in economic terms, there is a simple test in human terms. It would take place when a willing worker went into a place of employment and said, I'm ready to give you every ounce of ability and energy I have, and all I ask in return is a fair wage. "The goal of full employment will be achieved when there is indeed a place that man can go."[12]

Of course, there are ostensibly valid economic arguments against the implementation of a true national employment policy. However, it should be recognized that the value and validity of an economic theory does not lie in the persistence or reputation of its advocates but in its explanatory power, in its ability to help us understand how and why things happen. In this regard, neoclassical economic theory may be seen as leaving much to be desired in its application to the present employment environment, as evidenced by the growing numbers of contemporary economists who are challenging some of its most cherished premises.

Another series of problems that a national employment policy should deal with concerns the consequences of the growth of the nonstandard workforce and the economic and social implications of that growth discussed in an earlier chapter of this work. Some of the issues that need to be addressed concern the failure of labor legislation and regulation to keep up with developments in the employment environment. As some labor analysts have pointed out,

There are four primary gaps in labor law coverage that severely limit the protective effects of existing labor law for part-time and contingent workers. First, when the federal government establishes the 'bargaining units' that define who will be in a given union, nonstandard workers are often excluded. Second, current laws are ill-equipped to handle joint employment, as when a business hires workers through a temporary agency or subcontractor. Third, subcontracting of public sector jobs creates a gray area between public and private employment where the legal protections associated with either often do not apply. Finally, current labor laws are inadequate for high-turnover workforces.[13]

It would also seem that, at a minimum, there is a need to develop and implement fair labor standards that create wage and benefit parity between permanent and nonstandard workers. A national policy might also deal with the issue of how best to strengthen the enforcement of regulations intended to prevent employers from misclassifying employees as independent contractors to avoid paying social security taxes and benefits normally made available to permanent employees. These proposals, understandably, are likely to be rejected out of hand by those who are unalterably opposed to any further intrusion of government into the private-sector. That is, any government intervention that does not enhance the profitability of business. However, unless one is prepared to accept the notion that maximum private profitability, even at the expense of the public interest, is a founding principle of our society, such objections should not deter serious consideration of such measures.

This is not to suggest that the legitimate concerns of business should not be a factor of major consideration in dealing with these difficult issues. The challenge before us is to construct national policies that will reconcile the needs of nonstandard workers and their employers. The former need workplace protections comparable to those now accorded to standard core employees, without losing the ability to avail themselves of the flexible employment options is currently open to nonstandard workers. Businesses require a degree of workforce flexibility, that is, the ability to adjust the size and tenure of their non-core workforces, to enable them to remain competitive and profitable in an increasingly globalized economy.

As pointed out earlier, a national economic policy would not in itself provide a panacea for contemporary labor market problems. But, in combination with other public policy approaches, it could make a significant contribution to resolving the larger employment issues that face us. Those other public policy approaches include the effective use of fiscal, monetary, and trade policies to increase private-sector employment opportunities, approaches that will be discussed in the pages that follow.

NOTES

1. Stephen K. Bailey, *Congress Makes a Law: The Story Behind the Employment Act of 1946* (New York: Columbia University Press, 1950), p. 7.

2. *The Report of the Committee on Economic Security of 1935* (Washington, DC: National Conference on Social Welfare, 1985), pp. 3–4, 8–9.

3. Bailey, *Congress Makes a Law*, p. 42.

4. Ibid., p. 179.

5. "Building the Post-war Economy," Year-End Report of War Contracts Subcommittee of Committee on Military Affairs (Washington, DC: U.S. House of Representatives, 78th Congress, 2d Session, December 18, 1944).

6. House report no. 1520 (Washington, DC: U.S. House of Representatives, February 5, 1946).

7. Philip Harvey, *Securing the Right to Employment: Social Welfare Policy and the Unemployed in the United States* (Princeton, NJ: Princeton University Press, 1989), pp. 112–113.

8. Matthew Forstater, "Public Employment and Economic Flexibility," public policy brief highlights no. 50A (Anandale-on-Hudson, NY: The Jerome Levy Economics Institute of Bard College, February 1999).

9. Hyman P. Minsky, *Stabilizing an Unstable Economy* (New Haven, CT: Yale University Press, 1986), p. 308.

10. L. Randall Wray, *Understanding Modern Money: The Key to Full Employment and Price Stability* (Cheltenham, U.K.: Edward Elgar, 1998), p. 135. See also, Dimitri Papadimitriou, "No Cheers for Full Employment," *Challenge* (November-December 1999), pp. 92–99.

11. Stephen Herzenberg, John Alic, and Howard Wial, "A New Deal for a New Economy," *Challenge* (March-April 1999), p. 119.

12. Andrew Levison, *The Full Employment Alternative* (New York: Coward, McCann & Geoghegan, 1980), pp. 209–210.

13. Virginia L. duRivage, Francoise J. Carre, and Chris Tilly, "Making Labor Law Work for Part-Time and Contingent Workers," in *Contingent Work: American Employment Relations in Transition*, eds. Kathleen Barker and Kathleen Christensen (Ithaca, NY: Cornell University Press, 1998), p. 266.

12

NATIONAL ECONOMIC POLICIES

When we control business in the public interest, we are also bound to encourage it in the public interest, or it will be a bad thing for everybody and worst of all for those on whose behalf the control is nominally exercised.
—Theodore Roosevelt

In a highly relevant discussion of national economic policy from an international perspective, Ethan Kapstein of the Council of Foreign Relations wrote,

To meet the growing problems of working people, governments must develop a coherent package of economic policies and programs supported by international policy coordination that generates renewed growth. Such a strategy, which will require some fiscal relaxation, has some costs, but the consequences of doing nothing will be worse. . . . The starting point for any policy effort of this kind is the normative assertion that the appropriate goal of economic policy is to improve the lives of the citizenry. Monetary and fiscal policies should be structured in such a way as to ensure the fundamental promise that working people can earn a living wage. This means that in every industrial country, policies must be directed toward helping people cope with the consequences of economic change.[1]

Is contemporary economic policy in the United States designed to improve the lives of its citizenry? Does it ensure that working people can earn a living wage? Finally, does it help people deal with the consequences of economic change? In considering how to respond to these questions, one must consider the impact of current fiscal, monetary, and trade policy on the American workforce.

FISCAL POLICY

Considering current fiscal policy, it would be very difficult to answer these questions affirmatively, especially since existing tax policies do not appear to have been formulated with such normative goals in mind. Nonetheless, fiscal policy, appropriately modified or redesigned, can play a significant role in mitigating some of the negative consequences of developments in the contemporary labor market

It has been suggested both implicitly as well as explicitly that federal, state, and local tax policies can be used artfully to encourage job creation. Stated perhaps somewhat simplistically, fiscal policy currently provides considerably greater tax benefits and subsidies for business investment than it does for human investment. Were fiscal policies restructured to provide business with tax incentives for creating significant job opportunities, it seems reasonable to assume, given the financial benefits to be realized, that we would witness a positive impact on both aggregate employment and median income. This in turn would prove beneficial to the economy as a whole. In this regard, Robert Reich has suggested that corporate income taxes might be reduced or eliminated entirely for those firms that demonstrate a tangible commitment to keeping workers on their payrolls.[2] Part of the costs of such tax incentives would be recovered from the increased levels of personal income tax payments that would result from payroll expansion, which would also have a beneficial impact on payroll-based contributions to the Social Security and Medicare trusts. The remainder, presumably, would have to come from an increase in corporate taxes that would effectively reduce the profits of those corporations that do not demonstrate a commitment to retaining their workers. In other words, corporations that do not conduct their business in a manner supportive of the public interest would be penalized for their indifference.

To complement the approach of providing the "carrot" of fiscal incentives for promoting employment, a constructive fiscal policy would also apply the "stick" of eliminating or significantly reducing current fiscal benefits to businesses that no longer serve the public interest. It is estimated that current federal corporate tax and spending subsidies to business, none of which are directly related to job generation, amount to more than $100 billion annually. The Congress presently funds more than 125 programs that subsidize private businesses, a largesse that has come to be known as "corporate welfare." According to an in-depth 1995 report by the Cato Institute, "Every major cabinet department, including the Defense Department, has become a conduit for government funding of private industry. Within some cabinet agencies, such as the Department of Agriculture and the Department of Commerce, almost every spending program underwrites private businesses."[3]

Ironically, the justification for much of this corporate welfare is that it helps create jobs. Thus, Congress appropriated $5 billion for the U.S. Import-Export Bank over a six-year period to subsidize companies that sell goods and services abroad. As James A. Harmon, president and chairman of the bank put it, "American workers . . . have higher-quality, better-paying jobs, thanks to Eximbank's financing." But, as a *Time* special report on corporate welfare pointed out, "the numbers at the Bank's five biggest beneficiaries—AT&T, Bechtel, Boeing, General Electric and McDonnell Douglas (now a part of Boeing)—tell another story. At these companies, which have accounted for about 40% of all loans, grants and long-term guarantees in this decade, overall employment has fallen 38%, as more than a third of a million jobs have disappeared."[4]

Robert Shapiro of the Progressive Policy Institute notes that "scores of influential industries continue to succeed in protecting their subsidies from the budget ax."[5] For example, there still exists a subsidy program for agribusiness firms that assures them fixed payments, although some recent legislation promises to phase out some of these over the next several years. An egregious example of this sort of government largesse at public expense is the subsidies awarded to the giant $13 billion Archer Daniels Midland corporation. As pointed out in a 1997 article, "ADM is one of the largest beneficiaries of federal sugar subsidies—in the form of guaranteed price supports that keep out foreign sugar and thus raise food prices. The General Accounting Office says that sugar price supports gouge consumers out of an estimated $1.4 billion a year in inflated food prices."[6]

There are also federal subsidies for utility companies as well as for ranchers, mining companies, security firms, and arms exporters, as well as federal funding for foreign advertising by American firms. In addition, the government provides huge tax breaks and shelters for commercial advertisers and ethanol producers, as well as special tax subsidies for cattle breeding, timber, certain energy producers and exporters.

Similarly, at the state and local level, substantial amounts of public largesse are directed to businesses in the hope that such expenditures will produce additional employment. According to one 1996 study, "special state and local tax loopholes, tax credits, and tax abatements to business (generally referred to collectively as 'tax expenditures') now total billions of dollars annually. For example, data for just 11 states indicate that their corporate income tax breaks alone totaled more than $6.3 billion in 1992. Tax expenditures now easily dwarf all the other money spent on state and local economic development programs."[7]

Beginning in the 1990s, state governments have competed with one another to attract businesses by increasingly offering a new type of financial incentive that is rather uncharacteristic of a free market economy, namely, wage rebates. The wage rebate is a taxpayer financed subsidy that allows companies to recover a portion of their labor costs. Such subsidies were offered by only 8 states in 1989 but by 21 states in 1998, notwithstanding the fact that the country experienced a tight labor market for several years, making such wage rebates a windfall for business at taxpayer expense. Van Doorn Ooms, research director for the business-supported Committee for Economic Development, bluntly pointed this out. "In a high-unemployment situation, wage rebates are useful as a stimulus for creating jobs. In a tight labor market, they are more likely to simply pass on some of the cost of labor to the taxpayer from the employer."[8]

According to the *Time* special report on corporate welfare, "There are no reasonably accurate estimates on the amount of money states shovel out. That's because few want to know . . . All that's certain is that the figure is in the many billions of dollars each year—and it is growing, when measured against the subsidy per job." In 1991, Indiana gave United Airlines $451 million in economic incentives to build an aircraft-maintenance facility that would employ some 6,300 workers. This amounted to a subsidy of $72,000 per job. In 1997, Pennsylvania gave a Norwegian engineering and construction company, Kvaerner ASA, $307 million in economic incentives to open a shipyard in Philadelphia that would employ 950 people. This amounted to a subsidy of $323,000 per job. Assuming that each of these jobs pays an average $50,000 a year and that each worker will pay an average of $6,700 in state and local taxes, it would take more than 48 years for the state to recover the money expended to create these jobs. And even this assumes that the workers are not state residents who are already paying taxes.[9]

Despite all this public largesse, there is very little evidence that such "tax expenditures" have any significant effect on corporate decision-making or on raising employment levels. The reallocation of even a part of these governmental subsidies for direct job creation would have enormous impact on the general well-being of the American labor force. Moreover, Shapiro observes: "Market economics tells us that no government activity does greater injury to growth, for no overriding social purpose, than industry-specific subsidies that misdirect economic resources and insulate the companies receiving them from the market pressures that normally drive higher efficiency and productivity."[10] It does not seem far-fetched to suggest that increasing aggregate employment as well as median wages might well constitute an "overriding social purpose" that would justify redirecting a substantial share of the spending and tax subsidies that are presently being awarded to businesses for rather less compelling social purposes.

The bizarre character of corporate welfare has led to a number of highly controversial proposals to effectively curb it, at least at the state and local levels. One proposes the enactment of a federal excise tax on the incentives awarded to companies that would equal the amount of those incentives. That is, according to Arthur J. Rolnick of the Federal Reserve Bank of Minneapolis, "you have to make the tax confiscatory, a 100% tax, to take away the incentive."[11] Needless to say, any such proposals will be fought tooth and nail by the business welfare community.

There is also a certain perversity to tax policies that effectively encourage the transfer of jobs from the United States to overseas labor markets at a time when millions of Americans face unemployment and underemployment. The tax code facilitates this in two ways, through foreign tax credits and deferrals. A U.S.-based company that invests overseas and pays taxes to a foreign government is given preferential treatment over a company with only domestic operations that pays taxes to the state within which it does business. The former is permitted to deduct the entire amount paid in foreign taxes from the firm's federal tax liability, whereas the latter can only deduct the amount paid in state income tax from its federally taxable income. In effect, the company that transfers jobs overseas will likely pay less in federal taxes than a similar company that provides jobs here.

This anomaly is further exacerbated by a foreign tax deferral privilege that permits a U.S.-based corporation with a foreign subsidiary to defer payment on any earnings of the subsidiary unless and until the profits are repatriated to the United States. This, in effect, is equivalent to an interest-free loan from the American taxpayers to a company that may wish to expand overseas and reinvest its earnings abroad without paying any U.S. taxes on its profits. It has been estimated that if these tax benefits were eliminated it might mean as much as $17.5 billion in additional federal tax revenues.[12] It might also result in the creation of additional domestic employment.

The social logic of providing tax write-offs for capital investment, which in a high technology era tends to dramatically increase worker displacement, without providing similar tax benefits for finding ways to alleviate the employment consequences of such investment, surely leaves something to be desired. Presumably, the public interest is served by providing tax incentives for investments that will increase productivity. It is not clear, however, why this should apply to investments in machinery and equipment but not to investments in human resources for the same purpose. As argued in a *Washington Post* editorial, current tax laws "discriminate against equity financing and in favor of debt. The effect is a bias in favor of safe, high-yield ventures that lenders prefer and against the kind of long-term and often riskier investments that only equity—owners' money—will support. It's generally only equity that can be put into intangible investments, such as training. Yet training is now at least as important as the conventional investments in factory equipment that conventional tax benefits encourage."[13] It has also been suggested that tax policy could make a significant contribution to improving the quality of the workforce if government stopped treating company-provided tuition reimbursements as taxable personal income, and generally treated college tuition as tax-deductible.

Some have argued that existing federal tax policies effectively exacerbate current labor market problems, pointing out that the federal tax code prohibits educational deductions for those engaged in retraining for a new occupation, while permitting deductions for those who improve their skills within their present occupation. In effect, the tax system supports life span development of human capital only if necessary to meet the requirements of the current employer. A middle-aged or older worker threatened with the loss of a job who seeks to enhance his or her employability by acquiring new marketable skills is not permitted to deduct the costs of such training. "What we have in effect is a tax code that subsidizes the mobility of financial capital but not the mobility or development of human capital. . . . The tax code then reinforces an inherent bias toward the status quo: keeping people in their current jobs."[14] The problem, of course, is that many of those current jobs are disappearing.

There is reason to believe that if businesses were offered the same kind of tax write-offs for job creation that they may receive for capital equipment investments, the net result of which may be increased job destruction, significant levels of new and substantial employment opportunities might be realized. This would especially be true in the case where increases in capital investment might be expected to produce only marginal benefits in terms of increased productivity. Such human investment would be encouraged further if a means were found to link a reduction in capital gains taxes to investments that produced employment opportunities. The deployment of venture capital, which would receive a big boost from a capital gains tax cut, is a proven method of creating jobs. A 1996 study by Venture One Corporation and the National Venture Capital Association found that 495 venture-capital-backed companies generated 75,240 new jobs between 1989 and 1993.[15]

One of the more creative approaches to dealing with these issues was suggested in early 1996 by Congressman Jeff Bingaman in draft legislation that would have used fiscal policy to reward corporations that invest in employees and communities. A new class of "responsible corporations," the R Corp., would be created and would receive especially favorable tax treatment—a corporate tax rate of 11 percent as compared to 18 percent for conventional corporations. To qualify as a R Corp., a firm would be required to contribute 3 percent of its payroll to a portable pension plan, allocate 2 percent to employee training, pay half the costs of a qualifying health plan, and have an employee stock-ownership or profit-sharing plan. In addition, a qualifying company would have a "community responsibility agreement" and other employee-friendly features.[16] The current prognosis for this approach to dealing with stakeholder concerns is not promising. It directly contravenes the widely cherished notion of autonomous market forces, and may therefore not be salable in the contemporary domestic political environment. Nonetheless, it represents a reasonable alternative to allowing the continuing turbulence in the labor market to go unchecked, subsidized in part by blatantly pro-business tax policies.

The fiscal policy approach to job creation will unquestionably prove to be highly controversial, particularly because it appears to be predicated on the notion that it is advantageous to deliberately slow the growth in productivity in order to increase employment levels. This idea would seem to be borne out in fact by a comparison of the United States and Europe over the last two decades. Productivity growth in the United States has been about half that in Europe, with about half the unemployment rate. Nonetheless, many economists, perhaps even most, will take umbrage at the idea of attempting to do this as a matter of public policy. They will argue that, in the long run, such an approach will result in a lower standard of living, since the latter is directly related to growth in productivity.[17]

However, although there may be broad agreement with this argument in theory, it is by no means clear just how long the "long run" is likely to be. Moreover, it is by no means self-evident that one should reject the fiscal policy approach to decelerating technology-based productivity to produce greater employment opportunities on the basis of its "long run" impact on the standard of living. One might also reasonably consider the effect on the standard of living for most people of a continuing annual decline in median wages that has generally persisted for more than a decade, a decline that is directly related to the disjunction between productivity and employment.

Finally, it may be worth considering that the presumed direct linkage between productivity and the standard of living does not have as strong a theoretical basis as many assume. At best, improvement of the standard of living is but an *unintended* possible consequence of higher levels of productivity—firms do not invest in labor saving machinery and equipment in order to increase the standard of living, but to increase their profit margins. It is only when some of those profits are diverted to the workers in the form of increased wages or benefits that the standard of living rises. The standard surely does not rise for those experiencing a net decline in real wages at the same time that productivity is increasing. Encouraging higher productivity through public subsidization of capital investment is not necessarily a prescription for realizing a higher standard of living, or even for maintaining the current standard.

In the final analysis, the argument over what will happen in the long run may be understood as an argument over whether or not the future will be a repetition of the past. If one assumes that the application of high technology to achieve continually increasing productivity will follow the pattern of past technological changes, then there is ground for a certain degree of complacency concerning long-term expectations in this regard. However, if one assumes that a new post-industrial revolution is taking place, the net result of which will be a continuing decline in the relationship between labor and productivity, some long cherished economic theories may need drastic revision. Market forces, as we understand them, will ultimately resolve the problem under the first assumption, but will accomplish little in ameliorating the problem if the second assumption proves to be the more prescient. No one can be absolutely certain which of these fundamental assumptions will eventually prove to be the more valid, even though, as discussed earlier, the infrastructural implications of the cybernation revolution are becoming increasingly evident. In any case, prudence alone would seem to suggest that our approach to public policy in this arena be hedged to mitigate the consequences of the growing disjunction between labor and productivity.

MONETARY POLICY

The role of monetary policy in addressing the question of aggregate employment is probably the most controversial of the possible policy alternatives under consideration. It is in this area of public policy where conventional wisdom seems to be most deeply embedded, where traditional economic assumptions are considered almost sacrosanct, even in the face of contradicting realities. Nonetheless, monetary policy may prove to be among the most potent weapons in the public policy arsenal for dealing with the problem.

By effectively controlling the supply of money and credit through the regulation of interest rates to major borrowers and lending institutions, the Federal Reserve System exercises enormous influence on the expansion or contraction of the national economy. What is often poorly understood, however, is that, notwithstanding its name, which many construe as indicating that the "Fed" is a government agency, it is in fact a private corporation the stockholders of which are private commercial banks.

The Federal Reserve System consists of a board of governors, twelve regional Federal Reserve Banks, and the Federal Open Market Committee. The board of governors, which has overall responsibility for the system, consists of seven members drawn almost exclusively from the financial community, that are nominated by the President of the United States and confirmed by the Senate. These Governors are appointed for a 14-year period and cannot be dismissed except for gross incompetence or criminal conduct. The twelve regional Federal Reserve banks are locally owned and controlled, one-third of the board of directors coming from the regional banking community and a third from the regional business community. As a result, regional banking and industrial interests effectively control the Federal Reserve Banks. The Federal Open Market Committee, which determines the national monetary policy and sets interest rates, includes the seven members of the board of governors and five of the presidents of the regional Federal Reserve banks, giving the financial community great influence in the deliberations and decisions of the committee. The net result is that monetary policy in the United States is heavily biased in favor of the financial community's perceptions of the national interest, perceptions that do not always comport with the interests of the American labor force and their families.

Because business operations generally, and business expansion in particular, depend heavily on borrowing, the interest rates on capital are becoming an increasingly critical factor in business decision-making. In recent years, the costs to businesses of interest on borrowed capital has continued to eat away at profits to the point where interest paid far exceeds the amount paid in corporate taxes. Back in 1951, the annual interest costs to American corporations amounted to 6.1 percent of net profits and were equivalent to 5.2 percent of the taxes paid on those profits. By 1991, however, interest costs had risen to 107 percent of net profits and 171 percent of taxes on profits.[18] In other words, corporations spent 71 percent more on interest than they did on income taxes. As a result, the decisions of the Federal Reserve Board to raise or lower interest rates can have significant impact on the profitability of businesses and therefore on the growth of the economy.

Charged with the awesome responsibility of adjusting the supply of money and credit to assist in the control of inflation, the Federal Reserve is known to be making decisions on the basis of some theoretical economic assumptions that are increasingly being called into question. Of particular concern in this regard is the assumed theoretical relationship between inflation and unemployment. This relationship is based, ostensibly, on the so-called "Phillips curve," originated in 1958 by A.W. Phillips, an economist at the London School of Economics. In his study of the relation between unemployment and wage rates in the United Kingdom between 1861–1957, Phillips presented a curve showing a tendency for wage rates to rise more rapidly "when the demand for labor is high and there are very few unemployed." It also showed that wage rates tended to decline more slowly as unemployment increased.[19]

However, in his widely used and influential textbook *Economics*, Paul Samuelson adopted the Phillips curve but rather arbitrarily substituted price increases for wage increases, yielding a curve that now showed an inverse relation between prices and unemployment. This, in the view of some critics, represented a gross distortion of Phillips' argument. Nonetheless, the Samuelson version became a virtually unchallenged superstition that distracts one's attention from other factors that promote inflation, such as price fixing, price leadership, military spending, uncontrolled speculation, and the corporate welfare enjoyed by the dairy, cattle, tobacco, pharmaceutical and other industries. Ignoring the idea of wage-led productivity growth, the conventional economic wisdom continues to hail low wages as the key to growth, providing justification for Federal Reserve Board action to raise interest rates as a means of creating higher unemployment, thereby putting downward pressure on wages.[20]

The theory, in the form now accepted as the conventional economic wisdom, goes beyond the basic notion that higher wages will lead to inflation. It also asserts that full employment of the labor force will trigger an upward spiral of inflation, in effect assuming that inflation tends to become self-perpetuating if left alone. This is because full employment shrinks the supply of workers available for hire in an expanding economy, and where demand outstrips supply, it becomes a seller's market for labor in which the price of labor or wages will be bid upward. This in turn will raise the cost per unit of output, and therefore also the price of the goods and services sold to the public. But, as prices rise, the demand for wage increases will also rise, initiating an inflationary spiral which the public interest demands be brought under control. The theory therefore asserts that a substantial amount of unemployment is essential, as a safety valve, to constrain demand for higher wages and thereby to interrupt the otherwise self-perpetuating inflation. Accordingly, the common sense goal of full employment is considered to be contrary to the public interest.

However, the theory does not provide for the possibility, argued by some economists, that while wage increases may lead to inflation, they do not necessarily lead to an inflationary *spiral*. This leaves open the possibility that a given non-accelerating degree of inflation may be socially and politically acceptable as the price of full employment. As one commentator noted: "Life is full of tradeoffs. Consumers trade off spending today against saving for tomorrow. Congress trades off tax cuts against deficit reduction. And the Federal Reserve trades off inflation against unemployment."[21]

The theoretically desired amount of unemployment assumed to be necessary in order to prevent an inflationary spiral is designated as the "non-accelerating inflation rate of unemployment (NAIRU)." The NAIRU, which is often mistakenly identified with the so-called "natural rate of unemployment," an expression coined by Milton Friedman in 1968, is currently still pegged at about 6 percent of the labor force, or some 8 million unemployed.[22] It should be noted, however, that the NAIRU was considered to be around 3 percent in the 1950s and about 4 percent in the 1960s. Proponents of the theory have tried to explain why the NAIRU itself seems to keep rising over time. They attribute it, at least in part, to higher payroll taxes that increase the cost of labor and to other factors, such as real interest rates and the costs of energy, which put additional downward pressures on employment. However, this also suggests that appropriate public economic policies could have the effect of driving the NAIRU down, perhaps at some point in the future even permitting full employment at an acceptable level of inflation. In any case, it has become the challenge for the Federal Reserve Board to adjust the rate of growth in the economy to maintain the rate of unemployment as close as possible to the current estimate of the NAIRU. In other words, if the desired level of unemployment drops, interest rates must be adjusted upward to discourage borrowing and thereby to curtail business growth, effectively reducing the demand for labor and thus raising the level of unemployment to the NAIRU once again.

The problem is that this theoretical model is not sufficiently reflective of what is actually happening in the economy. Indeed, based upon a detailed study of inflation and unemployment from 1953–1992, economist Paul Ormerod asserted that "a single Phillips curve has not existed in America over the post-war period, and hence . . . there is not a clear relationship between inflation and unemployment. In fact, formal statistical methods indicate that, if anything, there has been a very weak *positive* relationship between the two over this data period. In other words, the evidence for the past forty years indicates that, on average, a rise in unemployment seems to have been associated not with a fall, but with a rise in inflation."[23]

To be sure, when interest rates go up, capital investment slows and the unemployment rate is driven up, and when interest rates are lowered businesses expand and the unemployment rate drops. However, the theory requires that when unemployment drops below the NAIRU, there should emerge a seller's market for labor bidding up wages and triggering an inflationary spiral. But this has not happened. As unemployment rates have dropped, the anticipated wage increases have not taken place. Thomas Plewes, an official of the Bureau of Labor Statistics, stated in 1995, "labor shortages are simply not translating into wage pressures. . . . If this were a normal recovery, one would have expected more wage pressure by now. But the world is not the old way anymore."[24] Although there were not insignificant wage increases between 1995 and 1998, the theoretically anticipated inflationary pressures had not materialized. This led investment economist David Levine to state: "It's widely believed that the old link between the employment rate and price inflation has been broken. But the link between unemployment and wage inflation is still solid."[25]

In fact, median hourly wages continued to erode for more than a decade without regard to the levels of unemployment or interest rates, leading some economists to question the validity and utility of the theory in the contemporary economy. As Wall Street economist Allen Sinai has pointed out: "In every business cycle, there are conventional wisdoms that prove to be myths—and the 6% NAIRU is proving to be a myth."[26] Some economists are suggesting that the unemployment rate would have to drop to about 4.5 percent (the point at which we found ourselves in 1999) for inflation to increase by about half a percentage point a year later.[27] Obviously, there are factors at work that are not covered by the theory.

For one thing, some economists argue that the anomaly can be explained in part by noting that the unemployment rate, as estimated by the Bureau of

Labor Statistics, is not adjusted to account for effects of an aging society. When the adjustments are made, unemployment is actually higher, possibly by as much as 10 percent of the reported rate. "The unemployment rate is low in part because groups that have historically had below-average unemployment rates [those between the ages of 25 and 44] are a larger share of the workforce than they were before. An aging population has contributed to the lowering of the unemployment rate." Accordingly, "if the age-adjusted unemployment rate is a better indicator of labor market 'slack' than the reported unemployment rate, there remains room for further expansion without fear of accelerating inflation."[28]

Evidently unwilling to let go of the NAIRU as a predictor of inflation, the 1997 *Economic Report of the President* attempted to re-conceptualize it in a manner that accounts for the inflation anomaly. "Although potentially transitory factors, such as a slowdown in the rise of employee health benefit costs and declining import prices, partly explain why inflation is subdued, the underlying reason is probably that the NAIRU has fallen substantially. The three main forces driving this decline are the changing demographics of the labor force, the delayed alignment of workers' real wage expectations with productivity growth, and increased competition in labor and product markets."

Of particular interest is the report's discussion of the changing demographics of the labor force:

Each demographic group can be thought of as having its own natural rate of unemployment: higher for teenagers than for adults, higher for women than for men, and so on. Even if these individual natural rates were constant, the overall NAIRU would change in response to changes in the proportions of these different groups in the labor force. If it is assumed that demographic changes had about the same effect on the NAIRU as they have had on observed unemployment, then about 0.5 percentage point of the decline in the NAIRU since the early 1980s can be attributed to demographic changes. The single most important demographic change is the aging of the baby-boom generation: the United States now has a more mature labor force, with smaller representation of age groups that traditionally have higher unemployment rates.

One may infer from this that the NAIRU may be expected to stabilize at its new natural level rather soon, at which time it will once again become a reliable predictor of inflationary trends. However, it is noteworthy that the NAIRU has also come under increasing attack from economists within the Federal Reserve System itself. Thus, in an in-depth analysis of the relationship between unemployment and inflation, economic researcher Roberto Chang has argued that "the concept of the NAIRU is of very limited use for predicting inflation, understanding its causes, or forming policy."[29] Another more recent analysis of the same issue concludes: "In the long run, there is no apparent relationship between inflation and unemployment."[30]

According to some theorists, there are at least two principal reasons why prices have not gone up, and another two that account for the failure of upward wage pressures to materialize. With regard to prices, global competition has effectively suppressed the ability of many companies to raise their prices, at the same time that higher productivity has slowed the growth of unit labor costs, which are increasing more slowly than wages. "By and large, companies have not passed along labor cost increases by raising prices; instead, they have bolstered productivity and accepted thinner profit margins."[31] As for wages, the decline of organized labor's bargaining clout has had a dampening effect on wage increases, at the same time that the sense of general economic insecurity has kept workers from demanding pay increases.[32] Moreover, as argued by James Challenger, "Corporate America has learned to use downsizing to thwart wage pressure. It controls wage pressure build-up by creating an environment of job insecurity and uncertainty where wages remain stagnant and employees are content just to have a job. . . . The workforce is aware that a request for a pay increase could be met with dismissal. Employees also know that any vacated position could quickly be filled by someone willing to accept the present wage."[33]

Another possible explanation of the anomaly is that, under current labor market conditions, the unemployment rate is not a reliable indicator of the actual state of the labor market. For one thing, the unemployment rate does not reflect the large numbers of people who are structurally underemployed, persons who are working at part-time, temporary, and other kinds of nonstandard jobs but who are available for full-time employment. It also does not reflect the hundreds of thousands of displaced workers whose unemployment benefits have been exhausted and are unable to find a job, and who therefore are no longer counted as participants in the labor force. Finally, it does not include the large numbers of those formally counted as self-employed (between 12 and 15 percent of the labor force) who actually constitute a reserve army of workers seeking full-time employment. In other words, concerns regarding the NAIRU are based on the current official unemployment rate, but not on the underemployment rate or on the actual number of persons available for work. The official unemployment rate therefore vastly underestimates what it would take to create a real labor shortage that could drive up wages and trigger inflation.

This would suggest that, if a lowering of interest rates helps to trigger inflation, it has little if anything to do with the state of the contemporary labor market. Accordingly, it would seem plausible that the still-in-vogue NAIRU hypothesis should be set aside. Instead monetary policy should be adjusted to encourage expansion of the economy to decrease the negative effects of unemployment and underemployment on the American labor force and their families, and thereby to mitigate the consequences for our society as a whole. In this regard, economist Robert Eisner calls into question "the use of the NAIRU as a justification for blocking fiscal and monetary policies that might bring 'full employment,' or distinctly lower unemployment than what is now widely viewed as acceptable."[34] Moreover, Eisner insists: "Neither God nor nature decreed that involuntary unemployment need always be with us, nor that there is a rate of unemployment below what is 'natural' but not below what is really full, which necessarily entails accelerating inflation. Once we accept that, it makes all the difference in what we can do to get our economy on the right, fast track."[35]

The key to creating more meaningful and well-compensated jobs, at least for the foreseeable future, is the expansion of the economy. (It should be noted that there are serious thinkers who argue against economic growth as a viable long-term strategy.) This point has been argued most forcefully by Felix Rohatyn. "Every major American social and economic problem requires stronger economic growth for its solution." Moreover, Rohatyn asserts that the majority of the business community believes that the current deliberately constrained rate of growth is "far short of our economy's real capacity for noninflationary growth."[36] And, it seems reasonable to add that, to the extent that monetary policy is designed to constrain such economic expansion on the basis of dubious theoretical considerations such as the NAIRU, policymakers should no longer consider the deliberate creation of unemployment as an acceptable public policy approach to inflation control.

What the appropriate rate of economic growth should be is surely an issue of the greatest importance to the well-being of our society. As one writer recently put it: "Healthy growth has been the glue that has held an otherwise diverse and often discordant people together since the nation's beginnings. Without it, a growing number of citizens feel, with good reason, that they are losing control of their lives. This is not business as usual in America. It is a reversal of our national experience."[37]

It is surely time to reconsider the traditional theoretical assumption regarding the relationship between employment levels and inflation and to begin exploring new and possibly more realistic approaches to the design and application of monetary policy in the public interest. Robert Eisner wrote in this regard: "There is no excuse for dooming the economy to lower employment and slower growth than their potential because of a suspect theory more and more contradicted by the evidence. Much of Main Street and the business community, as opposed to Wall Street and the financial community, seem to recognize this. The sooner everybody recognizes it, the faster we can move to sensible economic policy."[38] Paul Ormerod similarly attacked continued reliance by policymakers on the theory of the so-called natural rate of unemployment, a theory that "is not supported by the data." "The prime aim of anti-inflation policy should be to shift the economy from one inflation/unemployment path to another—to shift the curve, rather than try to move along it. . . . This is a task which ranges far beyond the narrow confines of conventional economic policy." Ormerod concludes his analysis with an assertion quite remarkable for an economist, "Economic policy is far too important to be left to economists."[39]

TRADE POLICY

In 1971, the United States experienced its first trade deficit of the post-World War II period, primarily as a result of competition from Germany and Japan. Since 1974, the annual trade deficit has been a regular feature of the U.S. economy. It has been estimated that the annual overall net trade deficits have been more than $100 billion for some two decades, and that number is increasing dramatically. It more than doubled by 1998, reaching some 3 percent of GDP, and rose to $265 billion in 1999, a level that former U.S. Trade Representative Charlene Barshefsky suggested would be "politically unsustainable."[40] The deficit was estimated to reach about $360 in 2000.[41] Although there has been some suggestion that a substantial amount of U.S. exports go unreported because of the systems used by the government, thereby skewing the figures in an unfavorable direction, it seems unlikely that correcting the reporting system will invalidate the growing concerns over the current and growing trade imbalance.[42]

One estimate by Tim Congdon of Lombard Street Research in London "calculates that if recent trends continue the current account deficit will rise to 4% of GDP within five years, and 5% by 2010."[43] The aggregate trade deficit over the past 15 years has reached some $2 trillion, transforming the United States from the world's largest creditor nation into the world's largest debtor.

Moreover, it is important to note that the net annual *merchandise* trade deficit is substantially higher than the overall trade deficit ($167 billion in 1996 and $248 billion in 1998), and it is the latter that has the greatest impact on domestic employment. In other words, for many years the country has been exporting about $150 billion less of domestically produced goods than it is importing from abroad. If it were possible to rectify that imbalance, the positive impact on unemployment as well as underemployment would be very substantial. Expanding domestic production to achieve $150 billion more in exportable goods would probably reduce unemployment by more than a full percentage point or provide as many as one-and-a-half million jobs. There is also evidence that exporting firms expand employment much faster than non-exporting companies and are significantly less likely to fail. Moreover, the effect on wages would also be significant since export-related jobs tend to pay, according to some perhaps overly optimistic estimates, from 12.5 to 18 percent more than the average wage. Accordingly, elimination of the external trade deficit would have a highly favorable impact on both domestic employment and wages.[44]

This optimistic analysis must be tempered by the recognition that export industries tend to pay higher wages primarily because they are mostly engaged in manufacturing, which is highly unionized. But manufacturing employment generally has been declining steadily over the years because of significant and continuing increases in both labor and capital productivity, and because of the trade imbalance. According to a 1997 report from the Economic Policy Institute, it is estimated that between 1979 and 1994 the trade deficit eliminated a total of 2.4 million job opportunities, about 2.2 million of these in the manufacturing sector. Trade thus accounted for 83 percent of the total 2.7 million jobs lost in manufacturing employment during that period.[45] It should be noted that some analysts suggest that "most of the decline in manufacturing's share of employment represents a shift in consumers' expenditure choices as they earn higher incomes," and therefore conclude that eliminating the trade deficit would have minimal effect on manufacturing employment.[46] However, the evidence for this conclusion seems rather dubious at best.

Trade deficits tend to have a generally adverse effect on wages because of the impact on the composition of employment. Workers displaced from the manufacturing sector usually wind up in service sector jobs paying lower wages. Moreover, the imbalance of imports, especially from low-wage countries, tends to put price pressure on domestic products, forcing U.S. businesses to cut costs. This usually means reduction of wages or cuts in staffing.[47] Finally, even economists who are proponents of free trade have been forced to conclude that the trade deficit is responsible for 20 to 25 percent of the increase in income inequality over the past twenty years.[48]

The optimistic assessment also assumes that the United States can capture a growing share of the international market, an assumption that is rather contentious, given that many exporting firms would be delighted if they could simply manage to maintain their market share, let alone increase it. Finally, it is important to recognize that a substantial part of the trade imbalance problem is self-inflicted. Robert Reich pointed out in a 1991 book,

much of America's stubborn trade imbalance during the 1980s was due not to the predations of foreign nations and corporations, insistent on selling more to us than we sold to them, but to American-owned firms making things abroad (or, more precisely, contracting with foreigners to supply them with particular goods and services, which the firm then sold in the United States). This cosmopolitan practice accounted, for example, for more than one-third of Taiwan's notorious trade surplus with the United States during the 1980s, and more than 20 percent of the U.S. trade imbalances with Mexico, Singapore, South Korea, and even Japan.[49]

A more recent example of this was the substantial increase in the export of spark plugs (from 16 million in 1993 to 21 million in post-NAFTA 1994) to Mexico. According to Senator Ernest F. Hollings, these exports "went to

American and foreign automotive plants that are using Mexico as a low-wage production platform to ship cars back to the United States."[50]

The causes of the trade imbalance are several and complex. In general, however, one might reasonably assert that one of the principal problems is that, while the United States touts the principles and benefits of free trade, some of its biggest trade partners practice managed trade. That is, they effectively restrict the import of foreign goods that are likely to be competitive with their domestic manufactures or preferred sources for imports. One example of this is the explosion of U.S. anger resulting in tariff retaliation in March 1999 against the new European Union's managed trade policies. The ostensible straw that broke the camel's back was the EU's banana-import rules that favored imports from former colonies in the Caribbean, distributed by European firms, over bananas from Latin America that were distributed by American companies. However, the issue over managed trade ran much deeper, including American anger over European subsidies for Airbus, a major competitor to U.S. companies in the aerospace industry, and proposed rules on aircraft noise that clearly discriminate against American firms with large fleets of older aircraft.[51]

The situation is especially serious in the case of trade with East Asia, which has produced a lion's share of the U.S. trade deficit. "East Asian countries are increasingly reluctant to press ahead with plans to free regional trade, or to argue for another round of talks at the WTO [World Trade Organization]. Many are cannily raising taxes on luxury goods, which are mostly imported, or pushing up tariffs in ways that do not breach WTO rules."[52] Perhaps the most egregious example of this is China, which maintains very heavy import restrictions. In 1997, imports from China amounted to $63 billion whereas exports to China were a mere $13 billion, resulting in a $50 billion bilateral trade deficit. One net result of such trade imbalances has been that the United States is flooded with high value goods produced overseas at the same time that large numbers of skilled workers in the United States are facing cutbacks and dislocation.

A recent study indicates that the 1996 trade deficit of $36 billion with China alone translated into more than 600,000 lost job opportunities.[53] Moreover, these job losses have affected every economic group, including the college-educated. It has been estimated that the 460,000 new jobs that were created by exports for college-educated workers between 1979 and 1994 were offset by the 750,000 job opportunities that were sacrificed to increased imports. The net result was a loss of some 290,000 jobs for the college educated.[54] Needless to say, those with only a high school education or less were affected in even larger numbers.

A second major problem concerns the matter of worker rights in the countries with which the United States does business. It needs to be recognized, in this regard, that there is a significant difference between domestic trade, which takes place with a common social and economic system, and international trade, which may take place with countries possessing significantly different domestic systems. As argued by Thomas Palley, "Where one country's lower costs are the result of superior productive efficiency, all is well and good. However, where lower costs are the result of pauperized wages, oppressed workers, and an absence of concern for social and environmental well-being, the result is disastrous. In this case, systems competition becomes the law of the lowest standard, because it forces countries with high standards to lower them in order to stay competitive."[55]

The Omnibus Trade and Competitiveness Act of 1988, which authorized participation in the Uruguay Round of negotiations on the General Agreement on Tariffs and Trade (GATT), set forth the principle negotiating objectives of the United States. With regard to the issue of worker rights, the United States was to seek to "adopt, as a principle of the GATT, that a denial of worker rights should not be a means for a country or its industries to gain competitive advantage in international trade." Unfortunately, little has been accomplished since passage of the Act to improve worker rights abroad. Indeed there has been a substantial increase in the worldwide growth of export processing zones where governments use restrictions on worker rights as a trade and investment incentive.[56] The fact is that multinational corporations manufacture in Asia because wages there are meager by western standards, ranging from $3 a day to as little as 30 cents.[57] Moreover, many of such corporations are principally U.S-owned and operated. The issue was described in a 1987 letter to the House Ways and Means Committee from then Labor Secretary Bill Brock. "Those countries which are flooding world markets with goods made by children, or by workers who can't form free trade unions or bargain collectively or who are denied even the most minimum standards of safety and health are doing more harm to the principle of free and fair trade than any protectionist group I can think of."[58]

Sadly, and notwithstanding the formal position of the U.S. government on this issue, employers and the governments of most of our trade partners use low wages for high productivity labor as a legitimate method of competition. It is argued by some that this constitutes a peculiar "neo-liberal" model of international trade, and that wage competition between domestic and foreign workers will continue to worsen until a model of international trade is adopted that goes back to basic principles. Such a model would base competitiveness "on greater efficiency and improved product quality and design rather than on wage exploitation. The model developed by the original liberals, such as Ricardo and Mill, said that if companies specialize in producing what they are least inefficient in, world production from existing resources can be maximized. Today's neoliberals have distorted this theory, producing a globalized economy in which multinational enterprises specialize in exploitation, not in efficiency, and in which production is not maximized."[59]

Much of the debate about trade policy and jobs in the last decade of the twentieth century has focused on the North American Free Trade Agreement (NAFTA) that went into effect on January 1, 1994. It should be noted, however, that NAFTA appears to have actually exacerbated the already existing competition between relatively high-waged U.S. and low-waged Mexican workers for the same jobs. Following the 1982 economic crisis in Mexico and a major devaluation of its currency, Mexican wages were severely reduced in dollar terms. As a result, employment in the *maquiladora* plants and factories along the U.S.-Mexican border soared from 110,000 in 1982 to 300,000 in the mid-1990s.[60] Moreover, as corroborated by a 1992 study by the Congressional Office of Technology Assessment, the new multi-national plants along the border "have demonstrated levels of productivity and quality equal to those in the United States."[61] Not surprisingly, most of these new *maquiladoras* were U.S. owned. As pointed out by one analyst, "By moving their plants from the United States to Mexico, they obtained labor approaching the productivity of U.S. workers, but at about one-tenth the wage, which made their products very competitive and their businesses very profitable. The *maquiladoras* were able to approach First World labor productivity, pay Third World wages, and sell their products at First World prices."[62] However, the ability to sell these low-cost labor products at First World prices in the United States depended on low tariff access to U.S. markets. The combined interests of U.S companies in protecting their investments and expected profits, and the Mexican government's concern about attracting businesses to the country to provide work for its growing labor force, served as a spur to the development and adoption of the NAFTA idea.

What has happened since the passage of NAFTA? A 1997 study by the Economic Policy Institute employed a model specifically designed to overcome the methodological oversights in most estimates of NAFTA's effects on jobs. It indicated that, as a result of NAFTA, there were significant reductions in net exports to Mexico and Canada that eliminated 394,835 U.S. jobs in the three-year period from 1994–1996. That is, while increased exports to Mexico created 158,171 jobs, this was offset by a loss of 385,834 jobs as a result of increased imports from Mexico. Similarly, although increased exports to Canada created 244,309 jobs, these were offset by a loss of 411,481 jobs as a consequence of increased imports from Canada.[63] These estimates of net job loss for the first three years of NAFTA is double that given by the government for the first four years of the agreement.

Moreover, the differences between imports from and exports to Mexico and Canada since the inception of NAFTA have substantially increased the trade deficit. In 1993, before NAFTA went into effect, the U.S. had a trade surplus (in constant 1987 dollars) of $635 million with Mexico. Three years later this trade surplus was transformed into a $18.8 billion deficit. In the case of Canada, the existing trade deficit increased from $16.7 billion to $29.5 billion over the same period.[64]

The trade balance problem has been exacerbated by continuing erosion of U.S. competitiveness resulting from shifting currency exchange rates, leading to a further decline in exports. In 1998, this affected almost all product groups, agricultural, industrial and capital goods, as well as services. Part of this downturn may be attributed to changes in international currency exchange rates, which have had a significant impact on comparative global labor costs. A 1998 Labor Department report indicated that in 1995 the United States was the principal low-cost industrial producer in the world, with an hourly compensation rate of $17.19. This was well below Germany's $31.85, Switzerland's $29.30, Japan's $23.66, and France's $19.34. By 1997, however, changes in currency exchange reduced Japan's labor costs to a mere 6 percent above those of the United States, and the premium costs of European labor dropped from 29 to 12 percent above the costs of American labor. There has even been a small drop in labor costs among the "Asian Tigers," namely, Hong Kong, Korea, Singapore and Taiwan. And in Mexico, where manufacturing compensation costs increased significantly in 1997, costs were still only one-tenth of U.S. costs.[65]

As a consequence of these factors, one cannot discount the possibility that policies that are designed to reduce imports may be as important, if not more so, than policies to increase exports if the concern is with job creation. Of course, this smacks of "protectionism," an approach to trade policy that is anathema to most neoclassical economists, even though it is clearly practiced to good effect by many of our international trading partners. In this regard, Senator Hollings wrote, arguing for absolute reciprocity in trade relations,

We must disenthrall ourselves from the idea that "protectionism" is evil. The fundamental duty of government *is* to protect. We have the army to protect from enemies without, the FBI to protect from enemies within. We have Medicare to protect from ill health and Social Security from the ravages of old age. We have environmental laws to protect the air we breathe, the water we drink and the food we eat. And safety and other provisions to protect the worker. These protections all go into the cost of production. This is the American standard of living. This standard must be protected.[66]

To keep this issue in perspective, the observations of Dani Rodrick of Harvard University seem particularly apropos. "It's surprising how much of the agenda of trade negotiations has been driven by business and how much of existing trade rules reflect the interests of business as opposed to labor or consumer or environmental interests." He notes further that "there is an interesting paradox in the whole GATT-WTO system is built on the notion that we have to avoid regulatory capture by special interest groups so that we do not slide down the slippery slope toward protectionism. Yet in practice it turns out that the agenda of globalization, trade expansion, and trade pacts has been captured largely by business interests."[67]

Although Federal trade negotiators have tried repeatedly to reach agreements with managed trade countries to open their markets, there have been few positive results from these efforts to date. As a result, there is an emerging cry from across the political spectrum that the United States take more active measures to protect against the further loss of jobs that can be attributed to the trade imbalance. As argued by Peter diCicco of the AFL-CIO, "This country needs a trade policy that recognizes the national interest in preserving our industrial base, instead of one that promotes the export of American ingenuity and know-how. By pushing U.S. industry off-shore, we are helping Mexico, China and other developing nations build manufacturing export platforms. So what if we get cheaper goods if we are, at the same time, undermining our middle class and exiling millions of American workers to the underclass?"[68]

All proposed protectionist measures are, understandably, highly controversial, especially that of imposing punitive import tariffs, which are opposed by many in the business community. On the other hand, many continue to argue, as does Robert Scott of the Economic Policy Institute, that "imports destroy jobs just like exports create them."[69] Ravi Batra, an avid advocate of what he calls "competitive protectionism,"[70] writes that import tariffs "would redirect American demand away from foreign goods and toward home goods. As imports fall, domestic manufacturing will hum again. The trade deficit will be immediately eliminated, and at least 2.6 million new manufacturing jobs will be created. A sharp pickup in labor demand will first raise real wages in manufacturing, and those workers who have been migrating to services since 1980 will go back to their old jobs. This will create labor shortages in services, raising their wages as well."[71]

Notwithstanding the controversy over protectionism, it seems clear that appropriate policies for rectifying the trade imbalance could make a significant difference with respect to the job outlook in the United States. They therefore should not be dismissed out of hand as incompatible with what may prove to be an overly idealistic notion about the benefits to be realized from free trade in the contemporary business environment. The issues engendered for our society by increasing globalization are very complex, and it does little good to oversimplify them by making purist arguments for free trade versus protectionism. Bearing this in mind, the words of Dani Rodrick are a fitting conclusion to this discussion,

Globalization is not occurring in a vacuum. It is part of a broader trend that we may call marketization. Receding government, deregulation, and the shrinking of social obligations are the domestic counterparts of the intertwining of national economies. Globalization could not have advanced this far without these complementary forces. The broader challenge for the 21st century is to engineer a new balance between market and society, one that will continue to unleash the creative energies of private entrepreneurship without eroding the social basis of cooperation.[72]

NOTES

1. Ethan B. Kapstein, "Workers and the World Economy," *Foreign Affairs*, May/June 1996, p. 31.

2. Robert B. Reich, "How to Avoid These Layoffs?" *New York Times*, January 4, 1996.

3. Stephen Moore, and Dean Stamsel, "Ending Corporate Welfare As We Know It," policy analysis no. 225 (Washington, DC: Cato Institute, May 12, 1995).

4. Donald L. Bartlett, and James B. Steele, "Corporate Welfare," *Time* (November 9, 1998), p. 38.

5. Robert J. Shapiro, "End Corporate Welfare," *Washington Post*, December 1, 1995.

6. Stephen Moore, "Corporate Welfare Queens," *National Review* (May 19, 1997).

7. Robert G. Lynch, "Do State and Local Tax Incentives Work?" (Washington, DC: Economic Policy Institute, 1996).

8. Louis Uchitelle, "Taxes Help Foot the Payrolls as States Vie for Employers," *New York Times*, August 11, 1998.

9. Donald L. Bartlett, and James B. Steele, "Corporate Welfare," *Time* (November 9, 1998), p. 39.

10. Robert J. Shapiro, "End Corporate Welfare," *Washington Post*, December 1, 1995.

11. Bartlett, and Steele, "Corporate Welfare," *Time* (November 30, 1998), p. 78.

12. Sheila Collins, Helen Lachs Ginsburg, and Gertrude Schaffner Goldberg, *Jobs For All* (New York: New Initiatives for Full Employment, 1994), p. 73.

13. "Why Wages Aren't Rising," *Washington Post*, November 17, 1995.

14. Harry R. Moody, *Abundance of Life: Human Development Policies for an Aging Society* (New York: Columbia University Press, 1988), p. 235.

15. Michael Y. Granger, "Cut Capital Gains Tax, Boost Black Jobs," *Wall Street Journal*, April 4, 1996.

16. Robert Kuttner, "Rewarding Corporations That Really Invest In America," *Business Week* (February 26, 1996).

17. *Economist* (November 25, 1995), p. 67.

18. "Economic Report of the President" (February 1994).

19. A.W. Phillips, "The Relation Between Unemployment and the Rate of Change of Money Wage Rates in the United Kingdom, 1861–1957," *Economics* (n.s., November 1958), pp. 283–289.

20. This issue was discussed in a draft paper by Bertram Gross and Charles Henry, presented at the Smithsonian Institution in Washington, DC on February 20, 1996 at a conference on "Economic Security and Progress: Past, Present and Future."

21. Gregory Mankiw, "Alan Greenspan's Tradeoff," *Fortune* (December 8), p. 36.

22. According to economic theorist Edmund S. Phelps, "It is a mistake to think of the natural rate as the 'nonaccelerating inflation rate of unemployment," "Scapegoating the Natural Rate," *Wall Street Journal*, August 6, 1996. In a 1996 article, Milton Friedman reaffirmed that "the natural rate is not a fixed number," and expressed his distress at the term's "widespread misuse and misunderstanding," *Wall Street Journal*, September 24, 1996.

23. Paul Ormerod, *The Death of Economics* (New York: St. Martin's Press, 1994), p. 128.

24. Louis Uchitelle, "Labor Costs Show Small Increase," *New York Times*, February 1, 1995.

25. Sylvia Nasar, "Wages Turn Hot for Workers, with gain of 1.2%," *New York Times*, October 30, 1998.

26. Dean Foust, "Can the Economy Stand a Million More Jobs?" *Business Week* (November 27, 1995), p. 38.

27. Fred Bleakley, "Economists Not Worried About Inflation," *Wall Street Journal*, July 9, 1996.

28. Robert Horn and Philip Heap, "The Age-Adjusted Unemployment Rate: An Alternative Measure," *Challenge* (January-February 1999), p. 114.

29. Roberto Chang, "Is Low Unemployment Inflationary?" *Economic Review* (Federal Reserve Bank of Atlanta, First Quarter 1997), p. 4.

30. "Inflation, Unemployment, and the Phillips Curve," *Economic Trends* (Federal Reserve Bank of Cleveland, December 1997).

31. Nasar, "Wages Turn Hot for Workers."

32. James C. Cooper, and Kathleen Madigan, "Sizzling Job Numbers Won't Spark Inflation," *Business Week* (June 24, 1996).

33. "The Secret Purpose of Downsizing," *Business Ethics* (November/December 1996), p. 13.

34. Robert Eisner, "Our NAIRU Limit: The Governing Myth of Economic Policy," *The American Prospect* (Spring 1995), p. 62.

35. Robert Eisner, *The Misunderstood Economy: What Counts and How to Count It* (Boston: Harvard Business School Press, 1994), p. 194.

36. Felix G. Rohatyn, "Cut and Be Prosperous," *Wall Street Journal*, November 30, 1995.

37. Jeffrey Madrick, "Post-1973, the Era of Slow Growth," *New York Times*, January 16, 1996.

38. Robert Eisner, "Nothing to Fear but Fear of Good News," *Wall Street Journal*, July 9, 1996.

39. Ormerod, *The Death of Economics*, pp. 136–137.

40. "American Trade Policy," *Economist* (January 30, 1999), pp. 63–64.

41. M.Corey Goldman, "U.S. Trade Gap Hits Record," *CNN Financial News*, November 21, 2000.

42. Paul Magnusson, "The Slip-Up That's Slanting the Trade Deficit," *Business Week* (June 7, 1999).

43. "The Perils of Growing Faster," *Economist* (December 12, 1998), p. 28.

44. C. Fred Bergsten, "Globalizing Free Trade," *Foreign Affairs*, 75, no. 3, p. 118.

45. Robert E. Scott, Thea Lee, and John Schmitt, "Trading Away Good Jobs: An Examination of Employment and Wages in the U.S., 1979–94" (Washington, DC: Economic Policy Institute, 1997).

46. Edward E. Potter, "Corporate Codes of Conduct: The New Protectionism," *Fact & Fallacy* (Washington, DC: Employment Policy Foundation, May 1999).

47. Robert E. Scott (Economic Policy Institute), "U.S. Trade Deficits: Causes, Consequences, and Policy Implications" (testimony before the Senate Finance Committee, June 11, 1998).

48. Laura Tyson, "Inequality Amid Prosperity," *Washington Post*, July 9, 1997.

49. Robert B. Reich, *The Work of Nations: Preparing Ourselves for the 21st Century* (New York: Alfred A. Knopf, 1991), p. 134.

50. Ernest F. Hollings, "Ignore Adam Smith," Letter to the *Washington Post*, April 9, 1996.

51. "The Beef over Bananas," *Economist* (March 6, 1999), p. 65.

52. "Creeping Protectionism," *Economist* (September 19, 1998), p. 74.

53. Jesse Rothstein, and Robert E. Scott, "The Cost of Trade with China," issue brief no. 121 (Washington, DC: Economic Policy Institute, October 28, 1997).

54. Scott, Lee, and Schmitt, "Trading Away Good Jobs."

55. Thomas I. Palley, *Plenty of Nothing: The Downsizing of the American Dream and the Case for Structural Keynesianism* (Princeton, NJ: Princeton University Press, 1998), p. 157.

56. Mark A. Anderson, "Trade Agreements and Worker Rights," in *Through a Looking Glass Darkly: Building the New Workplace for the 21st Century*, ed. James A. Auerbach (Washington, DC: National Policy Association, 1998), p. 99.

57. "Sweatshop Wars," *Economist* (February 27, 1999), p. 63.

58. Anderson, "Trade Agreements and Worker Rights," p. 99.

59. William C. Doherty, "NAFTAmath: What Next for Trade and the Hemisphere's Workers," in *Through a Glass Darkly: Building the New Workplace for the 21st Century*, ed. James A. Auerbach (Washington, DC: National Policy Association, 1998), p. 103.

60. Christopher Palmeri, "The Flip Side of Devaluation," *Forbes* (February 13, 1995), p. 45.

61. *United States-Mexico Trade: Pulling Together or Pulling Apart?* (Washington, DC: U.S. Government Printing Office, October 1992), p. 11.

62. Doherty, "NAFTAmath," p. 101.

63. Jesse Rothman and Robert Scott, "NAFTA's Casualties," issue brief no. 120 (Washington, DC: Economic Policy Institute, September 19, 1997).

64. Ibid.

65. "International Comparisons of Hourly Compensation Costs for Production Workers in Manufacturing, 1997," USDL 98–376 (Washington, DC: U.S. Department of Labor, September 16, 1998).

66. Ernest F. Hollings, "Protectionist and Proud of It," *Washington Post*, March 17, 1996.

67. "Has Globalization Gone Too Far: Interview with Dani Rodrick," *Challenge* (March-April 1998), p. 94.

68. Peter diCicco, "NAFTA: Killing U.S. Jobs," *Washington Post*, July 12, 1997.

69. Ben Wildavsky, "Not Happy After NAFTA," *U.S. News & World Report*, January 11, 1999, p. 49.

70. Ravi Batra, *The Myth of Free Trade* (New York: Charles Scribner's Sons, 1993), pp. 192–197.

71. Ravi Batra, *The Great American Deception* (New York: John Wiley & Sons, 1996), pp. 227–228.

72. Dani Rodrick, *Has Globalization Gone Too Far?* (Washington, DC: Institute for International Economics, 1997), p. 85.

Conclusion

It would not be an exaggeration to suggest that American society is in the throes of a radical transformation of its economic life comparable in a number of respects to the Industrial Revolution of the 19th century. And, as in the case of the earlier reconstitution of the economic basis of society, the road ahead is fraught with problems and its ultimate destination is uncertain. From our present vantage point it is difficult to visualize where the current transformation is leading, even though the changes taking place may ultimately result in substantial long-term benefits for society. Over the next decades, however, it appears certain that, barring some substantial societal interventions, the dramatically changing employment environment will continue to cause significant dislocations in the workplace. These disruptions will continue to have serious consequences for American society as a whole, and will dramatically affect the future economic security of many of today's mid-life and older workers. As Robert Reich has pointed out: "The American public is basically pro-business. But that support rests on an implicit bargain. And business betrays that bargain every time it fires an older worker in order to hire a younger one at a lower wage, provides gold-plated health insurance to top executives while denying its workers health coverage, labels employees independent contractors in order to avoid paying them full-time wages and benefits, or discards its workers rather than invest in them when profits are booming."[1]

It is important to recognize that the dilemmas confronting American society are essentially global in character, affecting all industrialized societies and prospectively the developing world as well, although not all societies respond to these dilemmas in the same way. Moreover, the international aspect of these problems should be of significant concern to us because of the potential effects on world market demand for American-produced goods and services. Richard J. Barnet put the global dimensions of the problem in stark terms in the September 1993 issue of *Harper's*,

Across the planet, the shrinking of opportunities to work for decent pay is a crisis yet to be faced. The problem is starkly simple: an astonishingly large and increasing number of human beings are not needed or wanted to make the goods or to provide the services that the paying customers of the world can afford. Since most people in the world depend on having a job just to eat, the unemployed, the unemployable, the underemployed, and the 'subemployed'—a term used to describe those who work part-time but need to work full-time, or who earn wages that are too low to support a minimum standard of living—have neither the money nor the state of mind to keep the global mass consumption system humming. Their ranks are growing so fast that the worldwide job crisis threatens not only global economic growth but the capitalist system itself. What this suggests is a deepening disjunction for many people between income and employment, a problem that is exacerbated by the restructuring of the economic sector in a way that tends to eliminate full employment as a vehicle for income redistribution, and therefore as the economic basis for the discretionary consumption of goods and services by a continually growing number of people.

Acknowledging that there is a serious problem confronting our society is the first step towards finding the means by which to ameliorate the situation. Formulating a long-term solution may well require a major paradigm shift in how we conceive the relationship of the public and private-sectors with respect to the societal challenges that are emerging as the unintended consequences of the dramatic changes taking place in the labor economy. As Hedrick Smith put it, "America needs a new mindset to compete and to build ourselves a really bright future. Developing our new mindset means, literally, rethinking every major thing we're doing—whether it's how we educate our children; how we train workers; how we get a long-term vision from corporate managers; how we approach the relationship between labor and management or what kind of relationship exists between government and business. It means giving up old ways and opening up to new ideas and new techniques that meet the demands and challenges of a global economy."[2]

Sooner or later we must, as a society, come to grips with these challenges. The sooner that happens, the fewer will be the number of those who will have been subjected to the economic convulsions now being experienced by many of the more than 135 million workers in today's labor economy, as a consequence of the radical changes taking place in the employment environment.

Although the employment picture described in these pages may appear unremittingly gloomy, there is little reason to believe that it cannot be made substantially brighter in the years ahead. Unless we, as a society, succumb to the fatalism engendered by a blind faith in The Market and its economic determinism, we are capable of resolving, or at least mitigating the most serious consequences of, the problems emerging from these trends and developments in the contemporary labor economy. To do so, however, requires that we be very clear about the problem we wish to address and what it is that we hope to achieve. As Wolman and Colamosca put it, "if the U.S. government doesn't devise imaginative new economic approaches and become effective in working with its major international trading partners, Americans who earn their living from work—be it with muscle, intelligence, or wit—are running in a race they cannot possibly win."[3]

In this regard, it seems reasonable to conclude that the quintessential problem to be addressed is that of declining aggregate opportunities for well-compensated employment. Most of the unfavorable impacts on the labor force identified earlier could be significantly ameliorated by an overall increase in the number of jobs that paid enough to allow people to maintain their standard of living. Moreover, workers need to be enabled to plan and invest in their future, and that requires the prospect of reasonably continuous employment with livable wages. As observed by David Fagiano of the American Management Association: "It is simply a matter of enlightened self-interest to create as much employment as possible. We cannot continue firing our customers without giving them the possibility for the income they need to become customers again. We cannot become a nation of consultants because we cannot be each other's clients."[4]

At the outset of this book, we posed the question of whether it is realistic to defer retirement on the assumption that there will be an abundance of jobs that will permit older workers to remain in the workforce for longer periods. The answer at this point cannot be affirmative. However, it can be made so if we would but put our minds and wills to it, that we will require a readiness to set aside much of the conventional policy wisdom that shapes our current approaches to the issues of employment and livable wages. We need to amass the courage to explore new options, some of which have been suggested here, that have reasonable potential for dealing with the practical issues and concerns of creating an employment environment in the 21st century that is hospitable to an aging society.

NOTES

1. Cited by Morton Kondracke, "After GATT: Job Training's The New Issue," *ROLL CALL* (December 5, 1994), p. 6.

2. *WETA Magazine* (January 1994), p. 7.

3. William Wolman, and Anne Colamosca, *The Judas Economy: The Triumph of Capital and the Betrayal of Work* (New York: Addison-Wesley Publishing, 1997), p. 9.

4. David Fagiano, "Employment Contract Myth," *Management Review* (July 1996), p. 5.

SELECTED BIBLIOGRAPHY

BOOKS

Aronowitz, Stanley, and William DiFazio. *The Jobless Future*. Minneapolis, MN: University of Minnesota Press, 1994.

Auerbach, James A., ed. *Through a Looking Glass Darkly: Building the New Workplace for the 21st Century*. Washington, DC: National Policy Association, 1998.

Auerbach, James A., and Joyce C. Welsh, eds. *Aging and Competition: Rebuilding the U.S. Workforce*. Washington, DC: National Planning Association, 1994.

Bailey, Stephen K. *Congress Makes a Law: The Story Behind the Employment Act of 1946*. New York: Columbia University Press, 1950.

Barker, Kathleen, and Kathleen Christensen, eds. *Contingent Work: American Employment Relations in Transition*. Ithaca, NY: Cornell University Press, 1998.

Barley, Stephen R. *The New World of Work*. London: British-North American Committee, 1996.

Batra, Ravi. *The Myth of Free Trade*. New York: Charles Scribner's Sons, 1993.

———. *The Great American Deception*. New York: John Wiley & Sons, 1996.

Berle, Adolph A., Jr. *Power Without Property*. New York: Harcourt, Brace & World, 1959.

Cappelli, Peter, et al. *Change at Work*. New York: Oxford University Press, 1997.

Castells, Manuel. *The Network Society*. Oxford: Blackwell, 1996.

Collins, Sheila, Helen Lachs Ginsburg, and Gertrude Schaffner Goldberg. *Jobs For All*. New York: New Initiatives for Full Employment, 1994.

Databook on Employee Benefits. Washington, DC: Employee Benefit Research Institute, 1992.

Downs, Alan. *Corporate Executions.* New York: American Management Association, 1995.

Drucker, Peter F. *Managing for the Future: The 1990s and Beyond.* New York: E. P. Dutton/Truman Talley Books, 1992.

———. *Post-Capitalist Society.* New York: HarperCollins, 1993.

Eisner, Robert. *The Misunderstood Economy: What Counts and How to Count It.* Boston, MA: Harvard Business School Press, 1994.

Estes, Ralph. *Tyranny of the Bottom Line: Why Corporations Make Good People Do Bad Things.* San Francisco, CA: Berrett-Koehler Publishers, 1996.

Frank, Robert H., and Philip J. Cook. *The Winner-Take-All Society: How More and More Americans Compete for Ever Fewer and Bigger Prizes.* New York: Free Press, 1995.

Galbraith, James K. *Created Unequal: The Crisis in American Pay.* New York: Free Press, 1998.

Galbraith, John Kenneth. *The New Industrial State.* Boston, MA: Houghton Mifflin, 1985.

Gordon, David M. *Fat and Mean: The Corporate Squeeze of Working Americans and the Myth of Managerial "Downsizing."* New York: Free Press, 1996.

Handbook of Labor Statistics. Washington, DC: U.S. Department of Labor, August 1989.

Handy, Charles. *The Age of Unreason.* Boston, MA: Harvard Business School Press, 1990.

———. *Beyond Certainty: The Changing Worlds of Organizations.* Boston, MA: Harvard Business School Press, 1996.

Harrison, Bennett. *Lean and Mean: The Changing Landscape of Corporate Power in the Age of Flexibility.* New York, NY: Guilford Press, 1997.

Harvey, Philip. *Securing the Right to Employment: Social Welfare Policy and the Unemployed in the United States.* Princeton, NJ: Princeton University Press, 1989.

Judy, Richard W., and Carol D'Amico. *Workforce 2020: Work and Workers in the 21st Century.* Indianapolis, IN: Hudson Institute, 1997.

Kosters, Marvin H. *The Effects of the Minimum Wage on Employment.* Washington, DC: AEI Press, 1996.

Levison, Andrew. *The Full Employment Alternative.* New York: Coward, McCann & Geoghegan, 1980.

Lyons, Max R. *Part-Time Work: Not a Problem Requiring a Solution.* Washington, DC: Employment Policy Foundation, 1997.

Mace, Myles L. *Directors: Myth and Reality.* Boston, MA: Harvard Business School Press, 1986.

Mandel, Michael J. *The High-Risk Society: Peril and Promise in the New Economy.* New York, NY: Times Books, 1996.

McNulty, Paul J. *The Origins and Development of Labor Economics.* Cambridge, MA: MIT Press, 1980.

Minsky, Hyman P. *Stabilizing an Unstable Economy.* New Haven, CT: Yale University Press, 1986.

Mishel, Lawrence, Jared Bernstein, and John Schmitt. *The State of Working America 1996–1997.* Armonk, NY: M. E. Sharpe, 1997.

Moody, Harry R. *Abundance of Life: Human Development Policies for an Aging Society.* New York: Columbia University Press, 1988.

Morse, Dean. *The Peripheral Worker.* New York: Columbia University Press, 1969.

Nader, Ralph, Mark Green, and Joel Seligman. *Taming the Giant Corporation.* New York: W. W. Norton, 1976.

Ormerod, Paul. *The Death of Economics.* New York: St. Martin's Press, 1994.

Palley, Thomas I. *Plenty of Nothing: The Downsizing of the American Dream and the Case for Structural Keynesianism.* Princeton, NJ: Princeton University Press, 1998.

Pfeffer, Jeffrey. *The Human Equation: Building Profits by Putting People First.* Boston, MA: Harvard Business School Press, 1998.

Pollin, Robert and Stephanie Luce. *The Living Wage: Building a Fair Economy.* New York: The New Press, 1998.

Reich, Robert B. *The Work of Nations: Preparing Ourselves for the 21st Century.* New York: Alfred A. Knopf, 1991.

Rifkin, Jeremy. *The End of Work.* New York, NY: Putnam, 1995.

Rodrick, Dani. *Has Globalization Gone Too Far?* Washington, DC: Institute for International Economics, 1997.

Roosevelt, Franklin D. *Public Papers and Addresses.* Vol. VII. New York: Random House, 1937.

Roszak, Theodore. *America the Wise: The Longevity Revolution and the True Wealth of Nations.* Boston, MA: Houghton Mifflin, 1998.

Rudolph, Barbara. *Disconnected: How Six People from AT&T Discovered the New Meaning of Work in a Downsized Corporate America.* New York: Free Press, 1998

Sennett, Richard. *The Corrosion of Character: The Personal Consequences of Work in the New Capitalism.* New York: W. W. Norton, 1998.

Smith, Hedrick. *Rethinking America: Innovative Strategies and Partnerships in Business and Education.* New York: Avon Books, 1996.

Terry, Roger. *Economic Insanity: How Growth-Driven Capitalism Is Devouring the American Dream.* San Francisco, CA: Berrett-Koehler Publishers, 1995.

Tilly, Chris. *Half a Job: Bad and Good Times in a Changing Labor Market.* Philadelphia, PA: Temple University Press, 1996.

Winpisinger, William W. *Reclaiming Our Future.* Boulder, CO: Westview Press, 1989.

Wolman, William, and Anne Colamosca. *The Judas Economy: The Triumph of Capital and the Betrayal of Work.* Reading, MA: Addison-Wesley, 1997.

World Employment 1995. Geneva, Switzerland: International Labour Office, 1995.

Wray, L. Randall. *Understanding Modern Money: The Key to Full Employment and Price Stability.* Cheltenham, U.K.: Edward Elgar, 1998.

ARTICLES AND REPORTS

Altman, Morris. "A High Wage Path to Economic Growth and Development." *Challenge*, January-February 1998.

Anderson, Sarah, and John Cavanaugh. "CEOs Win, Workers Lose: How Wall Street Rewards Job Destroyers." Washington, DC: Institute for Policy Studies, April 1996.

Appelbaum, Eileen, Peter Berg, and Dean Baker. "The Economic Case for Corporate Responsibility to Workers." Washington, DC: Economic Policy Institute, 1996.

Belous, Richard S. "The Rise of the Contingent Workforce: Growth of Temporary, Part-Time, and Subcontracted Employment." *Looking Ahead*. Washington, DC: National Policy Association, June 1997.

Bergsten, C. Fred. "Globalizing Free Trade." *Foreign Affairs*, 75, no. 3.

Bernstein, Jared. "America's Well-Targeted Raise." Washington, DC: Economic Policy Institute, September 1997.

———. "Another Modest Minimum Wage Increase." Washington, DC: Economic Policy Institute, February 1998.

Blanchflower, David G. "Changes Over Time in Union Relative Wage Effects in Great Britain and the United States." Working paper no. 6100. Washington, DC: National Bureau of Economic Research, July 1, 1998.

Brown, Lester R., Gary Gardner, and Brian Halwell. "Impacts of Population Growth." *The Futurist*, February 1999.

Brozen, Yale. "Minimum Wage Rates and Household Workers." *Journal of Law and Economics*, October 1962.

"Building the Post-War Economy." Year-End Report of War Contracts Subcommittee of Committee on Military Affairs. Washington, DC: U.S. House of Representatives, 78th Congress, 2nd Session, December 18, 1944.

Caudron, Shari. "The Changing Union Agenda." *Personnel Journal*, March 1995.

Challenger, John A. "There Is No Future for the Workplace." *The Futurist*, October 1998.

Chang, Roberto. "Is Low Unemployment Inflationary?" *Economic Review*, First Quarter 1997. Atlanta, GA: Federal Reserve Bank of Atlanta, 1997.

"The Changing World of Work and Employee Benefits." EBRI issue brief no. 172. Washington, DC: Employee Benefit Research Institute, April 1966.

Chen, Yung-Ping. "Income Security for the Third Age." *Research Dialogues* (TIAA-CREF), no. 53, December 1997.

Cohany, Sharon. "Workers in Alternative Employment Arrangements: A Second Look." *Monthly Labor Review*, November 1998.

Cohen, Stephen S. and John Zysman. "The Emergence of a Manufacturing Gap." *Transatlantic Perspectives*, Autumn 1988.

Cole-Gomolski, Barb. "Reliance on Temps Creates New Problems." *Computerworld*, August 31, 1998.

"Contingent Workers and Workers in Alternative Work Arrangements." Issue brief no. 207. Executive summary. Washington, DC: Employee Benefit Research Institute, March 1999.

Couch, Kenneth A. "Distribution and Employment Impacts of Raising the Minimum Wage." *Economic Letter*. No. 99–06. San Francisco, CA: Federal Reserve Bank of San Francisco, February 19, 1999.

Cox, Harvey. "The Market as God." *The Atlantic Monthly*, March 1999.

Daviss, Bennett. "Profits from Principle." *The Futurist*, March 1999.

"Declining Job Security and the Professionalization of Opportunity." Research report no. 95–04. Washington, DC: National Commission for Employment Policy, May 1995.

Downs, Alan. "The Truth About Layoffs." *Management Review*, October 1955.

Drucker, Peter. "The Future That Has Already Happened." *The Futurist*, November 1998.

Eaton, Leslie. "Cloudy Sunset." *Barron's*, July 12, 1993.

"The Effects of the Minimum Wage on Teenage Employment." Washington, DC: National Center for Policy Analysis, 1996.

Eisner, Robert. "Our NAIRU Limit: The Governing Myth of Economic Policy." *The American Prospect*, Spring 1995.

"Employee Benefits, Retirement Patterns, and Implications for Increased Work Life." Issue brief no. 184. Washington, DC: Employee Benefit Research Institute, April 1997.

Encouraging Employee Self-Management in Financial and Career Planning. Report no. 976. New York: The Conference Board, 1991.

Ettorre, Barbara. "Empty Promises." *Management Review*, July 1996.

Fagiano, David. "The Legacy of Downsizing." *Management Review*, June 1996.

———. "Employment Contract Myth." *Management Review*, July 1996.

Fierman, Jaclyn. "The Contingency Workforce." *Fortune*, January 24, 1994.

Forstater, Matthew. "Public Employment and Economic Flexibility." Public policy brief highlights no. 50A. Anandale-on-Hudson, NY: The Jerome Levy Economics Institute of Bard College, February 1999.

Franklin, James C. "Industry Output and Employment Projections to 2005." *Monthly Labor Review*, November 1995.

Freedman, Audrey. "The New Look in Wage Policy and Employee Relations." Report No. 865. New York: The Conference Board, 1985.

Gendell, Murray. "Trends in Retirement Age in Four Countries, 1965–95." *Monthly Labor Review*, August 1998.

Grossman, Robert J. "Short-Term Workers Raise Long-Term Issues." *HRMagazine*, April 1998.

Harari, Oren. "Let the Computers Be the Bureaucrats." *Management Review*, September 1996.

"Has Globalization Gone Too Far?: Interview with Dani Rodrick." *Challenge*, March-April 1998.

Harrison, Bennett. "The Dark Side of Business Flexibility." *Challenge*, July-August 1998.

Hertz, Diane E. "Worker Displacement Still Common in Late 1980s." *Monthly Labor Review*, May 1991.

———. "Work After Early Retirement: An Increasing Trend Among Men." *Monthly Labor Review*, April 1995.

Herzenberg, Stephen, John Alic, and Howard Wial. "A New Deal for a New Economy." *Challenge*, March-April 1999.

Hiatt, Jonathan P., and Lynn Rhinehart. "The Growing Contingent Workforce: A Challenge for the Future." *The Labor Lawyer*, 10, no. 143 (1994).

Hipple, Steven. "Contingent Work: Results from the Second Survey." *Monthly Labor Review*, November 1998.

Hogarty, Donna Brown. "New Ways to Pay." *Management Review*, January 1994.

Horn, Robert, and Philip Heap. "The Age-Adjusted Unemployment Rate: An Alternative Measure." *Challenge*, January-February 1999.

"Inflation, Unemployment, and the Phillips Curve." *Economic Trends*. Cleveland, OH: Federal Reserve Bank of Cleveland, December 1997.

"Into the Dark: Rough Ride Ahead for American Workers." *Training*, July 1993.

Jacoby, Sanford. "Downsizing in the Past." *Challenge*, May-June 1998.

"Job Creation and the 7(A) Guaranteed Loan Program." Washington, DC: Small Business Administration, Office of the Inspector General Inspection Report, November 1994.

"Job Loss in a Booming Economy." Washington, DC: Employment Policies Institute, January 1998.

Kapstein, Ethan B. "Workers and the World Economy." *Foreign Affairs*, May/June 1996.

Kimmel, Jean, and Karen Smith Conway. "Who Moonlights and Why? Evidence from the SIPP." Upjohn Institute Staff working paper 95–40. W.E. Upjohn Institute for Employment Research.

Klein, Ethel, and Guy Molyneux. "Corporate Irresponsibility: There Ought to be Some Laws." Washington, DC: Preamble Center for Public Policy, July 29, 1996.

Labich, Kenneth. "The New Unemployed." *Fortune*, March 8, 1993.

Larson, Jan. "Temps Are Here to Stay." *American Demographics*, February 1996.

Lips, Brad. "Temps and the Labor Market: Why Unions Fear Staffing Companies." *Regulation*, Spring 1998.

Lynch, Robert G. "Do State and Local Tax Incentives Work?" Washington, DC: Economic Policy Institute, 1996.

Mankiw, Gregory. "Alan Greenspan's Tradeoff." *Fortune*, December 8.

Miller, Preston J. "The New Economics of a Minimum Wage Hike." *Fedgazette*. Minneapolis, MN: Federal Reserve Bank of Minneapolis, October 1995.

Mishel, Lawrence, and Jared Bernstein. "The Joyless Recovery: Deteriorating Wages and Job Quality in the 1990s." Briefing paper. Washington, DC: Economic Policy Institute, September 1993.

Mishel, Lawrence, Jared Bernstein, and Edith Russell. "Who Wins with a Higher Minimum Wage?" Briefing paper. Washington, DC: Economic Policy Institute, 1995.

Monroe, Anne. "Getting Rid of the Gray." *Mother Jones*, July/August 1996.

Moore, Stephen, and Dean Stamsel. "Ending Corporate Welfare As We Know It." Policy Analysis No. 225. Washington, DC: Cato Institute, May 12, 1995.

Munk, Nina. "Finished at Forty." *Fortune*, February 1, 1999.

Neumark, David, and William Wascher. "The Effects of Minimum Wages on Teenage Employment and Enrollment: Evidence from Matched CPS Surveys." *Research in Labor Economics*, 1996.

Oliver, Byron D. "Retirement Blues." *Management Review*, May 1996.

Olson, Craig A. "Health Benefits Coverage Among Male Workers." *Monthly Labor Review*, March 1995.

Palley, Thomas I. "Building Prosperity from the Bottom Up." *Challenge*, September-October 1998.

Palmeri, Christopher. "The Flip Side of Devaluation." *Forbes*, February 13, 1995.

"Part-Time Work: Characteristics of the Part-Time Work Force, Analysis of the March 1992 Current Population Survey." Working paper P–55. Washington, DC: Employee Benefit Research Institute.

Peak, Martha H. "All Pain, No Gain." *Management Review*, July 1996.

Phillips, A. W. "The Relation Between Unemployment and the Rate of Change of Money Wage Rates in the United Kingdom, 1861–1957." *Economics*, n.s., November 1958.

"Policy Challenges Posed by the Aging of America." Washington, DC: Urban Institute, May 1998.

Polivka, Anne E. "Contingent and Alternative Work Arrangements, Defined." *Monthly Labor Review*, October 1996.

Polivka, Anne E., and Thomas Nardone. "On the Definition of 'Contingent Work.'" *Monthly Labor Review*, December 1989.

Popkin, Joel, et al. "Business Survival Rates by Age Cohort of Business." Small business research summary—RS no. 122. Washington, DC: U.S. Small Business Administration, n.d.

Potter, Edward E. "Corporate Codes of Conduct: The New Protectionism." *Fact & Fallacy*. Washington, DC: Employment Policy Foundation, May 1999.

"Promoting Employment." Report of the Director-General, International Labour Conference, 82nd Session. Geneva, Switzerland: International Labour Office, 1995.

Reed, Lawrence W. "Minimum Wage Hurts Jobless by Making Work Illegal." Viewpoint on public issues no. 97–SRI. Midland, MI: Mackinac Center for Public Policy, February 24, 1997.

Reich, Robert B. "Frayed-Collar Workers in Gold-Plated Times: The State of the American Workforce 1995." Address to the Center for National Policy, Washington, DC, August 31, 1995.

———. "A Better Way to Raise the Minimum Wage." The Electronic Policy Network, February 23, 1998.

"Report and Recommendations of the Commission on the Future of Worker-Management Relations." *Daily Labor Report*. Special supplement, no. 6, January 9, 1995.

The Report of the Committee on Economic Security of 1935. Washington, DC: National Conference on Social Welfare, 1985.

Reynolds, Larry. "Potential Pension Disaster." *Management Review*, November 1992.

Rothstein, Jesse, and Robert E. Scott. "NAFTA and the States." Issue brief no. 119. Washington, DC: Economic Policy Institute, September 19, 1997.

———. "NAFTA's Casualties." Issue brief no. 120. Washington, DC: Economic Policy Institute, September, 19, 1997.

———. "The Cost of Trade with China." Issue brief no. 121. Washington, DC: Economic Policy Institute, October 28, 1997.

"Runaway CEO Pay." *Executive Pay Watch*. Washington, DC: AFL-CIO, 1998.

Salisbury, Dallas L. "Preparing for the Baby Boomers Retirement: The Role of Employment." Washington, DC: U.S. Senate Special Committee on Aging, July 25, 1997.

Salisbury, Dallas L., and Nora Super Jones, eds. *Retirement in the 21st Century . . . Ready or Not*. Washington, DC: Employee Benefit Research Institute, 1994.

"Saving for Retirement: How Are Women Doing?" *Working Age* (AARP), November/December 1998.

Schiller, Bradley R., and Philip Crewson. "Entrepreneurial Origins: A Longitudinal Inquiry." Research summary—RS no. 152. Washington, DC: Small Business Administration, February 1995.

Schwab, K., and C. Smadja. "The New Rules of the Game in a World of Many Players." *Harvard Business Review*, November 1994.

Scott, Frank A., Mark C. Berger, and Dan A. Black. "Changing Characteristics of the Self-Employed." Research summary—RS no. 185. Washington, DC: U.S. Small Business Admininstaration, April 1998.

Scott, Robert E. "U.S. Trade Deficits: Causes, Consequences, and Policy Implications." Testimony before the Senate Finance Committee, June 11, 1998. Washington, DC: Economic Policy Institute.

Scott, Robert E., Thea Lee, and John Schmitt. "Trading Away Good Jobs: An Examination of Employment and Wages in the U.S., 1979–94." Washington, DC: Economic Policy Institute, 1997.

"The Secret Purpose of Downsizing." *Business Ethics*, November/December 1996.

"Self-Sufficiency and the Low-Wage Labor Market: A Reality Check for Welfare Reform." Washington, DC: Urban Institute, Summary of Conference, April 12–14, 1994.

Slevin, Barry S. "Defined Contribution Plans for Multiemployer Funds." *Employee Benefits Journal*, 21, no. 2, June 1996.

"State Employee Layoffs: Final Results of a Joint Survey Project of The Council of State Governments' State Policy and Innovations Group and The National Association of State Personnel Executives." Washington, DC: The Council of State Governments, February 1992.

"The State of Working America 1996–1997." Executive Summary. Washington, DC: Economic Policy Institute, 1996.

Steinberg, Bruce. "The Temporary Help Industry Annual Update." *Contemporary Times*, Spring 1994.

Stiglitz, Joseph. "Quis Custodiet Ipsos Custodes?" *Challenge*, November-December 1999.

Stowe, Eric. "Workforce—The Critical Challenge." American Chamber of Commerce Executives, May 1998.

Straka, John W. *The Demand for Older Workers: The Neglected Side of a Labor Market.* Publication no. 13–11776 (15). Washington, DC: Social Security Administration, June 1992.

"Strike Headlines and Union Decline." *Fact & Fallacy*. Washington, DC: Employment Policy Foundation, September 1998.

Tan, Jan. "Who Gets Assistance?" *Current Population Reports*. P70–58. Washington, DC: Bureau of the Census, July 1996.

"Too Close for Comfort." *Executive Pay Watch*. Washington, DC: AFL-CIO, 1998.

United States-Mexico Trade: Pulling Together or Pulling Apart? Washington, DC: U.S. Government Printing Office, October 1992.

Useem, Michael. "The Impact of American Business Restructuring on Older Workers." *Perspective on Aging*, October-December 1993.

Walters, Jonathan. "The Downsizing Myth." *Governing*, May 1993.

Waterman, Robert H., Jr, Judith A. Waterman, and Betsy A. Collard. "Toward a Career-Resilient Workforce." *Harvard Business Review*, July-August 1994.

"Where the Jobs Go—and Why." *World Press Review*, December 1995.

Wiatrowski, William J. "Small Businesses and Their Employees." *Monthly Labor Review*, October 1994.

Wilson, D. Mark. "Increasing the Mandated Minimum Wage: Who Pays the Price?" Backgrounder no. 1162. Washington, DC: Heritage Foundation, March 5, 1998.

INDEX

About the Author

MARTIN SICKER is a private consultant and lecturer who has served as a senior executive in the U.S. government and has taught political science at American University and George Washington University. He has also served as a director at the American Association of Retired Persons, dealing with workforce issues and programs, and as a consultant to the National Older Worker Career Center. Sicker is the author of 20 earlier books on political science and international affairs.